Current Issues in Project Analysis for Development

Edited by

John Weiss

*Professor of Development Economics and Associate Dean,
Research, University of Bradford, UK*

David Potts

*Senior Lecturer, Bradford Centre for International
Development, University of Bradford, UK*

Edward Elgar
Cheltenham, UK • Northampton, MA, USA

Published by
Edward Elgar Publishing Limited
The Lypiatts
15 Lansdown Road
Cheltenham
Glos GL50 2JA
UK

Edward Elgar Publishing, Inc.
William Pratt House
9 Dewey Court
Northampton
Massachusetts 01060
USA

A catalogue record for this book
is available from the British Library

Library of Congress Control Number: 2012935268

ISBN 978 1 84844 535 2 (cased)

Typeset by Servis Filmsetting Ltd, Stockport, Cheshire
Printed and bound by MPG Books Group, UK

Contents

Contributors

P.B. Anand is Reader in Environmental Economics and Head of Division, Bradford Centre for International Development, University of Bradford, UK

Massimo Florio is Professor of Public Economics, Department of Economics, Business and Statistics at the University of Milan, Italy

Manabu Fujimura is Professor of Economics at Aoyama Gakuin University, Tokyo, Japan

Erhun Kula is Professor of Economics, Bahçeşehir University, Istanbul, Turkey

Elio Londero is a Consulting Economist and retired staff member of the Inter-American Development Bank

Chris Nash is Research Professor, Institute for Transport Studies, University of Leeds, UK

David Potts is Senior Lecturer, Bradford Centre for International Development, University of Bradford, UK

Silvia Vignetti is Director of the Evaluation Unit, Centre for Industrial Studies, Milan, Italy

Keith Ward is an economic consultant

John Weiss is Professor of Development Economics and Associate Dean, Research, School of Social and International Studies, University of Bradford, UK

1. Editors' introduction

David Potts and John Weiss

UNDERLYING THEORY

Project cost–benefit analysis (CBA) in the context of developing countries has its practical roots in the work on water resource planning in the US in the 1930s and its theoretical foundation in the new welfare economics of the 1940s (Little, 1950).[1] The key feature is the insight that in any economy 'social value' in the sense of the contribution of any item to social welfare need not be represented by an observable market price – either because real world features of markets depart from competitive optima or because a market does not exist for the item concerned. In this framework holding everything else constant, the social value (P) for item i becomes:

$$P_i = dW/dQ_i \tag{1.1}$$

where W is a measure of welfare, Q is output quantity and d denotes a small change.

Social values in this sense have been variously termed shadow prices, economic prices or accounting prices to reflect their unobservable nature. In this chapter we use the term 'shadow prices' although other chapters in the book sometimes use the other terms.

Social welfare itself needs defining. From its origins in welfare economics most project economic analysis takes as its starting point the individualistic social welfare function where total social welfare is the aggregation of individual preferences. Thus where consumers have access to more goods, their willingness to pay to obtain them defines social value.[2] Two exceptions to this rule have been incorporated into the literature although they are rarely applied in practice. These relate to a specification of social welfare based on judgements by planners or political decision makers regarding the desirability or undesirability of the consumption of particular goods ('merit wants') or on the desirability or undesirability of particular patterns of distribution of consumption or income ('distribution weights'). Since social welfare is defined in individualistic terms and it is conventional to assume that individual welfare is determined by levels of consumption, it is natural to measure social welfare in consumption units. Thus, assuming there are no items affecting welfare that cannot be measured in monetary terms, the broadest expression for the change in welfare dW is:

$$dW = dC + \sum m.dC(p_m - 1) + \sum r.dC(p_r - 1) \qquad (1.2)$$

where C is consumption, m is the share of this which goes on merit goods and r is the share that goes to those above or below mean consumption, p_m is the weight placed on merit goods, p_r is the redistribution weight placed on those with non-mean consumption and $\sum$ refers to summation over all merit goods and individuals.

Savings can be treated as postponed consumption which will accrue in the future. Where there is a savings shortage, by definition, a unit of income saved in the present will be worth more than one unit of consumption in present value terms and the present value of total consumption C will be composed of two components:

$$C = C_1 + S.P^F \qquad (1.3)$$

where C_1 is current consumption, S is current savings and P^F is the value of a unit of current savings in terms of future consumption. Therefore equation (1.2) can be rewritten as:

$$dW = (dC_1) + (dS.P^F) + \sum (m.dC_1 + m.dS.P^F)(p_m - 1) \\ + \sum (r.dC_1 + r.dS.P^F)(p_r - 1) \qquad (1.4)$$

This basic approach defines the way in which various objectives in addition to increasing consumption – such as favouring merit goods, redistributing benefits and raising savings – might in theory be incorporated in project level calculations. In practice, as we discuss below, these latter adjustments have rarely been made and the focus has been on estimating simply dC or the monetary equivalent where non-marketed benefits are involved.

Conversion of the effects of a project into the monetary equivalent of consumption draws on the basic principles of welfare economics. A project is viewed as a disturbance to a market, creating effects in terms of both demand and supply. In a simple competitive framework there are three possibilities depending upon whether the project is large enough to affect price in the market and whether project output is internationally traded or non-traded:

- the project may affect the balance of payments, in which case the world price provides the measure of value;
- the project may displace other supplies, in which case there is no additional consumption and cost saving measures output value;
- the project may add to consumption directly, in which case willingness to pay measures value.

Where traded goods are produced and the country is a price-taker on the world market there will be a given market price and a perfectly elastic horizontal supply line. Assuming no protection or trade costs and that the restrictions of the perfectly competitive model hold, extra project supply will be absorbed at this ruling price, and if domestic demand is insufficient then the residual supply will be exported. Under these limited conditions, ignoring trade margins, the world market price provides a measure of value. The theoretical link with consumption is that foreign currency values should be converted into domestic currency at an exchange rate that reflects consumer willingness to pay for foreign currency.[3] On the other hand, projects can impact on the domestic economy through their production or use of non-traded items. Where projects change domestic prices, then in welfare terms they create changes in consumer and producer surpluses whose value in terms of consumption determines the social value of the projects.

Figures 1.1 and 1.2 illustrate these points. A project is represented by an outward shift in the supply line from SS to SS_1. Where output is exported and we adopt the small country assumption, all project output can be sold at the world price P_0 and gross benefits will be the area ABQ_1Q_0 in Figure 1.1. Where, as in Figure 1.2, a good is sold domestically and does not affect international trade, the shift to SS_1 will bring price down to P_1 from P_2 and this will create both an increase in demand from Q_1 to Q_2 and a fall in other domestic supply from Q_1 to Q_3. The gross benefit at the demand margin is the area ABQ_2Q_1C, composed of both revenue (BQ_2Q_1C) and consumer surplus (ABC) and at the supply margin it is ACQ_1Q_3D or total cost savings composed of both revenue loss (CQ_1Q_3D) and producer surplus (ACD). Thus where prices change due to a project, social value is determined by the revenue effect, which is captured by the financial analysis of a project, and the change in consumer and producer surplus, which is not. To capture social value requires quantifying these surpluses and adding them on to financial effects. How far project output replaces other supplies or adds to demand will be determined by the size of the respective supply and demand elasticities at the pre-project price–consumption point.

In a perfect market with no trade barriers each definition of value would be equal. In a small open economy the world price will be the domestic

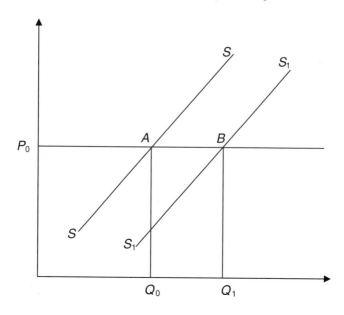

Figure 1.1   Project output exported at constant price

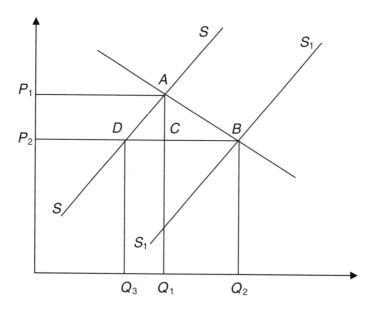

Figure 1.2   Project output sold domestically

price, and in the non-traded case the unit value at both the demand margin and at the supply margin is the average of the with and without project prices (P_2 and P_1). This is the so-called 'rule of half' which still figures in practical work in some sectors. This follows since, if we assume linear relationships, gross benefits at the demand margin are:

$$P_2*(Q_2 - Q_1) + 0.5*(P_1 - P_2)*(Q_2 - Q_1)$$

and rearranging:

$$(Q_2 - Q_1)*(P_2 + 0.5*(P_1 - P_2))$$

which reduces to $(Q_2 - Q_1)*0.5*(P_2 + P_1)$.

Similarly at the supply margin gross benefits are:

$$P_2*(Q_1 - Q_3) + 0.5*(P_1 - P_2)*(Q_1 - Q_3)$$

which reduces to $(Q_1 - Q_3)*0.5*(P_2 + P_1)$.

However, in real world conditions with taxes, subsidies, monopoly or monopsony power, uncertainty and externalities, there is no reason why the value of mean willingness to pay (at the demand margin) should equal mean cost saving (at the supply margin). In real world conditions there will be wedges (or 'distortions'), sometimes large ones, between these three bases for value, which practical analysis has to estimate.

As the starting point of the competitive market model is a gross simplification of reality, the test for project economic analysis is to find ways of approximating the 'true' or shadow price value of project items, where markets do not exist or where, if they do, they are strongly influenced by taxes, subsidies, monopoly or monopsony power, uncertainty and externalities. The framework underlying Figures 1.1 and 1.2, drawn from welfare theory, provides the starting point for the application of project economics concepts. However, as project economics deals with an imperfect world, its shadow prices are 'second best' prices as opposed to the 'first best' prices that prevail under restrictive theoretical conditions.

EVOLUTION OF THE LITERATURE

The early academic literature focused on adjusting for some of the most obvious market distortions, principally taxes and subsidies. However, the adjustments were asymmetrical as between costs and benefits. As transfers, taxes should be deducted from project costs or from benefits where, at the supply margin, these are defined in terms of cost savings. However, since taxes that are paid are part of willingness to pay, taxes on outputs should be included in benefits. The seminal figure in this literature was Arnold Harberger, who showed in a number of papers how relatively simple adjustments to market prices could generate approximate shadow prices.[4]

The work of Harberger focused on estimating the first term in equation (1.2) in what were termed 'efficiency' adjustments since they focused on the efficiency of resource use without incorporating growth, distribution or merit want objectives. This approach was expanded significantly to allow for a shortage of savings in the work of Feldstein (1964) and Marglin (1967). The insight here was that, where growth is constrained by lack of savings, a unit of income saved in the present can be treated as postponed consumption whose future value, when discounted back to the present, will exceed the original value of savings. This is the parameter P^F in equation (1.3) derived as the discounted stream of the future consumption generated by a unit of income saved in the present. In its simplest form, with a constant marginal productivity of investment, a constant proportion of the extra income generated in future years reinvested and a constant discount rate,

$$P^F = (1 - s)q/(i - sq) \qquad (1.5)$$

where q is the return on additional investment, s is the share of extra income saved and i is the rate at which society's valuation of future consumption declines over time or the 'social time preference' discount rate.

One of the important consequences of this approach was that where P^F is used, the appropriate discount rate should be not the opportunity cost of capital (q) – as in most operational work and Harberger (1973), for example – but a social time preference rate (i). As the latter is typically assumed to be in the range 2–8 per cent and the former is conventionally taken as 10–12 per cent for developing countries, this makes a major change in the weighting of future project effects.[5]

The introduction of merit wants displaces the individualistic basis for valuation and thus implies that social value, as determined by politicians or planners, is higher (for publicly desirable goods) or lower (for publicly undesirable goods) than that defined by the willingness to pay of individuals. Once a premium for merit wants or savings is incorporated in the analysis (as in $P^F - 1$ and $p_m - 1$ in equation (1.4)), a unit of account or numeraire is required, since items with a special weight must be compared with a reference item with a weight of unity. Given the focus on individual welfare, a natural unit is units of consumption as in equations (1.2) and (1.4). This is set out clearly in one of the key texts of the literature, UNIDO

(1972). Written by three of the then leading exponents of applied welfare economics, Partha Dasgupta, Stephen Marglin and Amartya Sen, the so-called UNIDO Guidelines combine academic rigour with an accessible non-technical style. They still stand as a classic statement of project economics.

Although it essentially restated the work of Marglin and Feldstein, UNIDO (1972) added to the literature by showing how distributional issues could be incorporated into project analysis, both through tracing the income flows created by a project and in addition by applying weights to the consumption of different groups to get a distribution weighted measure of project worth. Weights were to be either determined in a revealed preference approach, by examining past decisions to ascertain how far decision makers had in the past traded off gains in total income for gains to a particular group, or treated as an unknown in the form of a switching value calculation. The Guidelines held back from introducing value judgements on distributional issues but at the cost of fairly vague advice on how weights could be determined or used.

Whilst the consumption unit (strictly units of consumption to average consumers) introduced by UNIDO (1972) had an intuitive link with welfare economics, the other key strand of the project economics literature from the work of the Oxford economists Ian Little and James Mirrlees (Little and Mirrlees, 1968, 1974) superficially appeared to move in a quite different direction. Little and Mirrlees were concerned initially with devising a system that would identify projects that were financially profitable due to import protection but that were economically inefficient as project costs were high relative to the import price of the commodity. Much of their focus therefore was on traded good projects, where as noted above, under a set of assumptions, world prices provide the measure of social value.[6] Little and Mirrlees recognised the need for a numeraire or unit of account but adopted the opposite approach to that of UNIDO (1972). Whereas UNIDO opted for units of consumption, which it measured in domestic prices, Little and Mirrlees (1974) introduced as its unit government income measured at world prices. This appeared initially as a major departure from conventional approaches; however, syntheses soon appeared and, for example, equation (1.4) can be modified readily to convert it to an expression in Little–Mirrlees units. Assuming all government income is invested (or is used for equally valuable purposes) and that the average ratio of world to domestic prices – what Little and Mirrlees term the standard conversion factor – is SCF then, in their units, equation (1.4) becomes $(dW/P^F)SCF$.

Here the welfare change in consumption at domestic prices is first converted to an equivalent in units of government income by division by P^F and the resulting value in units of government income at domestic

Table 1.1   Choice of numeraire

	Little–Mirrlees	UNIDO
Units	Government income (equivalent to saving)	Average consumption
Price level	World	Domestic
Adjustments	Domestic to world prices (by multiplication by *SCF*)	World to domestic prices (by multiplication by *SER/OER**)
Adjustments	Consumption to savings (by division by P^F)	Savings to consumption (by multiplication by P^F)

Note: * OER is the official exchange rate.

prices is converted to world prices by multiplication by *SCF*. Once comparable adjustments and assumptions are made in both systems, they give the same accept/reject decision on a project although the resulting indicators of project worth will differ. Critical here is that the discount rate differs between the two systems with the social time preference rate used in UNIDO (1972) and an opportunity cost of capital rate reflecting the decline in the value of government income in Little–Mirrlees (1974). The latter follows since government income is normally treated as being equivalent to investment. In fact Ian Little stated on one occasion that their choice of numeraire was driven by the need to come up with a specification of the discount rate which would be compatible with practice in operational appraisals at the World Bank and elsewhere. Table 1.1 summarises the adjustments in the Little–Mirrlees and UNIDO approaches.

Early discussion of the Little–Mirrlees approach misinterpreted its applicability, thinking it could not be applied in the analysis of non-traded activities where, as we have seen, willingness to pay is the appropriate measure of value at the demand margin where project output adds to consumption in the economy. The approach was cumbersome in that willingness to pay estimates would still be needed, but an extra step of converting these from domestic to world prices was required.[7]

A notable synthesis of the UNIDO and Little–Mirrlees approaches (although it adopted the numeraire of the latter) was given by Squire and van der Tak (1975), who showed how distribution weighting would in principle affect all shadow prices. Unlike UNIDO (1972), which gave no advice on how weights should be derived, Squire and van der Tak (1975) showed how a value judgement on a single parameter, the rate at which the social value of consumption declines – the elasticity of the marginal social utility of consumption – can be used to derive consumption weights for different groups of consumers. The subjective nature of the judgement is hidden in an apparently technical formula where the weight on a unit of extra consumption to individual i is through a comparison of i's consumption with the national average and the application of the elasticity parameter. Thus:

$$p_{r_i} = (c_{av}/c_i)^n \qquad (1.6)$$

where p_{r_i} is the redistribution weight in equations (1.2) and (1.4), c_{av} and c_i are mean consumption and consumption of i respectively, and n is the elasticity of the marginal social utility of consumption.

PRACTICAL APPLICATIONS

Key users of the methodology were multilateral development banks who needed a means of checking that the projects they were proposing to fund were a sensible use of aid resources. Analysis of financial profitability alone was deemed inadequate in many cases due to a combination of factors:

- difficult to value sectors – either because goods were not sold on a market – such as free provision of health and education services – or where the sale was at prices that did not reflect willingness to pay;
- serious economy-wide controls and tax-subsidy interventions which rendered the market price of key variables – like the exchange rate, interest rates and a range of commodity prices – inappropriate guides to social value;
- inequality in income distribution and a concern that project aid should benefit the poor.

Squire and van der Tak were staff members at the World Bank, and various papers were drafted showing how the weighting approach they devised could be applied (for example Linn, 1977). However, in practice none of the major banks or agencies adopted the full range of adjustments. In terms of equation (1.2), the analysis incorporated only the first term on the right-hand side (or the 'efficiency effect').[8] In a retrospective piece looking back at project analyses in the World Bank, Squire in Deverajan et al. (1996) identified several reasons for this:

- inability to convince practical people;
- complexity of the data requirements;

- disagreement on how the subjective elasticity parameter driving the weights might be identified;
- a concern that distributional and savings issues would be better dealt with by fiscal or other direct policies rather than by project selection.

The rationale for this omission is that, if allocative efficiency effects can be picked up accurately, other policy instruments can be used to address other objectives. Well prepared project analysis of World Bank projects appears to be associated with the subsequent success of projects once they become operational (Jenkins, 1997; Deininger et al., 1998), so good economic analysis should increase the overall level of resources available for allocation and the distribution of those resources in turn can be influenced by appropriate policy measures.

The choice not to use a savings premium and distribution weights (P^F and p_r in equation (1.4)) was followed by other development agencies and multilateral development banks. In practice, therefore, the unit or numeraire applied in practical appraisal related only to a choice between measuring consumption effects at domestic or world prices, the alternative parameters needed to move between different price levels being the shadow exchange rate factor (in a domestic price analysis) or its inverse, the standard conversion factor (in a world price analysis). Manuals produced by international agencies usually did not specify a preference for one numeraire over the other, but noted their equivalence as the economic internal rate of return would be the same in both analyses provided identical assumptions were used.[9] Practice is still varied and there is a tendency for the price level chosen to be related to type of project – with analysts preferring to use a world price system in traded good projects (as in agriculture, for example) and a domestic price system for non-traded projects (as in water or transport). If distribution analysis is to be carried out, even with no application of consumption weights, there is clear advantage in conducting the initial appraisal at domestic prices.[10] This follows since distribution analysis traces the income changes for different groups created by a project, and this is operationalised by first estimating the changes created by the financial transactions of a project and then at a second step estimating the changes created by the difference between market and shadow prices. The first set of income flows must be at domestic prices, hence for comparability we need the second set of flows also to be at domestic prices. Hence having shadow prices at domestic rather than world prices is clearly an advantage.[11]

In recent years the bulk of aid-funded projects subject to economic analysis have been in non-traded sectors and the respective manuals have given considerable attention to the distinction between the demand

and supply margins highlighted in Figure 1.1 as these form the basis for valuation (see ADB, 1997; Belli et al., 2001; Jenkins and Harberger, 1994). ADB (1997) for example stresses the distinction between 'incremental output', which adds to consumption, and 'non-incremental output', which displaces other supply, with willingness to pay determining the value of incremental output, and cost saving the value of non-incremental output. Jenkins and Harberger (1994) add the further refinement of using elasticity weights to determine the proportion of project output that falls into the two categories. This is clearly the rigorous way to estimate project impact, although the accuracy of elasticity estimates available at the time of project appraisal may be open to question.

USE AND LIMITATIONS OF DISCOUNTED CASH FLOW ANALYSIS

CBA is a version of the broad approach of discounted cash flow, which compares future benefits and costs in a discounting framework. When CBA was first adopted in the US in the 1930s the main criterion used was the benefit–cost ratio (BCR). The origin of this indicator can be traced back to the work of Dupuit in the mid nineteenth century and arguably even further to early nineteenth-century US water projects (Hanley and Spash, 1993: 4). Two main variants of this indicator can be used. The first involves a comparison between total benefits and total costs:

$$BCR_1 = \sum_{t=1}^{n} \frac{B_t}{(1 + r)^t} \bigg/ \sum_{t=1}^{n} \frac{C_t}{(1 + r)^t} \qquad (1.7)$$

where B_t is the gross benefit in year t and C_t is the sum of capital and operating costs and r is the discount rate.

The second version involves a comparison of the present value of gross benefits net of operating costs with the present value of capital costs:

$$BCR_2 = \sum_{t=1}^{n} \frac{(NB_t)}{(1 + r)^t} \bigg/ \sum_{t=1}^{n} \frac{K_t}{(1 + r)^t} \qquad (1.8)$$

where NB_t is the gross benefit net of operating costs in year t and K_t is the capital cost.

Subsequent debates suggested that this indicator in either form is unreliable for any form of ranking of alternatives since it does not measure the absolute size of the net benefits. Furthermore, definitional problems as to what items were included in the denominator and the numerator meant that it could also not be regarded as a reliable indicator of efficiency in the use of resources. The consensus is that the net present value (NPV) is the most reliable indicator for mutually exclusive projects as long as the discount rate is known (see, for example, Layard, 1972: 51). The NPV can be defined by:

$$NPV = \sum_{t=1}^{n} \frac{(B_t - C_t)}{(1 + r)^t} \tag{1.9}$$

However, if the discount rate is not known and a capital rationing situation arises, the appropriate criterion should be to maximise the return to the scarce factor, in this case capital. In such a case the internal rate of return (IRR) provides a better criterion since it measures the return to capital. However, it suffers from the possibility that it may yield multiple roots and therefore could be indeterminate. Such cases are rather unusual but can occur where a project has a large negative value at the end of its life, examples being decommissioning of a nuclear power plant or restoration of an area degraded by a mine after the mine is exhausted. The IRR can be defined as:

$$IRR = r \text{ where } \sum_{t=1}^{n} \frac{B_t}{(1 + r)^t} - \sum_{t=1}^{n} \frac{C_t}{(1 + r)^t} = 0 \tag{1.10}$$

In arguing for the superiority of the NPV as a decision-making indicator, Hirshleifer (1958) pointed out that a pure capital rationing situation was rather unlikely in reality and therefore the argument for using the IRR rested on a rather extreme case.

A possible compromise that is sometimes recommended for capital rationing is to use the ratio of the NPV to the present value of capital costs (K): the NPV/K ratio. This is also a measure of efficiency in the use of capital but does not suffer from some of the problems associated with the IRR. However, it does require the specification of a discount rate. The NPV/K ratio can be defined as:

$$NPV/K = \sum_{t=1}^{n} \frac{B_t - C_t}{(1 + r)^t} \bigg/ \sum_{t=1}^{n} \frac{K_t}{(1 + r)^t} \tag{1.11}$$

In all of the conventional indicators of project worth the use of discounting means that the focus is on the returns to an initial investment, the assumption being that projects have an initial net outlay followed by a subsequent net benefit. However, the NPV is less vulnerable than other indicators to the possibility that the critical issue is not the initial investment but whether subsequent benefits will be greater than costs. This may be the case, for example, in some input-intensive agricultural activities where investment may be small relative to operating costs.

Conventional CBA calculations are normally based on values estimated in constant prices. The argument for doing this rests on the view that the results should not be distorted by whatever the rate of inflation happens to be. If CBA is done at constant prices it is also important that any comparison with lending rates should be with real rates, not nominal rates.

Use of constant prices makes sense in the economic analysis of projects but it is not always very helpful in financial analysis when the most important question is often whether the funds allocated to the project will cover the actual money outlays. In principle, financial analysis should therefore be undertaken at expected future prices allowing for general inflation as well as any changes in relative prices. For commercial projects this has the added advantage that the IRR of the project can be compared with the nominal rate of interest on any borrowed funds. However, to be able to compare a financial analysis conducted at current prices with an economic analysis conducted at constant prices, the financial analysis must be deflated by an appropriate inflation factor. This is particularly important if the results of the financial analysis are to inform an analysis of the distribution of benefits. There are a number of complications in ensuring full consistency, but they can be overcome (Potts, 1996c).

Values of costs and benefit items in expected future prices can be estimated by multiplying by an inflation factor (*IF*) relating to the expected rate of inflation *i* in each year up to the year in question. Thus:

$$IF_n = (1 + i_1)(1 + i_2)(1 + i_3). \ldots .(1 + i_n) \tag{1.12}$$

In principle, constant price values can be adjusted for any expected changes in relative prices but in practice such adjustments are rare, other than correcting for abnormally high or low prices at the time of planning the project. Adjustment factors (AFs) for changes in relative prices for a cost or benefit item *d* in year *n* can be made by dividing the inflation factor for *d* by the general inflation factor IF_n.
Thus with:

$$IF_d = (1 + i_{d1})(1 + i_{d2})(1 + i_{d3}). \ldots .(1 + i_{dn}) \tag{1.13}$$

$$AF_d = IF_d/IF_n$$

Best practice for cost–benefit analysis would therefore suggest that the financial analysis of projects should be conducted at expected future (that is, inflated) prices, while economic analysis should be conducted at constant prices with due account of relative price changes where the size and direction of these are expected with some degree of certainty. Decision making should be made on the basis of the NPV where the discount rate is known; however, there are a number of controversies in determining the discount rate. These issues are discussed by Kula in Chapter 7.

As noted earlier, a particularly important issue is the choice between a discount rate based on the opportunity cost of capital and one based on social time preference. In a situation of perfectly competitive capital markets the two would be the same but, as already indicated, conventional assumptions about these two indicators were that the former would be significantly higher than the latter, particularly in developing countries. Whether this is actually true or not is debatable, but it is clear that the choice of discount rate can have important implications for the choice of projects. The discount rate is not neutral in its impact on different kinds of projects or in the extent to which it gives due regard to the interests of future generations and the environment. A number of authors have argued that the 10–12 per cent rates typically used by development banks are potentially harmful.[12] In particular the evidence base for such high estimates of the opportunity cost of capital has not been demonstrated. Meanwhile there has been a major shift towards the use of social time preference rates in EU countries (Evans, 2007). The main rationale for using a higher rate in poor countries is that, where capital is scarce, returns to capital and therefore its opportunity cost will be higher. However, given the increased mobility of capital between countries that has occurred in recent years in response to capital account liberalisation this case may not be as compelling as in previous decades.

It is therefore clear that while there is a good deal of consensus about the situations in which to use particular indicators for discounted cash flow analysis, there is still significant disagreement about the value of the discount rate to be used in their calculation. Similar issues arise in relation to the estimation and use of shadow prices.

NATIONAL PARAMETER ESTIMATION

Two underlying assumptions of Little and Mirrlees (1968 and 1974) were that market prices in developing countries were sufficiently different from economic values to justify the use of shadow prices and that it would be possible for developing country governments to establish what they described as a 'Central Office of Project Evaluation' (COPE) that would have responsibility for their estimation. It was clearly recognised that it was neither realistic nor sensible to expect individual project analysts to estimate shadow prices beyond those that were very specific to the project in question. In particular the use of different conversion factors (where these are defined as the ratio of a shadow to a market price) for the same items in the appraisal of different projects would render the comparison of projects meaningless and therefore make systematic project selection virtually impossible. It was therefore considered necessary for the COPE to make periodic estimates of what came to be called 'national parameters' or economic values for key factors and sectors. In principle these parameters would then be used consistently for all projects until such time as they were revised.

While there have been many studies undertaken to determine shadow prices in different countries, it is unusual in practice to find a functioning system to ensure that they are updated on a regular basis.[13] Given that the estimation of shadow prices in the first place often depends on data that are one or two years old, it is clear that such estimates can easily become outdated and therefore of potentially limited value in project appraisal.

The main practical approach to estimating national shadow prices from the 1980s onwards has been through the use of semi-input–output analysis. A review of this method and some of the studies conducted using it is provided by Potts in Chapter 4. The number of studies undertaken suggests that the method itself is fairly robust, albeit subject to the limitations of the underlying assumptions and the data used. The key issues are therefore the extent to which such parameters are used in a systematic way, the stability of the parameters over time and the frequency with which they are updated. Unfortunately practice has been patchy at best in relation to the first and third issues and the second issue is relatively unknown because of the irregular updating of estimates.

A further issue that has influenced practice since the early 1990s has been the impact of economic liberalisation. Almost all countries have liberalised markets to a significant extent in the last twenty years. Arguably this might suggest that the need to use shadow prices might be lessened due to the reduced level of market imperfections. One of the main arguments used for applying shadow prices in developing countries was the level of market imperfection, which was contrasted with the situation in developed countries (Little and Mirrlees, 1974: 29–37). Do we need shadow prices if markets are liberalised? The consensus is that we do.[14] Most countries continue to impose some taxes on trade; unemployment and underemployment are still issues; and monopoly and discriminatory pricing still affect non-traded sectors. The implication is that at the very least there is a need to use a shadow exchange rate and shadow wage rates for different categories of labour as well as to remove taxes and subsidies when conducting economic analysis. A comprehensive discussion of the estimation of the shadow exchange rate is provided by Londero in Chapter 2 and an overview of issues relating to shadow wage rates is provided by Potts in Chapter 3.

Arguably a more important question is why shadow prices are not used more often in developed countries. The most recent EC Guide to Cost–Benefit Analysis for the regions (European Commission, 2008) proposes an approach that is very similar to that proposed by Squire and van der Tak (1975) in a developing country context. In Chapter 12 Florio and Vignetti describe the CBA method proposed for use in the EU regions as 'bridging the traditions'. A number of authors have either estimated shadow wage rates for developed countries or argued for their use and it is quite likely that the methodological distinction between CBA for developing countries and CBA in the developed world will become increasingly blurred.[15]

DIFFICULT TO VALUE NON-TRADED SECTORS

In recent years multilateral development banks have concentrated their project support on sectors providing either physical or social infrastructure, which are of their nature difficult to value. As noted above, in theory, willingness to pay provides the basis for valuation of incremental non-traded output. Strictly what is required is the compensating variation in income terms that exactly offsets the price change created by a project, which differs from the conventional area under a demand curve. However, in practice, estimation is based typically on approximations of the latter. Here we highlight three approaches of varying degrees of sophistication which have been applied in some non-traded sectors, particularly in water, where serious efforts have been made in recent years to quantify willingness to pay.[16]

The simplest approach is to apply a version of the rule of half discussed above. Where a water project provides piped water to a previously unserved area, and serves households who had previously obtained water from vendors, the average vendor charge per m^3 provides the without-project price (P_1 in Figure 1.3). The proposed water tariff to be charged by the project is the with-project price (P_2 in Figure 1.3). With the project water consumption has risen from Q_1 to Q_2. Assuming a linear demand function, total willingness to pay can be approximated by $0.5*(P_1 + P_2)*(Q_2 - Q_1)$. The approach is crude and implies that vendor and piped water are identical commodities so that a single demand line is applicable.

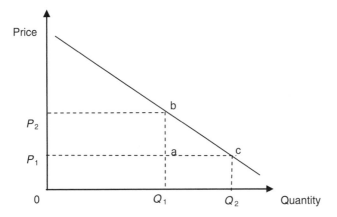

Figure 1.3   Simple rule of half

A slightly more rigorous approach extends the analysis to relax the linearity assumption.[17] The non-linear demand function can be defined as a semi-log function:

$$\ln q = \alpha + \beta p \qquad (1.14)$$

where ln is the natural logarithm and $\alpha > 0$, $\beta < 0$, q is quantity, p is price. The price elasticity (η_p) is given by:

$$\eta_p = (dq/dp)\,(p/q) = \beta p \qquad (1.15)$$

where d is the change in either quantity or price.

This functional form also has the desirable property that marginal willingness to pay rises exponentially as quantity supplied falls, as suggested by economic theory. The parameter α depends on income, the prices of substitutes, and other non-price variables that determine the demand. This functional form lends itself readily to calculating willingness to pay or economic benefit (EB), defined as the area beneath the demand curve between the existing and new outputs (q_1 and q_2), that is,

$$EB = \int_{q_1}^{q_2} p\,dq \qquad (1.16)$$

where q_1 to q_2 is the range of integration. Integrating with respect to q results in a willingness to pay of:

$$EB = q_2(p_2 - 1/\beta) - q_1(p_1 - 1/\beta) \qquad (1.17)$$

where p_1 and p_2 are prices corresponding to q_1 and q_2, respectively.

Use of equation (1.17) to estimate benefits requires information on β, the slope of the demand function. This requires estimation in an econometric demand model.

A further level of rigour is introduced by contingent valuation approaches that attempt to assess willingness to pay from specially designed surveys (Whitehead and Blomquist, 2006). In a closed-ended approach the respondent is asked whether they are willing to pay a specified amount presented as the value of the improved service. Prices for the service, or 'bids', are set within a range and distributed randomly to respondents. The yes/no answers to the question of willingness to use the service become the dependent variable in a probit regression model where they are related to household, area and service characteristics as well as the bid price. The probit model will be of the form:

$$Y = \alpha + \beta_1 X + \beta_2 B + \varepsilon \qquad (1.18)$$

where Y is the yes/no response, X is a vector of variables reflecting household, area or other characteristics, B is the bid price and ε is an error term.

Mean willingness to pay (WTP) is derived from the expression $(\Sigma(\beta_1 * X^a)/\beta_2)* - 1$ where X^a is the mean value of X variables.

Mean WTP is thus derived by first summing the product of the mean value for the explanatory variables and their coefficient from the probit analysis $\Sigma(\beta_1 * X^a)$ and then dividing this by the coefficient on the bid price (β_2). This expression is then multiplied by minus unity to give a positive number. Where there is a constant in the probit model (α) this must be added to the sum of the products to give $\alpha + \Sigma(\beta_1 * X^a)$ so that mean WTP becomes $(\alpha + \Sigma(\beta_1 * X^a)/\beta_2)* - 1$.

The same approach can be applied to derive mean WTP for specific target groups by replacing the average value for each variable X with the specific X value for the group concerned (for example for the very poor).

Measurement of benefits in the water sector can be regarded as potentially problematic but there are well established approaches for measuring the benefits of roads. These have been embodied in computer packages such as HDM-4. Various versions of this model link road quality with the cost of operating a vehicle to allow a specified road improvement to be converted into a saving in vehicle operating cost. In Chapter 9 Nash discusses the methods of measuring the benefits of road projects. At the simplest level vehicle operating cost savings provided the benefit for existing traffic with the rule of half applied using vehicle operating costs as proxies for consumer prices to value incremental traffic. Such benefits are more difficult to establish for rural roads where there may be little information on traffic or where roads previously did not exist. However, the role of rural infrastructure in improving the opportunities of the rural poor can be very important.

Similarly well established methods are available for appraising energy projects, especially where one source of energy is replaced by another such that the economic value is derived from cost saving from energy substitution. However, the energy sector faces similar problems of demand estimation to the water sector in the rural areas and similar methods may be used to value incremental demand.

Both the transport and energy sectors can involve particularly heavy investment costs and as a result they are the most likely sectors to be subjected to more sophisticated approaches to risk management. However, all projects are subject to some degree of risk or uncertainty and so methods are required to assess the potential sources and scale of risk and potential strategies to deal with possible negative outcomes. The analysis of risk is discussed by Weiss and Ward in Chapter 6.

VALUING THE ENVIRONMENT

The same contingent valuation survey approach described above in relation to water can be applied to other 'hard to value' activities, including aspects of the environment, although it is recognised that explaining to respondents the concept of paying for environmental amenities is not always easy and, if it is not fully understood, the utility of this approach is seriously undermined. The application of project analysis techniques to environmental issues has been a major growth area in recent years, principally in terms of how to place monetary values on environmental effects. However, there has also been a discussion of how conventional decision criteria on projects (including the discount rate) need to be modified to address issues of environmental sustainability (see Chapter 8). A majority of applications of environmental valuation have been in the context of developed economies; however, an increasing number of rigorous research-based case studies are now available for developing countries.[18]

All projects have environmental effects of some sort, and where serious damage is anticipated it is now standard to try to internalise this by incorporating mitigatory expenditure into project design. Problems for valuation arise where

- the project goal is to create an environmental benefit – such as restoring wetlands or removing air pollution;
- mitigatory activity can be only incomplete so there will be a residual negative externality;
- there is a risk of unforeseen environmental damage.

In discussions of environmental value it is conventional to distinguish between use and non-use value, since, unlike other goods, effects on environmental goods can have a value that is in addition to any benefit arising from direct use. The environment is valuable to users because it provides a range of services: the supply of natural resources, the assimilation of waste and the supply of aesthetic benefits, such as beautiful views or rare species. In addition, because of uncertainty regarding the future supplies of non-renewable or non-reproducible environmental resources, users may be prepared to pay a premium simply to guarantee that supplies will be available in future. This 'option value' is a form of insurance premium and, since it is related to future use of the environment, it is a form of use value. Option value is an important element in the argument for the preservation of biodiversity.

Non-use value arises because the environment and its resources may be deemed valuable in their own right independently of any use; thus individuals may value environmental resources or natural species (for example, tropical forests or a rare butterfly) not because they will ever use or even see them, but because they are judged to be of intrinsic value in their own terms. The motives here could be a mixture of genuine altruism and a sense of responsibility to future generations, including individuals' own families. This form of value is normally termed 'existence value', with a concern for one's own family in the future termed a 'bequest value'.

Total environmental value for the environment is composed of the sum of use and non-use values. However, not all potential sources of value can simply be summed to give total value, since some sources of value may be incompatible; for example, some direct uses of tropical forests may preclude the protection of rare wildlife and thus reduce existence value. Hence total environmental value must be based on a compatible set of environmental functions.

Chapter 8 by Anand discusses environmental issues in more detail but there are several approaches to environmental valuation. The most common approach in operational project work is to estimate the economic value of environmental use by the tangible goods and services whose availability is affected by a project's environmental impact. Since such goods and services are marketed in one form or another this approach is said to be 'market-based'. It can be related to both output loss through environmental impact or the mitigatory cost involved in negating that impact. The former case requires the establishment of a relationship between a project and certain environmental parameters (such as soil or air quality) and then a second relationship between these parameters and production. This is the 'dose–response' methodology, where an environmental change (a dose) is linked with a change in production (a response).

The most obvious examples of this approach relate to projects which alter the pattern of land use and thus change output; where output change results from the environmental effect of a project the economic value of this output gives the basis for use value. A timber project, for example, will reduce the products that can be obtained from the forest in its natural state. Their value may not always be easy to estimate, partly because some of the products may not be sold in a market, so that proxy values based on marketed alternatives must be used. Similarly, from a different perspective, planting of trees as shelter beds will be expected to raise crop yields, and the value of these crops will provide an estimate of environmental benefit from tree planting. The use of world prices to value internationally tradable outputs will be relevant where the goods concerned can be exported or sold to replace imports.[19]

A form of environmental use value that has received considerable attention in recent years is the carbon store function of tropical forests, since if forests are cleared, this carbon will be released into the atmosphere, contributing to global warming; the damage attributed to global warming in terms of lost output gives a measure of the effect from this form of use value of forests.[20] This benefit is global rather than national, and if the perspective for appraisal is that of a national economy, citizens of the economy in which the forests are located may gain little from this effect.

There will clearly be some environmental use value for which market transactions will not be relevant, since no market exists for the type of effects involved. The approach of 'surrogate markets' involves using data from existing markets as proxies for the relevant environmental values. The key requirement is that the market used must be influenced by environmental effects in a quantifiable way to allow a revealed preference approach to valuation. The two best-known revealed preference approaches to environmental valuation are the 'travel cost' approach and the use of property prices in the so-called 'hedonic price' model.

The idea of the travel cost approach is that individuals and their families incur costs in terms of travel in visiting sites of natural beauty and recreation, such as parks or beaches, and that this cost can be used as a means of eliciting what people are willing to pay for these environmental services, even when no access charges are imposed. Since these costs are actually incurred when visits are made, this is a revealed preference approach. Travel cost defined broadly to include the cost of time can be used to establish a demand curve for visits to a site of natural beauty where travel cost acts as the price to which demand is related.[21]

The thinking behind the hedonic pricing approach is that in some markets environmental factors will influence price, and if their independent influence can be identified, this should give an approximate estimate of willingness to pay for the environmental factor concerned (and hence a proxy for total economic value, not just use value). The approach is used most frequently in relation to property markets, where it is reasonable to assume that air and noise pollution, access to scenic sites and recreational facilities, as well as the location of environmentally hazardous facilities, impact on house prices. Property prices will be influenced by a range of factors: the characteristics of the property itself (such as age, size, number of rooms, aesthetics); the characteristics of the neighbourhood in which it is located (such as crime rate, availability of public transport, access to schools); and environmental factors (like noise and air pollution levels and access to recreation sites). In principle, a well-specified regression analysis can identify the separate impact of environmental measures on property values controlling for everything else.[22] Although a hedonic price approach has been used widely in a developed economy context it is probably only in the higher-income developing economies that property markets will be sufficiently well developed for it to be applied, since where markets are thin there is the risk that prices respond to speculative pressure rather than underlying market conditions. Further, there is the more serious restriction that for many environmental effects implicit markets will not be available. This applies particularly to biological resources relating to rare species and ecosystem diversity. Since markets that relate even indirectly to these natural assets do not exist, implicit markets offer relatively little help in the valuation problem, and a direct stated preference or survey approach will be required.

The valuation approaches discussed so far have the significant limitation that they address only the use value of the environment. If the other components of environmental value – that is, option and existence value – are to be quantified, this can be done only by direct survey techniques that elicit a subjective response to the value placed on the environment. This is the third of the possible approaches and involves contingent valuation studies on environmental effects. All such studies need to avoid sources of bias, but these can be particularly serious where valuation is for intangible environmental benefits. For example, if respondents think their answer has no impact on pricing but they want to obtain or preserve the resource, they may overstate their willingness to pay (strategic bias), whilst respondents may have difficulty distinguishing one part of an environmental resource from the whole, for example protecting one lake from a series of lakes (part–whole bias). Similarly respondents may be uncomfortable with placing a value on something they have never purchased. Hence the way in which the problem is explained to respondents may influence their answers (information bias). A considerable effort has been exerted in the literature to design surveys that minimise these and other sources of bias, but the potential for error must be borne in mind.[23]

Contingent valuation for environmental effects is now a widely accepted procedure in both academic and policy circles. A major step in its acceptance was the work on valuing the impact of the Exxon Valdez oil spill in Alaska in 1989. A special panel of distinguished academics appointed by the US government concluded that contingent valuation studies were sufficiently reliable to be used as evidence in the US judicial process in assessing environmental damage (Arrow et al., 1993). Furthermore there is also evidence of consistency of results over time, with studies showing a reasonably high correlation between willingness to pay estimates for environmental protection at different points in time (Carson et al., 2003). The UK government has also used contingent valuation techniques to aid decision-taking on environmental issues.[24]

Work on valuation of the environment has been given added impetus in recent years by the growing concern over climate change and the potential economic damage caused by alternative scenarios for temperature rise. The Stern Review (Stern, 2007) quantified the damage from various natural events triggered by climate change – such as drought, floods, sea level rise and typhoons – which will either necessitate mitigatory expenditure (valued at its cost) or create damage like loss of crops (valued at their export price) and broader impacts on health and ecosystems. A comparison between projected costs of adaptation and benefits in damage avoided becomes a very aggregate cost–benefit calculation which shows high returns in the very long term, although these results are sensitive to the discount rate chosen.[25]

DISTRIBUTION AND POVERTY OBJECTIVES

The focus of literature in the 1970s in relation to poverty objectives was on the use of distribution weights. Experiments were made with adjusting shadow prices, particularly the shadow wage rate for unskilled labour, using weights that reflected the trade-off between growth and distribution, but as noted above they were not widely adopted in practice. The alternative approach to dealing with distributional issues is to measure the distributive impact of projects. The way to do this was implicit in the 1972 UNIDO Guidelines and demonstrated more clearly in the subsequent Guide (UNIDO, 1978) and a book of case studies (UNIDO, 1980). A more comprehensive theoretical statement of the approach was developed by Londero (1996a). The essence of the approach is to work out not just the value of the economic NPV but also who gets the benefits and who pays the costs. In principle the financial analysis can identify the direct beneficiaries, and any adjustments made to account for externalities or differences between shadow prices and market prices can be attributed to particular stakeholders. For example, tax changes will affect government income and the difference between the shadow price of unskilled labour and the market price can mainly be assumed to be an income gain to workers. With the rapid development of spreadsheet capacity it is no longer a problem to derive an annual statement of the distribution of costs and benefits that matches the annual statement of the economic value of costs and benefits at shadow prices.

With such a distribution analysis the question of what distribution weights to use becomes less of an issue. The important policy issue is who gets the benefits (Potts, 1999). With the advent of the Millennium Development Goals the focus of international agencies on poverty reduction was emphasised. The question then arose as to the specific impact of projects on poverty reduction. The most prominent organisation involved in establishing how to identify the poverty impact of projects has been the Asian Development Bank (Fujimura and Weiss, 2000; ADB, 2001; Weiss, 2004). However, as with shadow pricing, practice falls behind the theory and while we know how to assess poverty impact it is relatively rare that it is actually done in a systematic way. In Chapter 5 Fujimura discusses the issues relating to and lessons learned from the conduct of poverty impact analysis.

It is often argued that an emphasis on social sector projects, particularly health and education, is pro-poor. However, these sectors are rarely subjected to systematic investment analysis and the use of CBA there is relatively rare. The work of Psacharopoulos and associates (Psacharopoulos, 1994; Psacharopoulos and Patrinos, 2002) has been used to argue that returns to education and primary education in particular are both relatively high, and are likely to have a positive impact on distribution. However, the validity of their methods has been criticised, particularly by Bennell (1996b). Educational cost–benefit analysis and the alternative use of cost effectiveness analysis (CEA) are discussed by Potts in Chapter 11.

CBA is even more rarely used in the health sector but in recent years the use of CEA in relation to health outcomes has become increasingly common. This has relevance to poverty reduction since the poor are disproportionately affected by high rates of morbidity and premature mortality. It can therefore be used to establish the potential impact on poverty reduction objectives (Weiss, 2003). The methods available for use in appraising the effectiveness of health sector projects and programmes are discussed by Weiss in Chapter 10.

The association of pro-poor projects with activities in the social sectors has been accompanied by a relative decline in the attention paid to agriculture. This may seem surprising given the prominence of agricultural and agro-industrial projects in the early literature on CBA in developing countries. A classic text developed originally in 1972 and subsequently extended in a second edition (1982) was Gittinger's *The Economic Analysis of Agricultural Projects*. Given the importance of agriculture as a source of livelihood for the majority of the world's poor it was not surprising that a significant proportion of World Bank funding in the 1970s and early 1980s should have been concentrated on the agricultural sector. The ideological shift in the donor countries in the 1980s that influenced subsequent structural adjustment policies regarded agriculture as a commercial activity that belonged in the private sector. As a result, donor funding of agricultural interventions declined. At the same time, donor funding also shifted towards sector programmes and budget support and away from projects. These two factors led to a relative neglect of both cost–benefit analysis (as a project related tool) and of the agricultural sector. For a long time development policies that proclaimed the importance of poverty reduction paid little attention to the sector from which, even in a rapidly urbanising world, the majority of poor people obtain an income.

While the general features of the technical approach to the economic appraisal of agricultural projects have not changed significantly since Gittinger's books were published, there have been changes in emphasis and in the issues addressed, and a substantial change in the capacity of spreadsheets and related software to deal with the complexities of the sector. The changes in emphasis and issues include greater attention to environmental sustainability, greater gender awareness and recognition of the importance of understanding rural livelihoods.[26] Particular features of the livelihoods approach include the attention paid to the different forms of capital employed by rural households and the diverse strategies used to sustain them. A further change in emphasis has been the almost universal withdrawal of the state from directly productive agricultural activities. As a result the economic analysis of agricultural projects is now largely confined to enabling projects oriented to small farmers and commercial projects funded by development banks, often with an outgrower component. Paradoxically, despite the decline in attention paid to the sector, the expansion of software capacity has made the analysis of diverse production systems and related issues of risk and the distribution of benefits much more feasible.

There are some signs that the tide is turning, both in relation to the use of cost–benefit analysis and in the attention paid to agriculture. The World Development Report for 2008 (World Bank, 2007) was titled *Agriculture for Development*, and this has been accompanied with an increase in funding to support the sector. A recent review of the use of CBA at the World Bank (World Bank, 2010) found that the proportion of World Bank projects for which CBA was undertaken had fallen from 70 per cent in the 1970s to 25 per cent in the early 2000s. About half of this decline was due to the shift in lending towards those sectors for which CBA is not usually undertaken. However, there was also a general decline in the use of CBA despite the observation that performance improvements were most evident in those sectors that do use CBA. It is, however, clear from the importance attached to the document that the World Bank is committed to the continued use of CBA in the sectors for which it is feasible and also to ensuring improvement in the practice of conducting such analysis.

CONCLUSIONS

Project CBA provides a framework that allows costs and benefits to be assessed consistently both for an individual project and across projects. As such, its validity depends upon how accurately costs and benefits can be identified and valued. The test for its usefulness is not comparison with an abstract classroom case study that assumes away information difficulties but with alternative ways of decision making under the uncertainty that prevails in the real world. In their different ways the chapters in this volume make the case that practical application of CBA offers an important aid to decision making that is superior to hunches, simple rules of thumb or multi-criteria approaches that list different project effects without converting these to monetary equivalents.[27]

Project CBA in the development context was developed initially as an aid to planning the participation of countries in international trade by stripping away the impact of a system of trade controls. Since traded outputs are valued at world prices (not at the world price plus the relevant import tariff) and the domestic resources needed to produce them are valued at their opportunity cost, CBA provides a means of making operational planning along the lines of comparative advantage. Activities with low opportunity costs relative to world prices – for example due to a labour surplus or abundant natural resources – appear attractive in cost–benefit terms. The removal of the majority of trade barriers in much of the developing world over the last two decades has lowered the divergence between domestic and world prices and made this aspect of CBA less critical, since in such liberalising countries trade protection now has a much weaker impact on financial profitability. However, the continued existence of unemployment and some taxes on trade in both developed and developing countries means that these issues cannot be entirely ignored.

Meanwhile other developments have increased the relevance of CBA. First, the poverty focus of aid initiatives over the last decade has brought the question of the poverty impact of projects to the centre of attention. It is not straightforward to trace who gains and who loses from a project and in practice it is typically only first round effects that can be estimated. However, project CBA provides a clear framework for undertaking this exercise. Knowing how a project is likely to affect the poor has become a critical question for many donors and even approximate estimates are welcome.

Second, developments in survey methodology now allow a much more sophisticated approach to estimate the value consumers place on a range of project outputs, some of which may not be sold in a market. The contingent valuation approach is being applied in a range of sectors and offers a practical solution to the problem of estimating willingness to pay. Again there are qualifications regarding the quality of survey design, the difficulty of transferring results from one location or context to another and the need to avoid various forms of bias. However, the increased application of such surveys has made possible practical valuation in what used to be thought of as intrinsically 'hard to value' activities, and in doing so has given a major boost to the use of CBA.

Finally, textbook discussions have always highlighted environmental effects as a classic form of externality overlooked in the financial analysis of a project. The debate on climate change and the environmental impact of new projects has underlined the need to include such externalities in project calculations and the very extensive and rapidly growing literature on environmental economics has provided the means of quantifying and valuing environmental effects. A full assessment of environmental policy requires much more than project-by-project calculations, but a useful starting point is a discussion of how far individual projects create effects, how far these effects are internalised by mitigatory expenditure undertaken by the projects themselves and how far they remain as externalities. The toolkit of project economists has been expanded significantly by drawing on development in the environmental economics literature (see Pearce et al., 2006).

In short, this volume argues that project CBA remains both valid and relevant for development many years after it was first recommended to developing countries. Priorities and challenges may look different today from fifty years ago, but a cost versus benefit comparison is central to any rational form of decision taking, and the CBA literature, with the modifications discussed in this volume, offers a practical and relevant framework to guide decisions on resource allocation.

NOTES

1. The 1936 Flood Control Act in the US mandated agencies working in the sector to justify investments on the grounds that benefits exceeded cost, where it was clear that as water was a largely non-marketed item financial analysis would not reveal the true picture (Marglin, 1967: 16–17).
2. Strictly, in the context of a price reduction, this should be based on compensating variation – the amount of money the consumer can receive and still be as well off as before the price reduction – rather than on the area under the demand curve.
3. The link between world prices and consumption benefits through a shadow exchange rate (SER) is made clear in UNIDO (1972, Chapter 16).
4. Harberger (1973) has a collection of these key papers.
5. The issues relating to estimation of the social time preference rate are discussed by Kula in Chapter 7.
6. The proposition that world (producer) prices provided the basis for social value was analysed in depth in Diamond and Mirrlees (1971) and found to hold under a range of scenarios.
7. Little and Mirrlees (1974) suggested that this could be done though an average conversion factor for consumption, although in principle this aggregate measure could be replaced by specific conversion factors for consumer groups. Ray (1984: 55–7) shows how willingness to pay figures in the Little–Mirrlees system.
8. Merit wants do not figure in Squire and van der Tak (1975), and after being raised in Marglin (1967) and UNIDO (1972) their inclusion was not pursued by others.
9. See for example ADB (1997).
10. This issue is discussed by Fujimura in Chapter 5.
11. Although the financial income flows can be adjusted to world prices this is an extra step which is often not well understood.
12. For a range of views on this issue see Markandya and Pearce (1988), Birdsall and Steer (1993), Cline (1993), Potts (1994), Livingstone and Tribe (1995), Price (1996a and 1996b).
13. For example both the editors of this book have been involved in studies to estimate national parameters for Ethiopia but the length of time between the first study and the second (about ten years) meant that, while some aspects of the methodology of the original study were relevant to the more recent study, the differences between the new estimates and the original values were often substantial.
14. See for example Belli et al. (2001: Chapter 5), Curry and Weiss (2000: 326–30), Potts (2002: 354–5), Campbell and Brown (2003: 13–14).
15. For example Del Bo et al. (2009, 2011) have made estimates for shadow wage rates in a number of European countries and regions. Kirkpatrick and MacArthur (1990) investigated the potential use of shadow wage rates in Northern Ireland and similar work has been done by Honohan (1998) in relation to the Republic of Ireland. Potts (2008) has argued that shadow wage rates could be used for appraisal and evaluation of regeneration projects in the UK. Swales (1997) and Wren (2005) have also argued for the use of shadow wage rates in the UK.

16. Whittington et al. (1991) is one of the path-breaking studies of contingent valuation in the water sector.
17. The discussion here follows Choynowski (2002) who illustrates the approach in relation to power.
18. For example Pearce et al. (2002) brought together 19 case studies mostly using a form of contingent valuation.
19. Dixon et al. (1994) has examples of this change in productivity approach.
20. Brown and Pearce (1994) was an early example of this estimation of the use value of forests based on the carbon store function.
21. For example, Day (2002) uses a travel cost approach to value game parks in South Africa.
22. A classic example of the hedonic approach is a study on house prices in Los Angeles by Brookshire et al. (1982) which estimated the impact of air quality on property values.
23. Pearce et al. (2006, Chapter 8) highlight the key issues.
24. The UK Department of the Environment and Transport commissioned a major survey to establish how much people both close to and distant from quarries would be willing to pay in higher taxes to see a quarry shut and the quarry site restored to its natural condition (HM Treasury, 2003).
25. The Stern Review used the PAGE2002 model developed at the University of Cambridge. A more recent rerun of this model showed the global costs of adaptation expenditure (for example construction of seawalls and development of drought-resistant crops) outweighing benefits until 2050, but with benefits significantly outweighing costs beyond that date (ADB, 2009: 90).
26. See for example Chambers and Conway (1992), Ellis (2000) and Scoones (2009).
27. For a brief discussion of multi-criteria approaches see Potts (2002, Chapter 13). For a more extended discussion see van Pelt (1994).

2. Estimating a shadow exchange rate

Elio Londero[1]

INTRODUCTION

This chapter largely avoids theoretical discussion, with formulae presented rather than derived formally. References to the literature where such demonstrations may be consulted are provided throughout. While the most important theoretical considerations are mentioned, emphasis is placed on the issues faced by practitioners when trying to estimate a shadow price of foreign exchange. However, the reader should keep in mind that estimating a shadow price or performing a cost–benefit analysis is an art, the exercise of which requires understanding the principles and assumptions underlying the formulae, procedures and shortcuts used. It is that understanding that allows the applied economist to correctly develop or adapt formulae and recommendations to the particular situations faced in practice.

PRINCIPLES AND OPERATIONAL FORMULAE

In applied work, the formulae and estimation procedures used are based on a partial equilibrium approach.[2] Under such approximation, the shadow price of foreign exchange (SPFE), like any other shadow price, is defined as the change in total economic welfare attributable to a unit change, in this case in the demand or supply of foreign exchange. A change in total economic welfare is conceived as the interpersonal aggregation of individual economic welfare changes. The criterion generally used to obtain an economic measure of a welfare change at the individual level is the compensating variation (Hicks, 1939a, 1939b, 1975; Mishan, 1981; Londero, 1996a, 2003a). It consists of comparing the situation resulting from the action being analysed (the with-project situation) with the situation that would exist if such an action would not be carried out (the without-project situation) in order to formulate the following question: what is the change in the monetary income of the affected person that is required for him/her to consider that he/she is enjoying the same welfare that would have been enjoyed if such an action would not have been carried out? Such an amount is, for that person, the compensating variation of the action being analysed, and it is used as a monetary measure of the individual's welfare change.

For example, if access to a park would increase Lucy's welfare, her compensating variation (CV) of free access to the park would be the reduction in her monetary income in the with-access situation that would be required to bring her to the welfare level she would have enjoyed without free access to the park. Such a reduction in her income would be the money-measure of her welfare change attributable to gaining access to the park. If the action consists of increasing the individual's monetary income, the measurement problem is a simple one: if the person receives a $100 transfer, the corresponding CV is obviously $100. When the action consists of changes in the demand for or supply of consumption goods, the measurement criterion uses the theoretical framework known as the 'theory of consumer behaviour'. Within this framework it is possible to demonstrate that the CV may be quantified with reasonable approximation using the individual's preferences as revealed by his/her demand function for the good in question.[3] In practice, estimates are based on changes in consumers' and producers' surpluses, which are considered good approximations to CVs for small price changes (Willig, 1976). In the case of changes in the demand or supply of intermediate goods, the measurement criterion relies on the ability of markets to reflect, through the demand for inputs, consumers' valuation of their consumption changes attributable to marginal changes in the use of those inputs. If goods are not traded in conventional markets (as in the case of pollution), measuring CVs is more difficult due to the absence of market data that would allow a direct measurement.[4]

From all of the above, the shadow price of foreign exchange is the interpersonal aggregation of the compensating variations attributable to a unit change in the demand or supply of foreign exchange. It may be expressed as:

$$SPFE = \frac{\sum_i u^i CV^i(\Delta f)}{\Delta f} \tag{2.1}$$

where u^i is individual i's welfare weight as derived from the social welfare function (Londero, 2003a), and $CV^i(\Delta f)$ is his/her compensating variation as a function of the change in the demand or supply of foreign exchange Δf generated by a project.[5] These compensating variations are measured in the markets affected by the additional demand or supply of foreign exchange, which are primarily those for marginally imported and exported goods. It is a comparative-static measure derived from comparing two

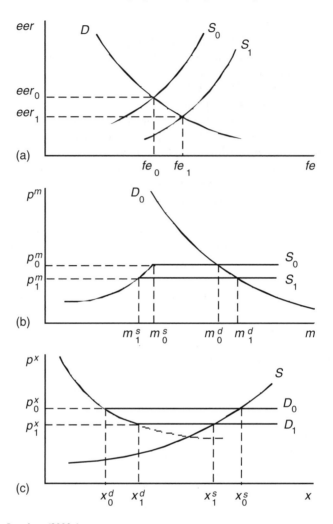

Source: Londero (2003a).

Figure 2.1   An increase in the supply of foreign exchange

long-run equilibrium positions, those without and with the additional
demand or supply resulting from the project concerned. Figure 2.1a
exemplifies this with an increase in the demand for foreign exchange. The
direct effect of the project's additional demand for foreign exchange is
to increase the equilibrium exchange rate (*eer*), and thus to generate two
main types of second round effect:

1. Increases in the domestic prices of marginally imported goods, thus reducing their domestic consumption (intermediate and final) and increasing their domestic production (Figure 2.1b).
2. Increases in the domestic prices of marginally exported goods, thus reducing their domestic consumption (final and intermediate) and increasing their production (Figure 2.1c).

The compensating variations attributable to changes in the consumption and production of traded goods are those included in expression (2.1). This theoretical expression is difficult to estimate, so in practice the SPFE is estimated, at least initially, in a partial equilibrium framework, assuming that changes in consumers' and producers' surpluses are good estimates of the individual's economic welfare changes, and further assuming that:

1. In the long run, adjustment to an additional demand for foreign exchange takes place through changes in imports and exports induced by changes in the real exchange rate.
2. If incentives or disincentives to import or export other than *ad valorem* taxes exist (for example due to quotas or other controls), they can be quantified as an equivalent *ad valorem* tax or subsidy.
3. The domestic prices of domestically produced but marginally traded goods adequately reflect their corresponding marginal costs at efficiency prices.
4. Domestic prices of imports at the custom gate, or custom-gate prices, equal CIF prices plus import taxes (so there are no port services costs or indirect taxes on traded goods).

Assumptions 2, 3 and 4 will be lifted later in the chapter, but are retained for the moment as they underlie many presentations on and practical estimates of the SPFE.

To simplify our presentation we use the distributional value judgement of so-called 'efficiency analysis'; that is, unit income changes to different individuals are equally valuable in the welfare function regardless of their income level.[6] The combination of the simplifying assumptions 1 to 4 and the efficiency value judgement results in equation (2.2):

$$SPFE = \frac{eer\left[\sum_i p_i^m \Delta m_i(1 + t_i^m) + \sum_j p_j^x \Delta x_j(1 - t_j^x)\right]}{\sum_i p_i^m \Delta m_i + \sum_j p_j^x \Delta x_j} \tag{2.2}$$

where *eer* is the nominal equilibrium exchange rate; p_i^m and p_j^x are, respectively, the CIF and FOB prices of imports and exports in foreign currency;

Δm_i and Δx_j are the quantity changes in the imports of i and exports of j attributable to a given change in the demand for foreign exchange, and t_i^m and t_j^x are the *ad valorem* equivalent rates for tax (e.g. tariffs) and non-tax trade interventions (e.g. import or export quotas, import deposits), while import and export subsidies (e.g. subsidised export credit) are treated as negative taxes. The denominator is equal to the change in the supply or demand of foreign exchange Δf, and shows that under long-run equilibrium conditions, the whole change in the demand (supply) of foreign exchange is used to finance changes in exports and imports.[7]

Changes in imports Δm_i and exports Δx_j are due to changes in both their domestic consumption ($m_1^d - m_0^d$ and $x_1^d - x_0^d$ in Figure 2.1) and their domestic production ($m_0^s - m_1^s$ and $x_0^s - x_1^s$ in Figure 2.1). The former would be valued at the welfare cost (benefit) of reducing (increasing) consumption, while the latter would be valued at the welfare cost (benefit) of increasing (reducing) production. Given the assumption that producer's prices[8] equal long-run marginal costs at efficiency prices (assumption 3), and the distributional value judgement allowing the CVs of different individuals to be simply summed without any welfare weighting, both costs (benefits) may be valued at the custom-gate prices of i and j; that is, including *all tax payments* required to take the products out of customs, and implicitly assuming that there are no port or customs real incremental costs attributable to the additional imports or exports (assumption 4). Equation (2.2) presents the efficiency price of foreign exchange in units of domestic currency per unit of foreign currency. In practice, however, it is customary to work with the ratio of the efficiency price to the prevailing exchange rate at the time of the transactions (*per*), which is the rate used to value project transactions. For the time being, we assume that the *per* is the same for all traded goods. We call that ratio the accounting price ratio of foreign exchange or the shadow exchange rate (SER), at efficiency prices:

$$SER = \frac{eer\left[\sum_i p_i^m \Delta m_i (1 + t_i^m) + \sum_j p_j^x \Delta x_j (1 - t_j^x)\right]}{per\left(\sum_i p_i^m \Delta m_i + \sum_j p_j^x \Delta x_j\right)} \qquad (2.3)$$

Equation (2.3) is often expressed by dividing the numerator and the denominator by the change in the demand for foreign exchange (Δf), where:

$$\Delta f = \sum_i p_i^m \Delta m_i + \sum_j p_j^x \Delta x_j \qquad (2.4)$$

thus obtaining:

$$SER = (eer/per)\left[\sum_i \alpha_i(1 + t_i^m) + \sum_j \beta_j(1 - t_j^x)\right] \qquad (2.5)$$

where α_i and β_j are, respectively, the changes in the value of imports and exports attributable to the additional demand for (supply of) foreign exchange, per unit of additional demand for (supply of) foreign exchange.[9] Under long-run equilibrium assumptions, the change in the demand for or supply of foreign exchange is used entirely to finance changes in imports and exports of goods and services (Figure 2.1). Equation (2.5) may also be presented using the price elasticity of imports and exports, η_i and ε_j, as:

$$SER = \frac{eer\left[\sum_i M_i^w \eta_i(1 + t_i^m) + \sum_j X_j^w \varepsilon_j(1 - t_j^x)\right]}{per\left(\sum_i M_i^w \eta_i + \sum_j X_j^w \varepsilon_j\right)} \qquad (2.6)$$

where M_i^w and X_j^w are the foreign currency values of imports and exports.

Equations (2.3), (2.5) and (2.6) correspond to the traditional formulae for the efficiency SER as presented by, *inter alia*, Harberger (1965, 1977). They differ only in that they take into account possible differences between the equilibrium and the prevailing exchange rates (Londero, 1996a, 2003a), an important aspect of applied work.

These expressions for the SER are conceptual and help clarify the issues involved in practical measurement. In practice, import and export price responses at the product level, be they in the form of partial derivatives or elasticities, are normally not available, forcing the analyst to estimate the SER as if all relevant elasticities were equal.[10] In this case, equation (2.6) simplifies to:

$$SER = \frac{eer(M + T^m + X - T^x)}{per(M + X)} \qquad (2.7)$$

where M and X respectively denote the domestic currency values of imports and exports of price-elastic goods and services valued at the *per*, and T^m and T^x are the associated total import and export taxes, including the *ad valorem* equivalent of non-tax trade interventions. Intuitively, if a US$100 additional supply of foreign exchange valued at the prevailing exchange rate of $10 per US dollar makes possible $1500 worth of additional domestic consumption valued custom-gate at the equilibrium exchange rate, then the *efficiency* price of foreign exchange would be $15 and the SER (at efficiency prices) would be 1.5.

This last formula provides a good insight into the main estimates required for an approximation to the efficiency SER: the equilibrium exchange rate and the *ad valorem* equivalents of trade interventions. Later we discuss other additional adjustments that may be necessary under some circumstances.

THE EQUILIBRIUM EXCHANGE RATE

The preceding discussion refers to the long-run equilibrium exchange rate *eer*; this is the nominal exchange rate resulting from achieving balance in both internal and external markets for *given* values of other fundamental variables, such as protection level, tax rates, labour laws, technology level and government spending, on which such an equilibrium position depends. Using long-run equilibrium prices is not the only possible approach, and this section briefly considers the alternative of using prevailing prices. We then discuss practical aspects of incorporating long-run equilibrium considerations in an approximate way.

A cost–benefit calculation is a comparative-static analysis aimed at assessing whether a project (or other action) represents a 'total economic welfare improvement'. To that effect, and from a rigorous point of view, the flows corresponding to two equilibrium situations, those with and without the project, are compared period by period over the life of the project. If the set of relative prices used to value project flows could be considered to reflect feasible long-run market equilibria, the comparison is not problematic since relative prices used correspond to an equilibrium situation in each year and the SER would need no *eer/per* correction.

But, what if that is not the case? An argument could be made for valuing flows at their prevailing market prices in each period and adjusting them to short-run shadow prices (reflecting the sum of compensating variations resulting from the existing situation in each period), rather than using expected long-run equilibrium prices. Such an approach involves the use of changing shadow price ratios each period and would require a simulation on how prices would evolve period by period as they move towards a long-run equilibrium. This would not only be extremely difficult to implement, but would also make the result dependent upon the starting moment for the project, which is normally unknown.

Alternatively, 'with' and 'without' comparisons could be made under long-run equilibrium conditions and project flows priced accordingly, making the results more independent of the date for starting the project. If necessary, separate consideration could be made for temporary situations affecting prices, such as short-run unemployment or international prices significantly different from their long-run values, but both results should be reported and the limitations of the short-run calculation spelled out. The approach implicitly followed in practice is long-run pricing, since constant relative market prices are normally used for preparing project flows at market prices, and constant shadow price ratios are applied to those market prices to determine economic welfare changes. The numerator of equation (2.2) for the SPFE is therefore based on projected long-run equilibrium values for all variables.

If the exchange rate is not a long-run equilibrium one, corrections normally rely on estimating a long-run equilibrium real exchange rate (*erer*). Given a long-run equilibrium level of world prices for traded goods, the *erer* may be expressed as:

$$erer = eer/P^{n*}$$

where *eer* is the nominal long-run equilibrium exchange rate, and P^{n*} is the long-run equilibrium price index for non-traded goods, all for given values of the other fundamental variables. It is implicit in this formulation that the *eer* has been calculated for the long-run equilibrium price index for traded goods P^{w*}, since the exchange rate is a function of world prices. A different measure of the same concept is often presented as the so-called relative price of tradables to non-tradables:

$$erer = eer P^{W*}/P^{n*} \tag{2.8}$$

This is the expression often estimated to assess the level of exchange rate misalignment.[11]

Once an estimation of the *erer* is available, we need to work our way backwards to the *eer*. If prices for traded goods are the long-run equilibrium ones, for prevailing prices equal to P^n all adjustment to restore relative price equilibrium between traded and non-traded goods would have to come from the *per* moving to an *eer*, thus bringing the prevailing real exchange rate (*prer*) to its long-run equilibrium level, the *erer*. In other words, if the *erer* is 20 per cent higher than the *prer*, the *eer* that would restore relative price equilibrium would be 20 per cent higher than the *per*. By so doing in equation (2.7), we are saying that after adjustment has been completed, the exchange rate will have increased 20 per cent with respect to domestic prices. In practice, that may happen by an increase in the nominal exchange rate higher than the increase in the prices of non-traded goods.

The situation is different if prices P^w are not long-run equilibrium ones. Under the small open economy assumption P^w is exogenous, but not necessarily always in equilibrium. For example, if the price of the main export, say good *a*, is temporarily very high, the domestic currency may appreciate. Ignoring the complexity of general equilibrium interactions, and for given prices of non-traded goods, the brunt of the adjustment to the *erer* would take place by a reduction in the world price of *a* and an increase in the nominal exchange rate relative to the domestic prices of non-traded goods. If this simplification is deemed acceptable, then the SER formula could be corrected by reducing the value of *a* exports in the numerator of expression (2.7), adjusting export taxes accordingly, and letting the remainder of the adjustment fall on the nominal exchange rate. Therefore, expression (2.7) would become:

$$SER = \frac{per(1 + \varphi_e)[M + T^m + (X - X_a) - (T^x - T_a^x) + (1 + \varphi_a)(X_a - T_a^x)]}{per(M + X)}$$

$$(2.9)$$

where φ_e is the expected rate of change in the *per* for a given P^n, φ_a is the expected rate of change in the price of *a*, both necessary to return to long-run equilibrium, X_a is the domestic value of *a*'s exports, and T_a^x is the domestic value of export taxes originating in *a*'s exports. In this case φ_e and φ_a carry opposite signs.

In practice, the real depreciation may change the composition of the traded goods basket due to different price elasticities and foreign exchange shares in marginal costs. For example, a real depreciation resulting from the reduction in the price of *a* may reduce *a* export volumes, increase export volumes of the other exported goods, and reduce import volumes. Such level of precision in estimation, however, is normally not possible, and the implicit assumption is that volumes do not change when relative world prices and the *rer* adjust to long-run levels. If the data is available, a better approach could be to calculate the SER for a recent year when relative prices were a better approximation to those expected to prevail in the long run. It is important to discuss these alternatives at the outset in order to minimise delays and estimation costs. The derivations of equations (2.3), (2.5) and (2.6) assume a flexible exchange rate. If the nominal exchange rate were fixed, say at κ, the correct formula would be $erer = \kappa \, P^{w*}/P^{n*}$. In this case, discrepancies between the prevailing and the equilibrium real exchange rates would require changes in the domestic prices of non-traded goods in order to restore equilibrium, since the nominal exchange rate is fixed and international prices are assumed to be independent of the country's situation (under the 'small open economy' assumption). These domestic price changes may conceivably originate in changes in relative productivity or in nominal wages, but in practice it is likely that nominal wages will carry the brunt of the adjustment.[12]

Developing countries are particularly exposed to significant exchange rate misalignment for various reasons. A common one is the application of unsustainable expansionary fiscal policies that lead to increases in the prices of non-traded goods relative to those of traded goods.

Another frequent origin of overvaluations is a commodity boom (e.g. oil, metals) in natural resource-rich countries often magnified by expansionary policies, rather than policies aimed at smoothing the cycle by saving to later finance compensatory policies when commodity prices decline. Finally, real appreciations often follow trade liberalisations when governments avoid the real depreciation normally associated with liberalisation by increased foreign borrowing, thus leading to over-indebtedness and the intergenerational transfers of costs.[13]

The importance of correcting for exchange rate misalignment is clear, as are the difficulties in obtaining good quantitative estimates of the degree of misalignment. The problems include controversies over how to measure the long-run equilibrium exchange rate *eer*, the complexity of modelling the economy in order to obtain a formula to estimate it, and the selection of the econometric approach to use.[14] However, reasonable estimates would be significantly better than ignoring the problem.

The difficulties in assessing the existence of exchange rate misalignment are not all purely technical. Governments would not want to recognise, much less implicitly declare, that the domestic currency is overvalued. The reasons go from propagandistic to the risks of implicitly announcing a forthcoming real depreciation, the need for which could be accelerated by the ensuing capital outflows looking to realise short-term profit. Moreover, by acknowledging an overvaluation financed by borrowing, the government would be acknowledging the transferring of costs to future generations. These problems may be even more difficult to overcome by analysts than purely technical ones. A case can be made for government planning agencies providing estimates of the SER that include the effects of exchange rate misalignment, but without disclosing the composition of the difference between the prevailing exchange rate and its shadow price.

Finally, if the exchange rate is misaligned, it is not just the relative prices of traded to non-traded goods that are affected, but the relative prices between non-traded goods as well, due to their different foreign exchange contents. These latter intra-non-traded effects are smaller than the traded–non-traded ones and are normally ignored. However, where they are significant and shadow prices for non-traded goods derived from input–output data are available, an approximate correction could be obtained using input–output techniques.[15]

WHAT GOODS AND SERVICES SHOULD BE INCLUDED?

The formulae presented for the SER estimate the welfare effects of *changes* in imports and exports of goods and services attributable to changes in the supply of or demand for foreign exchange. Coefficients α_i and β_j in equation (2.5) or price elasticities η_i and ε_j in equation (2.6) are based on partial derivatives of the type $(\partial m_i/\partial eer)(\partial eer/\partial f)$, implicitly assuming that markets govern all export and import changes. However, not all exported and imported goods may be allocated through market mechanisms.

The simple rule is to include in the calculation of equation (2.7) only goods and services whose imports or exports change when there is an additional demand or supply of foreign exchange. For example, it may be that only part of the additional foreign exchange is (and is expected to continue to be) allocated through the foreign exchange market, while the remaining part is (and is expected to continue to be) allocated using non-market rules ('as the emperor pleases'). In such a case, the calculation of the SER would include in the numerator the sum of the CVs attributable to changes in exports and imports originating in both allocation rules, market and arbitrary. This is simply a consistent application of 'second-best' principles, in which shadow prices reflect welfare impacts under the conditions expected to prevail in the future (so the emperor is expected to stay) rather than desired or optimal ones (Sen, 1972). We will now discuss two examples aimed at explaining the reasoning involved in analysing specific cases.

Import Quotas

Allocations based on the vagaries of an emperor may be an extreme situation, but there are other non-market-based allocations for foreign exchange, such as import quotas. They are often found in practice and present specific aspects that the analyst must take into account. As explained above, only quotas expected to change with changes in the demand for or supply of foreign exchange are to be included in the calculation, therefore we will concentrate on those. First, quotas may be temporary to compensate for a short-term disequilibrium, or may be of a more permanent nature, comparable to import taxes; in other words, quotas may or may not be part of the country's long-run commercial policy. This distinction is important when using the long-run approach to shadow prices, in which the numerator of the SER (or of any shadow price ratio) refers to the long-run shadow price and the denominator to the prevailing price. If the quantitative import restrictions are of a temporary nature, which is the most likely situation, the effects of removing them should be included in the *eer*. While the temporary restrictions are in place, the *eer/per* ratio will be higher, *ceteris paribus*, since the *per* will increase with their elimination. If, instead, those restrictions were considered a permanent part of commercial policy, then the *eer* corresponding to the 'with quotas' situation should be used and *ad valorem* equivalents to the quantitative restrictions need to be estimated and included in the numerator of the SER.[16]

Consider first the case of temporary quantitative restrictions. If the project were to import the good directly, project financial flows would record purchases at the *per*. Therefore, the project analyst could ignore the existence of a quantitative restriction as long as the SER included the corresponding effects through the *eer/per*. Domestic market purchases of goods subject to temporary quotas, instead, would be valued at market prices that include the rent of the quota in the distribution margins. In these cases the SER would continue to be based on the *eer* and normal tariffs, but it would be necessary to have special shadow price ratios for the distribution margins where rents from the temporary quotas are included, resulting in lower shadow price ratios for these distribution margins. In other words, imports would be decomposed into CIF value, tariffs, normal domestic distribution costs and rent from the quota, pricing foreign exchange at the above-described SER, pricing taxes and rents at zero, and normal domestic distribution margins at their shadow price ratios. This approach will result in a lower shadow value of the domestic distribution margin due to the omission of its rent (transfer) content. These principles are important to understand, but there will be cases in which the preceding approach is not practical, thus resulting in overvalued efficiency prices of imported goods subject to temporary quotas (since rents implicitly are treated as costs).[17]

When quantitative restrictions are permanent (as permanent as tariff levels), it is the *eer* resulting from the existence of these restrictions that should be used, since they are expected to remain in place for the analysis period. Thus, the *ad valorem* equivalent of the rents derived from those restrictions should be incorporated into the numerator of the SER in addition to import taxes paid; this applies, of course, only for goods whose imports or exports change with changes in the demand for or supply of foreign exchange. As a result, the *eer* would be lower than if quotas were temporary, but the numerator of equations (2.5), (2.6) or (2.7) would be higher since it would incorporate the *ad valorem* equivalent of the quantitative restrictions. As in the case of temporary quotas, this SER would allow for the proper pricing of traded goods imported or exported directly by the project. However, it would be more difficult to calculate the shadow value of the imported goods purchased wholesale if domestic margins cannot be decomposed and priced properly, since these margins will include the share of the quota rent captured by domestic intermediaries.

Three main questions need to be answered before estimating the *ad valorem* equivalents of quotas:

- Is the quota binding?
- Would the quota be changed in response to the additional availability of foreign exchange and by how much?
- How is the quota allocated, and consequently who appropriates the rents generated by it?

The first question is to eliminate non-binding quotas, since general import rules would govern prices and quantities of those goods. The first part of the second question determines whether the goods subject to the import quota enter into the formula for the SER, since a binding quota that is not affected by changes in the demand for or supply of foreign exchange would not affect prices or quantities consumed of the corresponding imported good.[18] How the quota is affected determines the weights that goods subject to import quotas would have in the formula for the SER (the Δm_i); the more the quota is increased (reduced) the higher (lower) the Δm_i would be, and thus the higher the weight in the overall calculation. The third question determines the approach to measuring the *ad valorem* equivalent of the quota and the distributional effects associated with it. For example, if the government auctions the import quota, the *ad valorem* equivalent to the auction price may be used as an approximation to calculating the difference between border and domestic prices. If, on the other hand, quotas are allocated on an ad hoc basis, estimating the *ad valorem* equivalent will be considerably more difficult since it will require specific studies to estimate the composition of market prices for these traded goods starting from market data, instead of the more simple approach of starting from trade data and adding estimates of the effects of trade intervention.

A final consideration to keep in mind when analysing quantitative restrictions is that the same good may have two market prices. One would be the price for those that import the good directly, authorised under the quota system, who may pay just the border price plus normal taxes; the other would be the market price for the remaining users who have to purchase from the direct importers, since that market price would include the rent created by the quota.

By-products of Non-traded Outputs

Some exports and imports may not be price elastic, and therefore would have to be excluded from the calculation. Consider for example the case of an exported good that is the by-product of a non-traded principal good[19] when the by-product is not consumed or processed domestically (all the by-product output is exported). Changes in the output of the by-product are determined exclusively by the production levels of the non-traded principal, which is not affected by changes in the *eer*;[20] formally, $(\partial x_i/\partial eer)$ $(\partial eer/\partial f) = 0$. The implication is that the export values and the corresponding trade taxes of these by-products have to be removed from the calculation of the SER. If, instead, the by-product is also sold domestically, changes in the *eer* will change export prices in domestic currency received by the producer and thus domestic prices, affecting domestic consumption and exports.

Removing by-products, however, should not be automatic, but rather the result of analysis. Take for example the case of an oil refinery that exports by-products of gasoline, whose production level is determined by domestic demand. If oil is non-traded at the margin, an increase in the *eer* may not affect gasoline production, and exports of the by-product will only be affected (increased) if there is domestic consumption and prices increase due to the increase in the *eer* (otherwise the producer would be engaging in price discrimination). If there is no domestic consumption, the by-product should be removed from the SER calculation. If, instead, oil is imported at the margin, and gasoline prices are determined by the *marginal* cost of oil, an increase in the *eer* will increase the price of gasoline and therefore reduce gasoline production, *reducing* the supply and exports of the by-products. Here, paradoxically, the by-product is an exported good, the exports of which decrease when the *eer* increases. It should be included in the SER calculation, but with the sign changed. Finally, if oil is exported at the margin but gasoline is non-traded, an increase in the *eer* may increase oil exports but will only affect exports of the gasoline by-product if higher oil export prices are transferred to gasoline prices, thus affecting domestic gasoline production.

TAX AND NON-TAX INTERVENTIONS

Some taxes on trade may be more difficult to identify, and the corresponding data harder to find, than other taxes. While traditional tariffs are normally recorded by customs and reported to government, other trade taxes charged on specific goods, resulting from special legislation or earmarking, may not be included with tariff collection and recorded in the trade data tapes used to calculate SERs. In order to identify all taxes, there may be a need to interview importers and exporters to find out all the financial costs that make up the difference between CIF or FOB and custom-gate prices.

One common non-tax intervention on the export side is a subsidised export credit programme. This incentive increases the factory gate price of exports and it is often estimated by the difference between the present value of the loan at the market interest rate and its present value at the subsidised interest rate, expressed as a proportion of the FOB value.[21]

Similarly, import deposits increase the custom-gate price of the marginally imported good, thus providing incentives to increase domestic production. The *ad valorem* equivalent to this financial cost may be estimated by the difference between the present value of investing the deposit at the market interest rate and the present value of holding the import deposit, all expressed as a proportion of the CIF value.[22]

Several other non-tax interventions may affect the domestic prices of traded goods, and consequently the SER. The creativity in designing non-tax interventions in foreign trade is significant, requiring an equivalent ingenuity on the side of analysts to identify these and estimate their corresponding *ad valorem* equivalents. Interviewing importers and exporters would also help identify most non-tax interventions.

RELAXING THE INITIAL ASSUMPTIONS

Multiple Exchange Rates

We have assumed up to now that all imports and exports are converted from foreign exchange to the domestic currency at the same *per*. That is not always the case. For example, certain goods may be imported at a 'preferential' exchange rate, rather than receiving a separate explicit subsidy. Say, for example, that there are two import exchange rates, per_1 and per_2, used for baskets of goods $[m_i^1]$ and $[m_i^2]$, that exports are liquidated at a third exchange rate, per_3, and that the multiple exchange rates are temporary (not a permanent part of commercial policy). Then, there would be only one SPFE described by equation (2.2), since the long-run equilibrium is one with a unified foreign exchange market, and three different SERs, one for each *per* ($h = 1, 2, 3$):

$$SER_h = \frac{eer\left[\sum_i p_i^m \Delta m_i (1 + t_i^m) + \sum_j p_j^x \Delta x_j (1 - t_j^x)\right]}{per_h\left(\sum_i p_i^m \Delta m_i + \sum_j p_j^x \Delta x_j\right)} \qquad (2.10)$$

Simplified equation (2.10) becomes:

$$SER_h = \frac{eer(M + T^m + X - T^x)}{per_h(M + X)} \tag{2.11}$$

Note that pricing traded goods would require knowing the exchange rate used in liquidating the transaction in order to select the corresponding SER_h.

Marginal export and import changes $p_i^m \Delta m_i$ and $p_j^x \Delta x_j$ in equation (2.10), as well as totals M, T^m, X and T^x in equation (2.11), correspond to the long-run situation and would differ from values calculated from current data. Correcting for these effects in order to use equation (2.11) would require estimates of import and export functions $M_i(per_i, t_i^m, \ldots)$ and $X_j(per_3, t_j^x, \ldots)$ in order to estimate the total value of imports, exports and trade taxes corresponding to the *eer*; that is, $M(eer)$, $X(eer)$, T^m and T^x.[23] However, good time series for import and export taxes and subsidies are hard to find in many countries,[24] making estimates difficult and less reliable, and resulting in the use of current data.[25]

Domestic Indirect Taxes on Traded Goods

Our initial presentation omitted the consideration of domestic indirect taxes applied on traded goods. In addition to tariffs, imports normally also pay domestic sales or value-added taxes before being released from customs. Therefore, their custom-gate prices include such indirect taxes. Under normal assumptions for the calculation of the SER, in particular that the custom-gate price of the imported good equals the producer's price of the identical domestically produced one, and that producer's prices equal long-run marginal costs at efficiency prices, the formula for the SER should include these domestic taxes.[26] In this case equation (2.7) becomes:

$$SER = \frac{eer(M + T^m + T^{md} + X - T^x)}{per(M + X)} \tag{2.12}$$

where $T^{md} = \Sigma_i M_i(1 + t_i^m)t_i^d$ is the indirect tax collection originated in imports at the custom gate, and t_i^d is the domestic tax rate for import i required to take it out of customs.

In the case of exports, the most common situation is that foreign sales are exempt from indirect taxes, but domestic sales of marginally exported goods are not. Therefore, equation (2.12) becomes:

$$SER = \frac{eer(M + T^m + T^{md} + X - T^x + T^{xd})}{per(M + X)} \tag{2.13}$$

where $T^{xd} = \Sigma_i \delta_j^x X_j (1 - t_j^x) t_j^d$, δ_j^x is the share of j's export changes due to changes in its domestic consumption, and t_j^d is the indirect tax rate on good j.

Non-traded Costs

During the preceding presentation it was implicitly assumed that custom-gate prices of imported goods were equal to producer prices of the domestically produced identical good, and that the differences between border and custom-gate prices were only taxes. Now we will reconsider these assumptions by following a more general model and explore the plausibility of the assumptions and their implications.

Starting with imports, the user's price of imported good i, p_i^{um}, and that of the identical domestically produced good, p_i^{ud}, may be presented as:

$$per \times p_i^{cif} \times (1 + t_i^m)(1 + t_i^d) + c_i^m + dis_i^m = p_i^{um}$$

$$p_i^p + dis_i^d = p_i^{ud} \tag{2.14}$$

where c_i^m is the port handling costs and other import fees paid by the imported good, dis_i^m and dis_i^d respectively are the non-traded domestic distribution costs (transportation, commerce, etc.) for the imported and the domestically produced good i, and p_i^p is the producer's price.[27] The most common assumption is that the user's prices of imported and domestically produced alternatives are equal for identical products;[28] from that equality it follows that:

$$per \times p_i^{cif} \times (1 + t_i^m)(1 + t_i^d) = p_i^p - c_i^m + (dis_i^d - dis_i^m) \tag{2.15}$$

Equation (2.15) shows that using just the border price plus taxes to estimate the SER amounts to assuming not just that custom-gate prices equal producer's prices and that producer's prices equal long-run marginal costs (LRMgC) at efficiency prices (our original assumption 3), but also that net port and distribution costs at efficiency prices are nil (our original assumption 4). Differences between market and efficiency prices of distribution services need to be assessed case by case, but the remaining assumptions may have larger effects and often do not match reality in developing countries. Domestic producer's prices do not equal long-run marginal costs at efficiency prices, and imported goods pay port service charges and tend to have higher distribution costs than domestic goods. Therefore, it may be useful to know how to deal with these problems so the analyst may judge whether the necessary adjustments make a significant difference to the final result for the SER.

If differences between domestic producer's prices and long-run marginal costs at efficiency prices are significant, correcting them requires a 'model' linking prices to costs. If the significant cases are just a few, there are simple procedures that can be applied by obtaining data on cost structures and revaluing costs at shadow prices.[29] If $\Sigma_k a_{ki} + \Sigma_h f_{hi} = 1$ describes the composition of the price for the domestically produced but marginally traded output i at producer's prices (where k are produced inputs and h are foreign exchange, non-produced inputs and transfers) and we have shadow price ratios (in the domestic numeraire) s_i and s_h for all inputs and transfers, then we could estimate the LRMgC as a share of the market price by calculating:

$$\sum_k s_k a_{ki} + \sum_h s_h f_{hi} = s_i \qquad (2.16)$$

The larger the absolute value of the difference $s_i - 1$, the larger the error of assuming equality between producer's prices and LRMgC at efficiency prices.[30] Say now that only imported good 1 shows large differences; then, we could reestimate equation (2.13) in an approximate manner by first decomposing from its numerator $M + T^m + T^{md}$ into:

$$M + T^m + T^{md} = \delta_1^m (M_1 + T_1^m + T_1^{md}) + (1 - \delta_1^m)(M_1 + T_1^m + T_1^{md})$$

$$+ (M_r + T_r^m + T_r^{md}) \qquad (2.17)$$

where δ_1^m is the share of changes in the production of good 1 in the total change in its consumption (i.e., $\delta_1^m = \Delta m_1^s / \Delta m_1$ from Figure 2.1) and r refers to all other goods apart from good 1; thus equation (2.12) can be rewritten as:

$$SER =$$

$$\frac{eer[\delta_1^m M_1 s_1 + (1 - \delta_1^m)(M_1 + T_1^m + T_1^{md}) + M_r + T_r^m + T_r^{md} + X - T^x + T^{xd}]}{per(M + X)} \qquad (2.18)$$

Equation (2.18) shows that in our example, for the correction to be worth the effort, not only does s_1 have to be significantly different from 1, but δ_1^m should be large as well. In practice, $\delta_1^m = \Delta m_1^s / \Delta m_1$ may have to be approximated by the average M_1^s / M_1. Then, the shadow pricing of the additional production may be written simply as $\alpha_1 M_1 s_1$ (where s_1 is the shadow price ratio for good 1 and α_1 is M_1^s / M_1).

If differences are large and widespread, and there are production cost structure data for domestically produced imported goods, a simplified approach could be followed by classifying total imports M *à la* Leontief (1956) into competing imports M_{co} and non-competing imports M_{nc} in order to calculate a weighted average of the cost structures for competing imports, with weights being the shares in total imports. The resulting cost structure for the basket of competing imports could then be used to calculate expression (2.16), thus obtaining a shadow price ratio for the basket or conversion factor s_{co}. Then, the new SER may be calculated as:

$$SER =$$

$$\frac{eer[\delta^m M_{co} s_{co} + (1 - \delta^m)(M_{co} + T_{co}^m + T_{co}^{md}) + M_{nc} + T_{nc}^m + T_{nc}^{md} + X - T^x + T^{xd}]}{per(M + X)} \tag{2.19}$$

Whether this adjustment would be worthwhile will depend on the difference between s_{co} and the alternative trade-taxes calculation, and the share of competing imports in total imports. If differences are large and widespread and there is a detailed input–output price model, consideration should be given to calculating the SER using such an approach. The presentation of this approach exceeds the scope of this chapter, but can be found in Londero (2003a).

Finally, distribution margins for traded goods may differ from margins for domestically produced ones, and port service costs should also be taken into account. As a result, from equation (2.15) it follows that:

$$per \times p_i^{cif} \times (1 + t_i^m)(1 + t_i^d) + c_i^m + dis_i^m - dis_i^d = p_i^p \tag{2.20}$$

Then, any of the simplified expressions for the SER may be corrected by adding estimates of port and incremental distribution costs to the numerator:

$$C^m + \Delta D^m = \Sigma_i m_i c_i^m + \Sigma_i m_i \Delta dis_i^m \tag{2.21}$$

Theoretically, these estimates should be added at shadow prices, in which case it needs to be kept in mind that C^m and ΔD^m should first be split into actual port and distribution costs and the marginal production costs of imports $(\Delta m_i = \Delta m_i^d + \Delta m_i^s)$ before shadow pricing each part with the corresponding shadow price ratios.

It should also be kept in mind that all these shortcuts are acceptable for an efficiency analysis that does not correct for the marginal cost of public funds or the accounting price of investment (UNIDO, 1972), where only the magnitude of the overall adjustment, not its distribution, is deemed important. If taxes are 'control variables' (Sen, 1972), accounting prices of investment are different from 1, or the distributional value judgement is different, then a more complex procedure should be used to avoid omitting distributive effects. In such cases, input–output approaches would help provide better estimates of the SER and the distributional effects than would analysis based on a partial approach.

Similar considerations apply to exported goods. In this case, the operational assumption is the producer's indifference between selling in domestic or foreign markets at the same basic price. Assuming that exports do not pay indirect taxes, which is the case in many countries, the expression for the operational assumption is:

$$per \times p_j^{fob} \times (1 - t_j^x) - c_j^m - dis_j^m = p_j^b = p_j^p/(1 + t_j^d) \qquad (2.22)$$

where c_j^m represents the cost of export port services and dis_j^m is the distribution cost (e.g., transportation from factory gate to port). The left-hand side is the basic price of the export and the right-hand side the one for the domestic sales. Then, the producer's price of j may be expressed as:

$$[per \times p_j^{fob} \times (1 - t_j^x) - c_j^m - dis_j^m](1 + t_j^d) = p_j^p \qquad (2.23)$$

It follows that assuming the equality between custom-gate prices, producer's prices and LRMgC at efficiency prices implies no domestic indirect taxes or export distributions costs:

$$per \times p_j^{fob} \times (1 - t_j^x) = p_j^b \Rightarrow t_j^d = 0 \text{ and } c_j^m + dis_j^m = 0 \qquad (2.24)$$

As in the case of imports, in practice this is not the case.[31]

Subsidies to the Production of Exported Goods

Thus far we have assumed that the LRMgC at efficiency prices of domestically producing the marginally traded goods are equal to their producer's prices. Often, however, these assumptions lead to significant errors. For example, exports of irrigated agricultural goods may be explained primarily by irrigation water provided at prices significantly below long-run marginal costs, thus making producer's prices for these goods much lower than long-run marginal costs; similarly, exports of energy-intensive goods may be explained by high subsidies to the domestic prices of the energy source. Significant discrepancies between producer's prices and costs may also originate in the first or second round manufacturing of exported primary goods subject to high export taxes (Bhagwati, 1988; Londero et al., 1998).

There are two main approaches to account for these subsidies. The first one is to correct for the effects of the production subsidy by estimating its amount, calculating its *ad valorem* equivalent and increasing the SER accordingly. In this case, care should be taken in adjusting the SER only to allow for the share of each *production* change (Δx^s in Figure 2.1) in total adjustment, since adjustment may also include changes in domestic consumption (Δx^d in Figure 2.1). This approach is helpful when these problems affect a small number of products of significant importance in marginal exports or imports.

The second approach should be considered when these market interventions are pervasive throughout the economy and quantitatively significant. Then, correcting the SER would require simulating the effects of market interventions on all prices through modelling the price system, for example using input–output techniques (see Londero, 1994).

SOME GENERAL EQUILIBRIUM CONSIDERATIONS IN ESTIMATING SHADOW PRICES

General equilibrium approaches to the derivation of shadow prices (*inter alia* Sieper, 1981; Squire, 1989; Fane, 1991; Dinwiddy and Teal, 1996) take into account that given an initial equilibrium situation, any change in government expenditure needs to be financed. For instance, using just investment financing as an example, increasing government investment would require reducing alternative government investments, reducing government consumption, increasing government tax revenue, or placing government bonds in the capital market. These alternative scenarios have important effects that are often neglected.

Discussions of the SER raise these wider considerations more frequently than those on other shadow prices because of the key role of foreign exchange, and for that reason this section briefly summarises the issues involved using investment financing as an example. If there is additional taxation *attributable* to financing project investment, there is a marginal welfare cost of raising the additional tax revenue (Atkinson and Stern, 1974; Squire, 1989; Sandmo, 1997), and such additional cost should be charged to the project. In practice, however, additional taxation and borrowing are rarely attributable to the individual project being analysed. Tax level and structure are explained by less technical considerations related to political power and the desired size of government, thus making government financing independent from *project* decisions and displaced government expenditure a more likely source of project finance.

Also, consumption and investment (public and private) may be affected by redistributions in monetary income, and such redistributions are important if the rate of discount differs from the marginal efficiency return on investments (UNIDO, 1972). Such considerations require estimating distributional effects according to marginal propensities to save and knowing the marginal efficiency return on investment of the affected groups (UNIDO, 1972; Londero, 1996a). Finally, net personal distributional effects (Londero, 1996a) are determined by net project effects, thus requiring information on the personal distributional effects of obtaining the financing. Note that this information would also be needed for the previous case if marginal propensities to save vary with income levels.

Wherever investment financing comes from, there would be a reduction in total demand equal to the domestic currency value of the project's investment, and the commodity composition of such reduction in the demand for other goods is defined by the financing of the investment at the margin. For example, if it is financed by reducing other government projects – the traditional assumption – the financing effects are included via the marginal rate of return of the alternative project. Say that doing government project A displaces government project B of identical investment cost and life span, described respectively by input and output vectors $[q_{it}^a]$ and $[q_{it}^b]$ ($i = 1, \ldots n; t = 1, \ldots .k$). Thus, project A's net demand for goods and services at time t would be vector $[q_{it}^a - q_{it}^b]$ and if A has a higher present value (PV) of costs and benefits than B, then:

$$PV(s_i p_i [q_{it}^a]) > PV(s_i p_i [q_{it}^b] = > PV(s_i p_i [q_{it}^a - q_{it}^b]) > 0 \quad (2.25)$$

where s_i is the shadow price of good i and p_i its market price. Thus, when working at 'efficiency' prices, a comparison with the marginally displaced government project in fact prices just project A's net demands.[32] Such is also the case if all investments are financed from a common source; the commodity composition of such financing would be the same for all projects and could thus be ignored in comparing net commodity effects. However, projects with different financing sources – for example one financed from general revenue and another financed from earmarked funds – would have to be compared on a net basis, thus requiring a knowledge of the commodity composition of the financing sources.

These issues, however, affect the estimation and use of all shadow prices, not just the SER. Therefore, they would be more productively discussed as general issues, outside the consideration of the specifics of estimating a SER.

THE FOREIGN EXCHANGE NUMERAIRE AND DISTRIBUTIONAL EFFECTS[33]

The treatment of foreign exchange has been closely associated with alternative methodological approaches to cost–benefit analysis (Little and Mirrlees, 1968, 1974; Squire and van der Tak, 1975) that led some economists to believe it was simpler to use foreign exchange expressed in the domestic currency at the prevailing exchange rate as the numeraire. Expressing an efficiency value in another numeraire only means using a different unit of account, as distances may be measured in miles or kilometres, and switching from one numeraire to the other should pose no significant problem or create any difference in the meaning of the final result. If in order to express an amount of foreign exchange (converted into the domestic currency at the *per*) in efficiency prices it is multiplied by the SER, any cost or benefit expressed in the consumption numeraire may be expressed in the 'foreign exchange numeraire' by dividing it by the SER, while imports or exports would be simply valued at the prevailing exchange rate (*per*). The use of one numeraire or the other would be just a matter of preference, and neither the sign or relative magnitudes of net present values, nor the rankings according to the cost–benefit ratios, nor the magnitude of internal rates of return would be affected by a genuine change in numeraire.

When performing an estimate of the distributional impact in the foreign exchange numeraire, care should be exercised in properly registering all the flows attributable to the project. Table 2.1 presents the case of imported good *s*, which is substituted by the project, under the assumption that both the imported and the domestically produced goods pay the same distribution margins. Then, the project output at market prices would be equal to the value of the substituted import, which is recorded as split into foreign exchange (100) and import taxes (30). The example in the top part of Table 2.1 corresponds to the consumption numeraire. Under the assumption that trade taxes make up the entire difference

Table 2.1   Distributive effects in two numeraires

	Project	Government	Total
Consumption numeraire			
Foreign exchange	100	20	120
Import taxes	30	−30	
Efficiency value	130	−10	120
Foreign exchange numeraire	130/1.2	−10/1.2	100

between the *per* and the SER, assumed to be 1.2, the additional foreign exchange available in the market would result in extra trade tax revenue for the government of (SER − 1) per unit value. Consequently, the project earns sales revenue (130), and the government is affected by the difference between the trade-tax revenue lost due to the reductions in the imports of *s* and the additional trade-tax revenue resulting from the alternative use of the foreign exchange released by the import substitution (−30 + 20).

As explained above, expressing these effects in the foreign exchange numeraire simply requires dividing the income changes by the SER, which is recorded in the bottom half of Table 2.1.[34] Therefore, it is unclear why anyone would use a foreign exchange numeraire when estimating distributional effects, since it involves an additional and unnecessary step.[35]

The example in Table 2.1 assumes that only trade taxes are responsible for the difference between the prevailing and the shadow exchange rates. If there were quotas and rents associated with them, then additional columns might be required in Table 2.1 to allocate the receipt of those rents as additional income. If the *per* differed from the *eer*, the required real depreciation would have important distributional effects, although it is likely that only a few very important ones could be estimated given the complex general equilibrium effects involved. Thus, it is important that the SER estimation details and records all different sources of discrepancy between the *per* and the SER.

Note that the effects captured in Table 2.1 are not the net attributable effects, that is, the effects of the project net of the effects attributable to the alternative course of action. For example, the without-project situation could be to avoid either a tax increase to finance it or displacing an alternative project. The net of the two would be the net attributable effects (see Londero, 1996a).

ROLE OF GOVERNMENT IN ESTIMATING THE SER

The discussion thus far should have made it clear that estimating the SER is not a task for an individual project analyst. First, having each project analyst make his/her own assumptions and judgements, for example on the *eer*, would not lead to good estimates or consistent comparisons amongst projects. Second, estimating equilibrium exchange rates and *ad valorem* equivalents of trade interventions takes time that is rarely available to analysts. Third, even with the necessary time, performing the estimations requires an overall understanding not only of applied welfare economics but also of the general equilibrium situation underlying the relative price system, and that is rarely the comparative advantage of project analysts, even if they are well-trained applied economists. Finally, there may be institutional pressures on analysts to come up with a favourable decision on a project. Regrettably, in practice, it is common to put project analysts in charge of estimating the shadow prices they need, including the SER, often leading to poor results.

The above reasons suggest that a single public institution should be in charge of estimating, updating and providing all shadow prices to be used in appraising public projects, including the SER. That responsibility, however, could be discharged by doing it directly, or by partially or totally subcontracting the job. There are clear advantages to doing it within the public sector, because it forces the discussion of important economic policy issues, the knowledge of which is often compartmentalised. There could, however, be risks derived from governments' reluctance to use or publicise estimates providing information on sensitive issues; for example, in the case of the SER, an overvaluation of the domestic currency or hidden export subsidies. These risks, however, will be present under any alternative. On the other hand, if the decision were to subcontract the estimates, the reasons suggesting the desirability of public sector estimates would call for the appointment of an able project manager in charge of designing the project, selecting the consultants, directing the execution, facilitating access to other public offices and to private firms, and ensuring that the right public officers participate in the discussion of critical issues. By so doing, the project manager helps in socialising the learning that always accompanies these estimations. In both alternatives, an independent technical advisor could help solve difficult technical problems and reduce pressures, thus leading to better estimates.

FINAL REMARKS

The traditional formulae for estimating the SER are simplistic, reflecting the simplistic nature of the assumptions from which they have been derived. These formulae are more of an educational than an operational tool. They become a better educational tool when their derivations are followed by brief discussions on the type of work required to abandon the most egregious simplifications of the real world. Knowing the simplifying assumptions and understanding the role of these assumptions, and thus the nature of the corrections that may have been omitted, allow the analyst to adapt these formulae to the case in hand and to call attention to the limitations of the estimates. Estimating shadow prices is, like cost–benefit analysis, an art based on a solid understanding of the principles and techniques involved. The quality of the artist is assessed by considering his/her judgement in selecting and applying the implicit model, the specific assumptions used to implement it, and the techniques employed to arrive at useful quantitative results that incorporate minimum bias.

In presenting the estimates, the analyst should discuss the assumptions used and pay special attention to those that may have the largest effects on the results, explaining why these simplifications were necessary or advisable. When simplifications were the result of the lack of data or time, but they are expected to have a significant impact on the result, the analyst should present these simplifications explicitly, assess the effects of abandoning some of the more constraining ones, and discuss the data and resources needed to obtain a better estimate.

It is important for the understanding and proper use of the estimated SER that the analyst documents the origin and nature of the differences between the shadow and the prevailing exchange rates, specifying sources and destinations of the transfers involved and discussing those where such specification has not been possible. This documentation becomes imperative when the SER is expected to be used in applied welfare economics involving the estimation of distributional effects, be they interpersonal, interinstitutional or even international.

Estimating a SER requires a combination of skills difficult to find in one person, thus making a team approach the preferred strategy. It also requires discussion of the general equilibrium implications of current and future policies, raising concerns about the short-term policy and political implications of disclosing the underlying reasons for a particular result. The combination of these characteristics often requires a team approach within the estimating organisation, as well as with other governmental and private organisations. That is particularly the case in less developed countries where highly specialised knowledge is scarce and difficult to access.

Methodological developments, more and better data, improved econometric techniques and software, and technical progress in computing power provide better conditions for processing trade data and estimating equilibrium exchange rates and other related parameters, thus dramatically improving the conditions for obtaining better estimates of the SER. Today we can expect significantly smaller estimation errors in estimating it, as well as in estimating other shadow prices.

A greater availability of more skilled economists, however, has not significantly changed the need for team work in applied welfare economics. Estimating a meaningful set of shadow prices to conduct actual project appraisals is no exception; it requires a range of skills that continues to be difficult to find in just one person. The estimation of a SER would require theoretical and practical knowledge on relative prices and general equilibrium issues, commercial policy, domestic taxation and domestic distribution costs, as well as access to sources that are not always willing to share their knowledge openly.

In many developing countries, however, there seem to be relatively fewer economists knowledgeable about shadow prices, and limited expertise on how to estimate them. Greater specialisation among applied welfare economists has not facilitated the appraisal of projects, and this greater specialisation may be itself the market outcome of less interest in the cost–benefit analysis of investments in general in favour of activities with more politically useful results.

Greater international competition and a more important role for markets in the allocation of resources in the economies of developed and less developed countries have not changed the need for *ex ante* cost–benefit analysis and a SER (and other shadow price ratios) to conduct it. In particular, in developed and less developed economies there continue to be misaligned exchange rates and many trade interventions resulting in relative market prices that significantly differ from relative shadow prices. The reason for avoiding the use of cost–benefit techniques is not that relative market prices adequately reflect relative shadow prices, but rather the lack of interest in knowing whether a measure of benefits to all exceeds the corresponding costs. Appraising investments, as well as other public expenditures, is a political decision that is not necessarily aligned with the electoral interest of politicians. If cost–benefit analysis is to remain an instrument to improve economic welfare, political forces other than political parties have to see it as an instrument for better resource allocation and demand its use in allocating public resources.

NOTES

1. Opinions expressed in this chapter are those of the author and are not intended to represent views of the institutions to which he is or has been affiliated. Authorisation to use materials previously published by the Inter-American Development Bank and Edward Elgar is gratefully acknowledged.
2. The reader may consult general equilibrium formulations in, *inter alia*, Sieper (1981), Drèze and Stern (1987), Squire (1989), and Dinwiddy and Teal (1996). Fane (1991) compares general and partial equilibrium approaches.
3. See introductory presentations in Winch (1975), Mishan (1981, Parts IV and V), and Londero (1996a), and a detailed mathematical one in McKenzie (1983); Freeman (2003) provides a good summary with environmental applications in mind. Sen (1973, 1977, 1987a) criticises the main assumptions.
4. Mishan (1988, Parts III and VI), and *Journal of Economic Perspectives* (1994).
5. Londero (2003a) provides a formal treatment.

6. Graaff (1957), Little (1950 [1960]), Mishan (1981, 1982), Ray (1984) and Londero (1996a, 2003a) discuss the distributional issues involved in applied welfare economics, and in cost–benefit analysis in particular.

7. Londero (1996a, 2003a) provides detailed derivations of this and other simple shadow price formulae taking distributional aspects into account.

8. In discussing different prices we use input–output conventions. Producer's prices are those at the factory gate; that is, prices charged by the producer at its factory including indirect taxes (net of subsidies) paid by the producer at the time of selling, thus excluding distribution costs (transportation and commerce) to reach the purchaser. Basic prices are those reflecting the net revenue received by the producer per unit sold, and are thus equal to producer's prices less the indirect taxes (net of subsidies) paid by the producer at the time of selling. Finally, user's or purchaser's prices are those paid by the purchaser, and are thus equal to producer's prices plus the distribution margins to reach the intermediate or final consumer.

9. More precisely, $\alpha_i = (\partial m_i/\partial eer)(\partial eer/\partial f)$ and $\beta_j = (\partial x_j/\partial eer)(\partial eer/\partial f)$.

10. Price elasticities for total exports and total imports, or for some major export goods, may be available and could be used, but not without a careful review of estimation procedures.

11. For a more detailed discussion of alternative measures of the real exchange rate see Harberger (1986), Edwards, S. (1988, 1989), Clark et al. (1994) and Hinkle and Montiel (1999).

12. See Keynes (1925), Harberger (1985) and Londero (1997, 2003b). A role for relative productivity increases in external adjustment may be expected in the case of trade liberalisation, but this role has often been overstated. Also, real depreciations following the combination of trade liberalisation and persistent overvaluation may have significant consequences for the structure of production and the commodity composition of trade (Londero, 1997, 2003b), thus creating many additional complications for the analyst including the classification of goods as traded and non-traded in long-run equilibrium.

13. For example, Argentina during the 1990s (Londero, 2003b).

14. Hinkle and Montiel (1999) provide an overview of the problems and the proposed solutions and approaches. Hinkle and Montiel (1999), Driver and Westaway (2004) and Lee et al. (2008) discuss estimation approaches, Londero (2003b) uses an alternative simpler approximation, and Abiad et al. (2009) provide a preliminary evaluation of IMF's Consultative Group on Exchange Rate Issues (CGER) assessments.

15. Londero (2003a, Ch. 7) includes a formal presentation, Londero and Soto (1987) provide a computer program to perform the calculations, and Cervini (2003) illustrates with an application.

16. Grennes (1984) and Vousden (1990) discuss trade restrictions and their equivalent tariffs under different scenarios. Also see Krishna et al. (1994, 1995) for the case of export quotas.

17. Import quotas also affect the estimation of shadow prices for non-traded goods; see Londero (2003a).

18. Except for minor effects in the *eer* ($eer_0 \rightarrow eer_1$ in Figure 2.1) normally ignored in calculating the SER.

19. For the conditions to classify an output as a by-product of another principal output see Londero (2001).

20. There may be minor effects since changes in the cost of producing the non-traded principal good may affect its price and thus its output level and that of the by-product, but those secondary effects would be generally ignored.

21. The implicit assumption is that there is a financial market able and willing to finance the importer, directly or via the producer; otherwise, an appropriate measure of opportunity cost would have to be used.

22. Cervini (2003) provides an example of estimates for quantitative restrictions, import deposits, and export financing.

23. Note that true estimates of T^m, T^{md} and T^x may require estimating import and export functions at a disaggregated level depending on price elasticities and the dispersion in tax and subsidy rates.
24. This is not to imply that such series cannot be produced, but that the time involved would be significant. The benefits would as well, since it would become possible to estimate export and import equations.
25. Also note that multiple exchange rates on imports could significantly affect relative shadow prices among non-traded goods as well.
26. See Londero (2003a).
27. Note the implicit assumption that the indirect tax is calculated over the CIF value plus tariffs, something that may vary from one country to another; for example, it may be calculated over CIF plus taxes, plus port fees.
28. If the imported and the domestically produced goods are not very close substitutes, the two goods become partially traded and require a special treatment. See Londero (1996b).
29. The following discussion requires some knowledge of estimating shadow prices for non-traded goods. See Londero (2003a).
30. Gómez (1979) and Mejía (1989) apply this method to estimating shadow price ratios for non-traded goods.
31. Londero (2003a, Ch. 3) provides an additional discussion of exports.
32. The complete discussion of this issue requires specifying the discount rate, the marginal rate of return at efficiency prices, and the specifics of the cost–benefit methodology used.
33. This section is based on Londero (1996a, Ch. 5, and 2003a, Ch. 2).
34. See Little and Mirrlees (1974: 149), where the tax revenue effects of the alternative use of the foreign exchange were omitted, and flows were not all expressed in the same numeraire.
35. The numeraire proposed by Little and Mirrlees (1974) is not simply foreign exchange, but 'present uncommitted social income measured in terms of convertible foreign exchange of constant purchasing power' (Little and Mirrlees, 1974: 151, 244–6, 251, 268–9; Squire and van der Tak, 1975: 135, 140). Little explains the reasons for selecting such a cumbersome numeraire in Schwartz and Berney (1977: 142–5). The assumption required to apply the Little and Mirrlees approach in the form it was proposed – that is, optimal allocation at the margin by the government between consumption and investment – is hard to find and eliminating it leads to a treatment very similar to that of UNIDO (1972).

3. Shadow wage rates in a changing world

David Potts

INTRODUCTION

This chapter outlines the issues involved in determining the shadow wage rate for different categories of labour. It starts off by looking at the surplus labour and migration theories that influenced early debates about the need to use a shadow wage rate and the kind of values that might be expected. It then looks in more detail at the factors that might determine the shadow wage for unskilled labour and the ways in which these may be taken into account, focusing on literature relating to the developing country context. Next it considers the different categorisation of labour and the factors that might influence the shadow wage rate in different regions and for different skill levels. Finally it looks at the potential use of shadow wage rates in the context of countries not normally described as 'developing' and asks whether the methods applied in developing countries are equally applicable in such contexts.

ORIGINS OF THE SHADOW WAGE CONCEPT: SURPLUS LABOUR THEORIES

The case for using a shadow wage rate can be traced back to the dual economy models of the 1950s and in particular to the work of W. Arthur Lewis (1954), who postulated the existence of 'unlimited supplies of labour' in some countries due to extensive rural underemployment. Lewis attempted to explain the coexistence of underemployment in the rural areas and relatively high levels of wages for unskilled workers in the urban areas on the basis that the marginal product of unskilled workers in the rural areas was at or close to zero, but that family members in the rural areas shared their income so that each received their average product. The implication was that additional unskilled labour could be recruited into the modern sector at little or no marginal economic cost but that the wage actually paid to labour would not fall below the average product in rural households. In such a situation it could be argued that the market wage rate paid in the modern sector significantly overstated the opportunity cost of labour and that investment projects that generated modern sector employment would yield additional benefits in the form of increased incomes to workers. While the private sector would presumably make decisions on the basis of market wages, it could be argued that public investment decisions and those of development-oriented international financial institutions, regulatory bodies and aid agencies should be based on economic values.

The simple assumption of an opportunity cost for unskilled labour of zero was criticised on a number of grounds. First of all, as argued by Schultz (1964), there may be seasonal variations in the availability of labour such that its opportunity cost is not zero at all times of the year. Harberger (1971: 560–63) argued against the idea that the opportunity cost of labour could be regarded to be close to zero on the basis of evidence on employment of landless labourers and difficulties in the recruitment of dam construction workers in India. Fitzgerald (1978: 51–3) discussed a variety of situations in which the opportunity cost of labour might vary on a seasonal basis with a significant positive value during peak periods. The marginal product of labour was therefore unlikely to be zero and its magnitude was an empirical question with results that could vary quite significantly both between different countries and between regions in larger countries with significant regional variation.

Secondly there are potential costs associated with the movement of workers from the relatively low-cost rural environment to the urban formal sector. Dixit (1968) argued that there may be a terms of trade effect between food and industrial products as a result of rural–urban migration. Rural–urban migrants would be paying more for their food than if they had stayed in the rural areas. Similar factors could apply to housing and transport costs and the external costs of migration-induced congestion (Harberger, 1971: 564–5; Perkins, 1994: 228–9).

Thirdly it can be argued (e.g. Sen, 1966) that there is some disutility of effort even at relatively low levels of income. This applies not just to the migrant worker but also to the family he/she leaves behind who have to take up the extra work previously done by the migrant. Lal (1973) argued that the social cost of this disutility should be disregarded on the grounds that the value placed on individual leisure does not have the same value to the government as to the individual. In a sense this is a philosophical question about what should enter into the social utility function, but it is not clear why such disutility should be ignored when it relates to poor people. The evidence pointed to by Harberger (1971) suggests that there is a reservation wage below which even poor people are not willing to work and therefore, at least from the individual point of view, there is some disutility of effort. Le (2009) presents empirical evidence from rural Vietnam confirming leisure as a normal good, therefore implying the existence of disutility of effort among rural households including the poor. A partial counter-argument might be that there is some positive individual utility in having a job in terms of self-esteem (Perkins, 1994: 226) as well as social utility in terms of the reduction of negative factors that tend to be associated with unemployment, such as crime. In practice both the disutility of effort to the individual and the potential gain in self-esteem have tended to be ignored in shadow wage estimates but this does not necessarily have to be the case, and in principle both effects should be taken into account.

Finally it has also been argued that the creation of one formal sector job results in more than one migrant from the rural area on the grounds that migrants are influenced by the probability of getting a job rather than the certainty of getting one (Harris and Todaro, 1970). Although it is not obvious that the migration factor is always more than 1, there is no particular reason why it should always be 1, and the issues raised by Harris and Todaro opened up the wider question as to where the ultimate source of the supply of additional formal sector unskilled labour comes from. Powers (1981: 39–41) indicated how this issue can be introduced into the shadow wage rate formula by multiplying the value of the forgone output of the worker by the number of migrants attracted per job created.

The issue of migration can be extended to challenge the conventional assumption that all formal sector unskilled workers are ultimately drawn from the surplus labour in the rural areas. Fitzgerald (1976) argued that movement of workers from urban informal sector occupations to the formal sector was important in the context of Latin American economies, but his argument applies much more generally in the twenty-first century. In 1960 about 76 per cent of the population in low and middle-income countries lived in the rural areas. By 2008 this had declined to 55 per cent. Even in a very poor and rural country like Ethiopia the proportion of the population living in the urban areas increased from 6.4 per cent to 17 per cent in the same period (World Bank, 2010). This change in the relative importance of the urban population is reflected in the increasing importance of the urban informal sector with the result that recruitment of formal sector unskilled workers is likely to include a significant proportion drawn from the urban informal sector. A study undertaken to estimate shadow prices for Ethiopia in the late 1990s took specific account of recruitment from informal urban sector sources in estimating shadow wage rates for different regions (MEDaC, 1998). If this is relevant in one of the least urbanised societies it is clearly even more relevant in the vast majority of countries that are more urbanised than Ethiopia. The significance of the urban informal sector also suggests that the issue of rural–urban migration is more complex than implied by a simple version of the Harris–Todaro model since the initial employment of migrants is often in the informal sector and this sector has its own dynamic that may be at least partially independent of what is going on in the formal sector.

The opportunity cost of formal sector unskilled labour is therefore likely to be a weighted average of the alternative earnings of both urban and rural informal sector workers, taking account of the potential impact of additional formal sector job creation on rural–urban labour migration as well as the additional costs associated with urbanisation and formal sector work. Estimation of the shadow wage rate can therefore be regarded as an empirical question that will yield different results in different situations, but it is unlikely to yield a result of zero.

While the opportunity cost of unskilled labour is not likely to be zero it may well be below the formal sector market price for two reasons. First of all the supply price may relate to average productivity in informal sector households rather than marginal productivity for the reasons suggested by Lewis. Secondly, institutional factors, such as the existence of a minimum wage legislation and pressure from trade unions, may hold the market price at a level that is above the level that would provide full employment. Although the total supply of unskilled labour can be regarded as fixed in the short run, with its expansion related to general population growth rather than the demand for labour (Perkins, 1994: 218), it can be regarded as highly elastic at the institutionally determined wage in the formal sector due to the existence of unemployment and underemployment. The opportunity cost of unskilled labour is therefore defined by its alternative use in the labour-losing sectors and is likely to be below the formal sector wage.

ESTIMATING THE SHADOW WAGE RATE

A first estimate of the shadow wage rate for labour category i can be made on the basis of:

$$SWR_i = x_i\left(\sum_{t=1}^{n} mr_{ti} + \sum_{t=1}^{n} wr_{ti} + zr_i\right) + y_i(mu_i + wu_i + zu_i) \quad (3.1)$$

where: x refers to the migration factor (i.e. the ratio of the number of additional workers migrating from the rural areas to the number of formal sector jobs created); mr refers to the marginal product of labour recruited from the rural areas; t refers to the time period of the year reflecting possible seasonal differences in the marginal product of labour in n time periods; *wr* refers to the disutility of additional effort implied in formal sector work which may vary by season for workers recruited from the rural areas; *zr* refers to the additional costs associated with moving from the rural areas to an urban formal sector environment; *y* refers to the proportion of workers recruited from the urban informal sector and not replaced by new recruits from the rural areas; *mu* refers to the marginal product of labour recruited from the urban informal sector; *wu* refers to the disutility of the additional effort implied in formal sector work compared to the urban informal sector; *zu* refers to the additional costs associated with moving from the urban informal sector to a formal sector environment (likely to be less than *zr*).

The above formulation assumes that the market price value of the commodities produced by unskilled rural workers is equal to its economic value. However, this may not be the case. In particular, with the assumption that formal sector unskilled workers are drawn from the rural areas, it may be assumed that *mr* is primarily in the form of reduced agricultural output.[1] Therefore in principle the value of *mr* should be adjusted by a conversion factor (*a*) reflecting the value of a unit of agricultural production in relation to a unit of the numeraire adopted.[2] Equation (3.1) therefore becomes:

$$SWR_i = x_i \left(\sum_{t=1}^{n} amr_{ti} + \sum_{t=1}^{n} wr_{ti} + zr_i \right) + y_i(mu_i + wu_i + zu_i) \quad (3.2)$$

Similar factors could also be applied to *w* and *z*, with *w* presumably being assumed to be valued as units of average consumption and the conversion factor for *z* relating to whatever additional costs are associated with living in the formal sector. Less attention has generally been paid to these factors because they are likely to be less important in the overall value of the shadow wage and because both may be conveniently assumed to be equivalent to units of average domestic consumption. A simple example can be used to illustrate the implications of the above formulation. Assume:

market wage rate in the formal sector (MWR) = 1250;
there are two agricultural seasons – the peak season (1) and the off-peak season (2). In the peak season agricultural workers do the same number of hours of labour as in the formal sector but in the off-peak season they work less;
$mr_1 = 400$;
$mr_2 = 225$;
$wr_1 = 0$;
$wr_2 = 150$;

$zr_{1+2} = 150$;
$mu = 700$;
$wu = 100$;
$zu = 50$;
$a = 1.1$ (this value is consistent with a country that has significant agricultural exports and relatively low protection of agricultural import substitutes).

If $x > 1$ as implied by the Harris–Todaro model (say 1.5), then there will be more workers recruited into the informal sector than leave the informal sector to join the formal sector, and y will be negative. In this example there will be a loss of welfare to the migrants who fail to get a job because the sum of their marginal product and the saving in effort and living costs ($mr_1 + mr_2 + wr_2 + zr_{1+2} - wu - zu = 400 + 225 + 150 + 150 - 100 - 50 = 775$) is greater than their urban marginal product (700). This is consistent with the idea that migrants move on the basis of the probability of gain but do not necessarily all actually gain. With these parameters $y = -0.5$ and $SWR = 1056$ and the conversion factor for labour is 0.845.

However, if $x < 1$ (say 0.5), the SWR falls to 919 and the conversion factor for labour is 0.735. Such an assumption would be consistent with an economy with an already large population engaged in the urban informal sector where the availability of additional formal sector jobs might have a lower impact on migration because the probability of a migrant getting the job would be lower. Assumptions about migration can therefore have significant implications for the shadow wage rate even with relatively small differences between income levels in the rural and urban informal sectors. It should be noted that in the above example the issue is not necessarily *who* gets the formal sector job but what the effect is on the total labour forces in the urban and rural informal sectors.

Systematic theoretical approaches to the estimation of shadow wage rates were developed in the late 1960s and early 1970s associated with the work of Little and Mirrlees (1968 and 1974) and Dasgupta, Marglin and Sen (UNIDO, 1972). A particular issue that arose was that of the use of the additional income earned by unskilled workers. In particular it was argued that, since unskilled workers were relatively poor, any additional income accruing to such groups was likely to be consumed. There was therefore a danger that excessive emphasis on labour-intensive development influenced by the use of low shadow wage rates might result in an inadequate rate of investment. In the context of economies with suboptimal levels of investment, additional consumption was therefore regarded to have a lower value than a unit of public investment because the social discount rate (i, described by Little and Mirrlees as the consumption rate of interest) would be lower than the opportunity cost of capital (q). The present value (v) of the annual consumption streams of q derived from a marginal unit of investment discounted over an indefinite period at a discount rate of i is greater than 1 when $q > i$. Furthermore if any proportion s of q is rein-vested, the additional investment will increase the value of v. Essentially the parameter v defines the trade-off between employment and growth.[3]

A further complication was the argument that on distributional grounds the social value of consumption by those who were relatively poor might have a higher value than consumption of those at the average level. Such considerations would increase the social value of the additional consump-tion of unskilled workers in relation to the value of the investment forgone as a result of paying them more than their opportunity cost. The methods associated with Little and Mirrlees and Squire and van der Tak (1975) attempted to build these distributional questions into the formulae for the shadow wage. Using the notation in equation (3.1) above, ignoring the dis-utility of effort and assuming that all incremental labour is recruited from the rural areas and that any seasonality factors are taken into account in the value of m, the standard formula for the shadow wage rate associated with Little and Mirrlees and Squire and van der Tak can be written as:

$$SWR_i = am_i + z_i + d_ib_i\frac{(c_i - m_i - z_i)}{v} \tag{3.3}$$

where: a is the conversion factor applied to agricultural output; b refers to the conversion factor for the consumption basket of the relevant labour category; c is the level of consumption expenditure of the worker in a formal sector occupation; z is the additional cost of moving from rural to urban areas and is assumed to be measured in units of the numeraire; d refers to the distribution weight attached to the additional consumption of the worker; and v refers to the value of a unit of average consumption in relation to a unit of investment (or uncommitted public sector income).

The approach associated with UNIDO (1972, 1978, 1980) treated the distribution question as a separate stage in such a way that distribution impacts were identified for specific groups before any attempt to attach weights reflecting distribution priorities. In terms of arithmetic the two approaches gave equivalent results with equivalent assumptions but the process was different and it can be argued that it is easier to derive infor-mation on distributional impact using the UNIDO stage-based approach and a domestic price numeraire (Londero, 1996a; Potts, 1999; Fujimura and Weiss, 2000).

The approach of including distribution weights in the estimation of shadow prices was criticised by Harberger (1978) on the grounds of the potential waste involved in implementing inefficient projects to deliver desired distribution objectives, and he argued for the separation of consideration of distribution questions from the process of estimating the NPV to be distributed. More recently the idea of including distributional issues in the calculation of shadow prices, which has rarely been adopted in any consistent way in practice, has also been criticised for lack of clarity in the presentation of the results of the analysis. It has been argued that too many objectives are conflated into a single measure for the project NPV and the important information on where the benefits of projects go is obscured (Potts, 1999). By making clear the distinction between the economic efficiency of the project and its impact on the welfare of different groups, an approach that specifies the income distribution impacts before any attempt to use income weights caters for Harberger's objection that economically inefficient projects could end up being justified on distribution grounds. In such an approach the resource cost of any decision influenced by distributional questions would be made clear.

SHADOW WAGE RATES AND MEASUREMENT OF DISTRIBUTION EFFECTS

If we are concerned about distributional impact but do not wish to follow the approach of including distribution weights in shadow wage rates we need to be able to measure the change in the income of workers associated with their movement from the informal sector to the formal sector. To do this we need to break down the market wage rate into its constituent parts including those opportunity cost elements that go into measuring the shadow wage rate and the income transfers that arise due to the difference between the opportunity cost of labour and its market price.

In principle the shadow wage rate is no different from any other shadow price in that it can be estimated by breaking down the market price value into primary factors and revaluing the components according to the values of the primary factors. The complication is that labour is itself normally considered as a primary factor. However, as we have seen, the market price value of labour can be broken down into:[4]

- the forgone output of the worker(s) (*xmr* and *ymu*);
- the additional costs of formal sector employment and urbanisation (*xzr* and *yzu*);
- the value of forgone leisure time (*wr and wu*);
- the additional benefit to the worker – the difference between the market wage rate and the above values.

Table 3.1   Breakdown of the opportunity cost of formal sector unskilled labour for Ethiopia (national average)

	Urban (%)	Rural (%)
Foreign exchange	16.8	31.8
Domestic consumption	62.5	30.9
Taxes and subsidies	1.7	−1.5
Changes in profits	0.8	−0.1
Income to unskilled workers	18.2	38.8

Note: The relatively low proportion of foreign exchange in the breakdown reflects the assumption made in the study that the principal cereal crop (teff), which accounts for a significant proportion of Ethiopian agricultural output, is effectively non-traded. The negative tax effect for rural unskilled labour relates mainly to the loss of export tax revenue from forgone coffee production.

Source: MEDaC (1998, Table 13.3).

Apart from the additional benefit to the worker, which is a transfer from the employer to the worker, the other elements can be broken down in the normal manner for traded and non-traded goods. As a result the market price of labour can be decomposed into:

- foreign exchange costs from the net loss of traded output;
- reduced domestic consumption as a result of loss of non-traded outputs and leisure;
- changes in transfer payments, particularly indirect taxes and excess profits;
- changes in the welfare of the worker.

Such estimates are most easily obtained if an extended semi-input–output approach to shadow price estimation is adopted (see Chapter 4). This approach allows the simultaneous derivation of breakdowns for all sectors and labour categories in such a way that both the direct and the indirect composition of any sector or labour category can be allocated to the above categories. It is then relatively straightforward to trace the distributional impact of the changes in employment arising from a project. A simplified summary of results from the 1998 study on Ethiopia for both urban and rural formal sector labour is given in Table 3.1. These figures give conversion factors for unskilled labour for urban and rural formal sector work of 0.81 and 0.66 respectively.

Such a table allows a fairly ready calculation of the indirect income effects derived from employment of additional unskilled labour. Of course national average values for relatively large countries like Ethiopia can be misleading if there are significant regional differences. For this reason the study made separate estimates for each of the regions as well as for different categories of labour. As might be expected there were significant regional differences with some very low shadow wage rate estimates in some of the poorer regions of the country.

DATA SOURCES AND THE ESTIMATION OF SHADOW WAGE RATES

In principle the estimation of shadow wage rates is derived from the factors described in equation (3.1). However, this raises the question as to where the data come from. In determining the shadow price of labour a distinction is sometimes made between approaches based on the supply price of labour and those based on the marginal product forgone (Edwards, A., 1989; Biçak et al., 2004). In principle they should arrive at the same result once factors such as the additional costs of urbanisation and the disutility of effort are taken into account in the marginal product forgone approach.

Much of the literature on shadow wage rates since the 1990s has been based on econometric studies of the small farming sector usually derived from rural household surveys (e.g. Jacoby, 1993; Skoufias, 1994; Menon et al., 2005; Barrett et al., 2008; Le, 2009). These studies investigate the allocation of resources in farm households through the estimation of household production functions. This can be regarded as a marginal product forgone approach in that these studies attempt to determine the marginal product of rural labour. While such studies generate considerable relevant information about the behaviour and rationality of rural households, including issues that have often been neglected, such as gender differences and the use of child labour, they are of limited applicability for the purpose of investment appraisal, partly because they were not generally conducted for that purpose. They tend to be confined to the farming sector and therefore tend not to take account of the urban informal sector. The valuation of leisure time in such studies is also potentially problematic. Is leisure time an objective with a value to be determined, or a constraint on the number of hours available for the activities specified in the objective function, including household maintenance?

Biçak et al. argue that the supply price approach, based on surveys of wages in uncontrolled (predominantly informal sector) labour markets, is easier in practice because the non-wage factors that may be difficult to determine are embodied in the supply price. This approach appears to be the most common in practice where estimation of shadow wage rates is undertaken for the purpose of investment appraisal (e.g. MEDaC, 1998; Biçak et al., 2004; Humavindu, 2008). Normally in empirical work a sample survey of new entrants into the formal sector labour force is conducted to determine their previous occupation. This may give an indication of the source of those who were successful in getting the job but it does not easily capture all the issues raised by models of rural–urban migration since it does not identify those who may have migrated but failed to get a job. It may also be difficult to identify the level and nature of the incomes earned in the previous occupations, especially if attempts are made to distinguish between the marginal and average product of members of a rural household, not all of whom may migrate. Furthermore it is unlikely that such studies will be able to pick up seasonality issues.

It could therefore be argued that the most reliable approach in a developing country context would be to combine the supply price approach with surveys of the marginal product forgone in rural areas and to make comparisons of the results to determine the extent to which consistent results are obtained. Through such a combination of approaches a better understanding could be obtained of the opportunity cost of the supply of both rural migratory labour and of workers from the urban informal sector and the margin of error in the resultant shadow wage estimate would almost certainly be reduced.

SHADOW WAGE RATES FOR DIFFERENT CATEGORIES OF LABOUR

Most of the literature on shadow wages concentrates on formal sector unskilled labour because this is the category perceived to be in excess supply and therefore to be likely to have a shadow price below the market price. However, for the consistent implementation of shadow prices it is also necessary to have shadow wage rates for other categories of labour.

The most straightforward categories are those that relate to the informal sectors (both rural and urban). These are straightforward in the sense that they provide the reference points for the valuation of formal sector unskilled labour and therefore the information sources are the same, with only the market price being different. For this reason the conversion factor for informal sector labour is likely to be close to the market wage and could even exceed it where rural workers produce a significant proportion of their output in the form of exportable products. In general the treatment of rural informal sector labour costs in agricultural projects is undertaken best through the use of farm models that try to trace the use of labour with and without the project. It is certainly not appropriate to assume that the conversion factor for formal sector unskilled labour, either rural or urban, can be used for the valuation of informal sector labour inputs. In the case of the Ethiopian study previously referred to, the national average conversion factor for rural informal sector labour was 1.08 compared to the national average formal sector value of 0.66 (domestic price numeraire version).

The situation applying to skilled labour is more complex. First of all there is the question of definition. What do we mean by skilled labour? If we define skilled labour as those categories that are not in excess supply, the definition is tautologous. If, however, we define skilled labour in terms of skills then there may be a number of different categories with different levels of scarcity. Particular distinctions may be made between skilled and semi-skilled labour and also between the public sector and the private sector.

The conventional approach to the value of skilled labour is to assume full employment and therefore that the shadow price and market price are the same (Powers, 1981: 41–2; Londero, 1996a: 81). However, while this may be approximately correct in the case of private sector skilled workers, there may be specific factors influencing the supply of and demand for public sector skilled workers. In some countries freedom of movement for graduates may be constrained by factors such as labour allocation or bonds relating to the costs of higher education. As a result it is possible that the market price of skilled labour could be held below the equilibrium level, particularly in situations where a relatively high proportion of skilled labour is employed in the public sector (Perkins, 1994: 221). Furthermore skilled workers often receive on-the-job training specific to their function. As a result the cost of replacing a skilled employee may be more than the salary paid to the replacement due to reduced efficiency and additional training costs. However, Irvin (1978: 124) has argued that the additional cost of training replacement workers should be estimated separately and not built into the shadow wage. One approach to estimating the shadow wage for skilled labour is to make direct comparisons of the salary levels of equivalent workers in the public and private sector, the underlying assumption being that private sector salaries are market-driven while public sector salaries are determined institutionally. This approach was used in studies in Lithuania and Latvia and yielded values of 17 per cent and 3 per cent (respectively) above the market wage for public sector skilled workers (Potts, 1995: 32; 1996a: 43).

A large and increasing proportion of the labour force in most countries can be regarded as semi-skilled in the sense that, while there may be no major formal barriers to entry, certain elements of skill or training are required (e.g. a minimum level of education or training for a specific skill).

In such cases it is possible that the workers might be regarded as scarce in some contexts and in excess supply in others. For example the Ethiopian study treated semi-skilled labour as scarce (i.e. equivalent to skilled) while the studies in Lithuania and Latvia treated semi-skilled labour as in excess supply and derived conversion factors of 0.61 and 0.63 respectively. These conversion factors were similar to the values for unskilled labour, reflecting the situation faced by semi-skilled workers in countries undergoing rapid transition to a market economy.

A special category of labour that can be important for some projects is that of expatriate workers. In most developing countries these are mainly confined to skilled workers although migrant unskilled workers are important in some oil-producing states as well as some developed countries. If the expatriate worker is not regarded as a member of the nation state then any benefits to the worker are not regarded as national benefits. However, any of the income of the worker that is taxed should not be regarded as a national cost. Biçak et al. (2004) provide an example of the estimation of the shadow price for expatriate labour in the context of South Africa. A similar approach is used by Humavindu (2008) for Namibia.

SHADOW WAGE RATES IN DEVELOPED COUNTRIES

The development of the shadow wage rate concept originated in the context of developing countries in which it was assumed that unskilled labour was abundant and skilled labour was scarce. However, there is a growing recognition that such a situation is not unique to developing countries and that the bipolar distinction between 'developed' and 'developing' countries is increasingly open to question. A number of studies have investigated the possibility of using a shadow wage rate in a developed country context (Kirkpatrick and MacArthur, 1990; Honohan, 1998; Swales, 1997; Saleh, 2004; Potts, 2008; Del Bo et al., 2009). There have also been a number of shadow pricing studies in economies in transition that are now members of the European Union (Dondur, 1996; Potts, 1995, 1996a, 1996b).

Florio and Vignetti (2004) have argued for a more consistent use of shadow wages in the EU as reflected in the most recent version of the EU cost–benefit analysis guide for the regions (European Commission, 2008). Del Bo et al. (2009) produced estimates of shadow wage rates for a wide range of regions of the EU with results suggesting that, in many of the poorer regions, the kind of conversion factor values obtained were very similar to those found in developing countries. These results can be contrasted with their survey of the guidelines produced by EU member and other developed country governments where there appears to be relatively little guidance provided on the use of shadow wage rates and no evidence of common practice other than non-use. It can therefore be argued that since there is no particular difference in principle between 'developed' and 'developing' countries in the approach to the estimation of shadow wage rates, there is a need for a more systematic approach to their use in the developed country context.

CONCLUSION

The use of shadow wage rates can be traced back to the dual economy models of the 1950s. While the cruder assumptions of zero opportunity cost of labour have been discredited there is widespread evidence that the opportunity cost of formal sector unskilled labour is significantly below the market price in most developing countries as well as a significant number of regions in the developed countries. In most large countries there are regional differences so, while a national average estimate of the shadow wage rate might be calculated, it is advisable also to have regional estimates.

In recent years markets in general have been liberalised and this also applies to labour markets to some extent. This raises the question as to whether market wages are now closer to opportunity cost than previously, therefore reducing the potential importance of using shadow wage rates. This is largely an empirical question, but some of the original issues pointed out by Lewis in relation to rural households still apply at least to some extent in many countries. Involuntary unemployment exists all over the world and rural underemployment is common in countries facing land shortages or with significant seasonal variations in the demand for labour. Nearly all countries maintain a minimum wage to protect low-paid workers and this provides a floor for formal sector earnings. It is therefore likely to continue to be important to estimate and apply shadow wage rates for investments involving some form of public sector or international agency intervention.

Recognition of the need to use shadow wage rates in the appraisal of public sector investment projects is not matched by consistency in estimation and application. Part of the reason may be traced to the tendency in the 1970s to develop complex formulations that tried to include too many objectives in a single expression of the shadow wage. While there is recognition of the need to separate distributional issues from shadow wage estimation in the literature on distribution analysis, there is not yet sufficient common practice for a consistent mode of application to be observed.

Most of the attention in the literature has been focused on formal sector unskilled labour but there is also a need to pay attention to the situation of skilled and semi-skilled labour. The latter category in particular may in some countries face similar conditions to those facing unskilled workers.

There is no particular difference in principle in the estimation of shadow wage rates between developing and developed countries. What is needed is some degree of consistency in use in all countries.

NOTES

1. It will not be entirely in the form of agricultural output. There is increasing recognition in the literature on rural livelihoods that people in the rural areas are engaged in a wider range of activities than agriculture.
2. In this chapter all results from empirical studies will be reported in domestic price numeraire equivalent values to facilitate comparison of different studies that may have adopted different numeraires.
3. A commonly cited formula for v developed by Marglin (1967) and used by UNIDO (1972) and Squire and van der Tak (1975) is $v = (1 - s)q/(i - sq)$. This formula assumes that the savings shortage implied by the difference between i and q continues indefinitely.
4. A more comprehensive outline of these general principles and their distributional implications can be found in Londero (2003a, Chapter 3).

4. Semi-input–output methods of shadow price estimation: are they still useful?

David Potts

INTRODUCTION

Semi-input–output (SIO) analysis has been used extensively in the estimation of shadow prices, particularly in the 1990s. It has the advantage of providing a comprehensive and internally consistent model of the economy and can provide the framework for more detailed work on individual items. However, like all techniques it rests on assumptions and is subject to their limitations. A particular problem associated with the use of any form of prices in cost–benefit analysis is that assumptions are made about an uncertain future. Given the rapid changes associated with globalisation, as well as the impact of liberalisation in reducing the difference between economic and market price values, we might ask whether the method is still useful. This chapter sets out to answer the question by investigating first the origins, main features, assumptions and limitations of the method, then by reviewing the practices used in studies in a number of countries. The potential ways in which the estimates produced by the method can be used are then discussed before considering its usefulness in present day circumstances.

ORIGINS AND MAIN FEATURES OF THE METHOD

The SIO method can be traced to the work of Tinbergen and Bos (1962: 82–3). The most important feature is the distinction between what were originally described as 'national' and 'international' sectors and what are now described as traded and non-traded sectors. In a conventional input–output table all of the intersectoral linkages are traced but, since traded goods can be either imported or exported, the effect of using or creating one more unit of a traded good is primarily felt on the trade balance and the value can be derived from the border price. The SIO method was used by Cornelisse and Tilanus (1966) to analyse a Turkish cement project using a 17-sector model, but the first widely known use of the method for estimating shadow prices was by Scott in relation to Kenya (Scott et al., 1976). Valuable outlines of the standard version of the method are provided by Powers (1981) and Weiss (1988). Simplified examples of SIO tables can be found in Curry and Weiss (2000) and Potts (2002).

A matrix of coefficients can be constructed consisting of an '*A*' matrix of inputs from other domestic sectors (including various average conversion factors for use where more detailed data are not available) and an '*F*' matrix consisting of factor payments and foreign exchange. By inverting the *A* matrix and multiplying by the *F* matrix, a new *T* matrix can be derived in which the unit output value of each sector is broken down into primary factors. A vector *S* is then set up with seed values for the conversion factors for primary factors. The *S* vector is then multiplied by the *T* matrix to derive a first vector of conversion factors *CF*. The procedure is then repeated until the *S* and *CF* vector values converge. The conversion factors for transfer payments are zero by definition and in a world price numeraire system the conversion factor for foreign exchange is 1.0 by definition. In the example outlined below, average domestic consumption was included in the *A* matrix so the only conversion factors to be solved by iteration are those for the labour categories.[1] Once the first set of results is established, the vectors in the *T* matrix giving the sector breakdowns for the opportunity cost of the labour categories are multiplied by the first sector conversion factor estimates in vector *CF* to derive a revised estimate for the labour conversion factors. The procedure is then repeated until convergence is reached. Only a few iterations are required to reach convergence. Thus:

$$(I - A)^{-1}.F = T \tag{4.1}$$

$$S.T = CF \tag{4.2}$$

Originally most studies adopted a world price numeraire approach; however, it is relatively easy to adapt the results to a domestic consumption numeraire by multiplying all the conversion factors by the reciprocal of the conversion factor for average domestic consumption. The structure of a standard SIO table is illustrated in Figure 4.1.

Clearly the major practical issues lie in the collection of data for the direct coefficients and the determination of the number of sectors to be included. A major advantage of the SIO table is that, since it is not going to be used for macroeconomic projections, it does not necessarily have to cover all sectors, and the level of aggregation can vary according to data

	a_1 .... a_n
Sector a_1	a_{11} .... a_{1n}
.	.
.	.
.	'A' Matrix
.	.
.	.
Sector a_n	a_{n1} .... a_{nn}
Primary Factor f_1	f_{11} .... f_{1n}
.	.
.	'F' Matrix
.	.
Primary Factor f_m	f_{m1} .... f_{mn}

Figure 4.1   Standard SIO table: direct coefficients

availability and priorities (Lucking, 1993: 114). In particular the SIO table is most likely to concentrate on the directly productive and infrastructure sectors that are most important in determining the costs and benefits of investment projects. These are also the sectors where tax and subsidy policies are most likely to cause differences between market prices and shadow prices. Average conversion factors for particular sectors and/or a standard conversion factor can be used for residual items for which information is not available, thereby allowing information gaps to be overcome.

There are some major advantages in the use of the SIO method. First of all, it should be internally consistent in that all the parameters are solved simultaneously and should therefore be consistent with each other. By providing a single reference source for the main national parameters it should also ensure that project analysts are using consistent estimates in their work, thereby making the comparison of different projects more reliable. Secondly, it provides the most effective way of accounting for the indirect effect of projects on other subsectors and through this on expenditure on different labour categories and on taxes and subsidies. If the potential of the method is used to the full it is then able to provide information on the impact of projects on critical economic indicators such as the balance of trade, fiscal balance and the incomes of particular groups associated with primary factor inputs. This can also enhance the potential for using the method to investigate the economic impacts of different patterns of investment expenditure, for example in the determination of sector priorities in relation to particular economic objectives such as conserving government income or improving the trade balance.

ASSUMPTIONS AND LIMITATIONS

The first and most obvious limitation is that it does not provide a substitute for good basic project analysis. Application of a consistent set of shadow prices to a poorly estimated set of market price costs and benefits is unlikely to have much added value. There are also limitations associated with the nature of the technique and its assumptions.

In common with all input–output techniques SIO has to assume constant returns to scale and it has practical limitations in terms of the extent to which sectors can be disaggregated, particularly if standard spreadsheet software is used with limitations on the maximum size for matrix inversion. An important issue for the non-traded sectors is treatment of the capital input into the sector output. Normally the data available will be derived from accounting sources and are therefore likely to be taken from depreciation estimates. Such estimates do not allow for a return to capital and are based on historic costs that may be well below replacement cost if there has been any significant inflation between the purchase or last revaluation of the assets and the time at which data collection is undertaken. These factors can be taken into account by using a depreciation adjustment factor (DAF) which updates historic costs to replacement values and adjusts the depreciation value using a capital recovery factor at the rate of discount used for economic analysis. Assuming updated historic costs and straight line depreciation, this factor can be expressed for capital input i as (Potts, 2002: 214):

$$DAF_i = CRF_i * IF_i * AL_i \qquad (4.3)$$

where CRF is the capital recovery factor for the life of the asset at the relevant discount rate, IF is an inflation factor to bring the historic cost value to replacement cost and AL is the assumed life of the asset. In equation (4.3) multiplication of the straight line depreciation of the asset by the asset life gives the original value of the asset which is inflated by IF_i. The

CRF then reduces the capital value to an annual equivalent value at the chosen discount rate.

While the above procedure is clearly preferable to using depreciation figures that do not allow for any cost of capital, there are implied limitations for the purist. The resulting coefficient is specific to the particular discount rate used and in principle use of any other discount rate (e.g. in the estimation of an IRR) would imply a different coefficient. In practice the difference is unlikely to have much effect in most sectors but it could be significant for more capital-intensive sectors such as energy, especially where output value does not cover full economic costs.[2]

The conventional assumption for all sectors is that supply of all goods and services is elastic and that there is no long-run excess capacity in any sectors. Part of the justification for this assumption is that projects are normally long-term investments and for most goods and services it is reasonable to assume that long-term supply is elastic but that long-run marginal cost implies capacity expansion and therefore has to include coverage of capital costs. In principle alternative assumptions could be made. In an SIO study for Lithuania in the 1990s (Potts, 1995) it was originally assumed that, in the context of the breakdown of the Soviet energy distribution system, there was long-run excess capacity in nuclear energy for as long as the existing nuclear power station continued in operation. The shadow price for electricity was therefore estimated on the basis of short-run marginal cost. However, subsequent investment in electricity transmission connections with Poland resulted in electric power becoming a traded good. Similarly it would be possible in principle to value non-traded goods assumed to be in fixed supply on the basis of willingness to pay but it would be difficult to justify an assumption of long-run shortages that would never be addressed.

Another important limitation of SIO studies is the tendency for them to become out of date. Usually the data used for constructing the table are a year or two out of date before the study is completed and it is rare for studies to be updated as frequently as they should be. While it can be argued that coefficients are less likely to vary as much as absolute values, estimates for any economy subject to significant changes in economic policy or the external economic environment may become out of date if not regularly updated.[3]

EARLY EXAMPLES

Scott's SIO study of Kenya, published in 1976, was followed by a number of studies of varying complexity for India (Lal, 1980), Ecuador, Barbados,

El Salvador and Paraguay (Powers, 1981) and Egypt (Page, 1982). These studies were reviewed by MacArthur (1994) along with other studies that were conducted by researchers associated with the University of Bradford for the Philippines (Johnson, 1987), Brazil (da Silva Neto, 1993), Botswana (Saerbeck, 1988), Ethiopia (Weiss, 1987), China (Weiss and Adhikari, 1989) and Sri Lanka (Curry and Lucking, 1991). The method was also used by Dondur (1996) in a study of shadow prices for Hungary. With the exception of the China study all the early studies used a world price numeraire. Although the study by Scott, MacArthur and Newbery (1976) was used to investigate distribution issues, and the Powers study (1981: 49–59) mentioned the possibility of extending the method to derive 'social accounting prices', most of the early studies did not make use of the potential for using the SIO method to derive indirect impacts on stakeholder incomes. An exception was the Brazilian study (da Silva Neto, 1996). The potential for using shadow price estimates for the derivation of indirect income effects was explored by Londero (1996a) using an average domestic consumption numeraire. His approach is elaborated further in Londero (2003a) where the rationale for the use of the domestic consumption numeraire is discussed (pp. 54–7) and details are provided of an SIO study for Colombia undertaken by Cervini et al. in 1990.

In most examples using a world price numeraire the value of average domestic consumption (the reciprocal of the shadow exchange rate in the domestic price numeraire system) was determined endogenously through the matrix inversion process by including average consumption as a sector. Sometimes a variety of different consumption conversion factors were included reflecting factors like the income levels of the recipients and/or location (rural/urban). In the domestic price numeraire system used in Cervini et al.'s study of Colombia the shadow exchange rate was determined exogenously (Londero, 2003a: 206–9). Clearly there is some potential for inconsistency in the interpretation of different studies; however, the differences between the values obtained either exogenously or endogenously in practice are likely to be well within the margin of error of the data used.[4]

RECENT STUDIES

Although the majority of available studies were undertaken in the 1980s and 1990s, SIO studies are still being undertaken and the technique remains the most systematic and comprehensive way of estimating shadow prices. More recently an SIO study for Spain is described in Nieves (2001). A study for Namibia was undertaken by Humavindu (2008) and an updated study for China based on the 2005 input–output table has also been undertaken (Zhao et al., 2009). There is significant variation in the number and choice of sectors included. For example the Spanish study has 70 sectors with an emphasis on manufacturing and services and only three primary agricultural sectors (agriculture, forestry and fishing). The Chinese study has 42 sectors, again mostly manufacturing and services. These studies can be contrasted with the 47-sector Ethiopian study which included nine primary agricultural subsectors but relatively little emphasis on services. In part the level of disaggregation in the studies depends on available data and in part it depends on the nature of the economy and priorities in public investment.

There is similar variation in the number of labour categories used. The Spanish study simply distinguishes between skilled and unskilled labour and the Chinese study appears to have only one labour category. By contrast, Humavindu (2008) estimated conversion factors for four categories of labour. The Ethiopian study also included four categories for the country as a whole, calculated through the SIO process, but separate calculations (i.e. outside the SIO framework but using the SIO parameters) were also made for urban and rural unskilled labour for each of 11 regions of the country. In the case of the Lithuanian and Latvian studies a distinction was made between skilled and semi-skilled labour and between public and private sector skilled labour. Such variations illustrate the potential flexibility of the tool to cater for country-specific circumstances.

A SIMPLIFIED EXAMPLE

A simplified example of a conventional SIO table is given in Table 4.1, partly based on aggregated figures from the Ethiopian study. The traded sectors in this table (agriculture and manufacturing) have been aggregated and include non-traded as well as traded goods. The values for the operating surplus are net of the annualised cost of capital in this case and therefore can be regarded as transfer payments.

The product of the inverted A matrix and the F matrix then provides the overall breakdown for each sector into primary factors (Table 4.2 – the T matrix) and through an iterative process the vector of conversion factors (CF) for all sectors and the conversion factors for different labour categories can be obtained.

It can be seen from the presentation of the results that the focus of the method is on determining the conversion factors, and the information is not presented in a way that can be used directly to determine indirect distributional impact, although much of the relevant information is there.

Table 4.1 *Simplified conventional SIO table: direct coefficients (A and F matrices)*

Sector		A	M	C	U	T	S	DC
Agriculture	A					0.873	0.013	0.528
Manufactured Products	M	−0.001	0.011	0.532	1.035		0.014	0.069
Construction	C		0.002	0.073	0.148		0.001	0.025
Utilities	U		0.001		0.033		0.005	0.009
Transport	T	−0.030	0.067	0.038	0.024		0.005	0.043
Services	S	−0.007	0.023	0.009	0.011	0.046	0.070	0.326
Domestic Consumption	DC	0.494	0.115	0.101	0.139	0.036	0.786	
Primary Factor								
Unskilled Labour	UL	−0.006	0.001	0.090	0.080	0.020	0.005	
Skilled Labour	SL	−0.001	0.001	0.097	0.140	0.135	0.016	
Foreign Exchange	FE	0.574	0.614	0.024	0.156			
Taxes and Subsidies	Tx	−0.023	0.145	0.012	−0.773	−0.116		
Operating Surplus (Public)	Pub	0.011	0.007				0.045	
Operating Surplus (Private)	Pri	−0.011	0.013	0.024	0.007	0.006	0.045	

Table 4.2   Simplified T matrix and CF vector

		UL	SL	FE	Tx	Pub	Pri	
Unskilled Labour	UL	−0.003	0.004	0.101	0.105	0.025	0.014	0.008
Skilled Labour	SL	0.011	0.017	0.125	0.192	0.153	0.050	0.035
Foreign Exchange	FE	0.982	0.796	0.618	1.263	0.762	0.774	0.886
Taxes and Subsidies	Tx	−0.020	0.149	0.087	0.174	0.015	0.010	0.007
Operating Surplus (Public)	Pub	0.027	0.013	0.026	−0.775	0.017	0.078	0.035
Operating Surplus (Private)	Pri	0.002	0.020	0.043	0.041	0.028	0.074	0.029

Primary Factors	UL	SL	FE	Tx	Pub	Pri
Seed Values	0.65	0.84	1.00	0.00	0.00	0.00

Sector	A	M	C	U	T	S	DC
Conversion Factors	0.99	0.81	0.79	1.49	0.91	0.83	0.92

Sector Breakdown of OCL	A	M	C	U	T	S
UL	0.363	0.105	0.084	0.000	0.000	0.167
SL	0.020	0.220	0.030	0.010	0.140	0.580

Labour Conversion Factors	
Unskilled Labour UL	0.65
Skilled Labour SL	0.84

In particular the sector breakdown for the opportunity cost of unskilled labour does not add up to 1.0 so it can be inferred that the difference is the income gain associated with additional employment, but this is not indicated explicitly.

EXTENSIONS OF THE METHOD

The process of estimating shadow prices and the potential for using SIO studies to investigate distributional impacts can be further enhanced by converting the SIO matrix into what was termed by the authors as an 'Extended Semi-Input–Output' table (Tan and MacArthur, 1995; Tan, 1997). In this version the A matrix is extended to include the various labour categories and factor incomes and the F matrix is confined to foreign exchange ($CF = 1.0$) and transfer payments ($CF = 0.0$). The process of matrix inversion then derives the conversion factors directly by multiplying the extended T matrix by an S vector with values of 1.0 and 0.0. The indirect income effects derived from the use of goods or services from any sector can be identified through the values of the transfer payment coefficients in the T matrix. These transfer payments include additional income to labour.

The version of the extended SIO system outlined above provides conversion factors in the world price numeraire system. This has the disadvantage that values are measured in units that do not correspond with the incomes received by different groups (Potts, 1999; Fujimura and Weiss, 2000; Londero, 2003a). It also fails to identify the income changes associated with changes in the availability of foreign exchange, in particular changes in taxes on traded goods. This can be resolved fairly readily by adopting a domestic consumption numeraire and multiplying foreign exchange components by a shadow exchange rate (SER) factor (see Chapter 2 for a discussion of approaches to the derivation of the SER). The SER can either be determined through the SIO system, normally as the reciprocal of the conversion factor for average domestic consumption, or exogenously.

The extended SIO system was applied to Malaysia by Tan with particular reference to measurement of the costs and benefits of foreign direct investment. Subsequently studies conducted in Lithuania, Latvia and Ethiopia (Potts, 1995, 1996a, 1996b; MEDaC, 1998) used this approach with a minor modification that the standard conversion factor (or average domestic consumption) was included in the F matrix. This allowed easy identification of indirect income effects since these consisted of the transfer payments identified in the breakdown given in the T matrix plus the

	$a_1 \dots\dots\dots\dots\dots\dots\dots\dots\dots\dots\dots\dots\dots a_n\ l_1 \dots\dots\dots\dots\dots\dots\dots l_m$
Sector a_1	$a_{11} \dots\dots\dots\dots\dots\dots\dots\dots\dots\dots\dots\dots\dots\dots\dots\dots\dots\dots\dots\dots\dots\dots l_{1m}$
.	
Sector a_n	$a_{n1} \dots\dots\dots\dots\dots\dots\dots\dots\dots\dots\dots\dots\dots\dots\dots\dots\dots\dots\dots\dots l_{nm}$
	A
Labour Category l_1	$l_{11} \dots\dots\dots\dots\dots\dots\dots\dots\dots\dots\dots\dots\dots\dots\dots\dots\dots\dots\dots\dots\dots l_{1m}$
.	
Labour Category l_m	$l_{m1} \dots\dots\dots\dots\dots\dots\dots\dots\dots\dots\dots\dots\dots\dots\dots\dots\dots\dots\dots\dots\dots l_{mm}$
Domestic Consumption	$d_{11} \dots\dots\dots\dots\dots\dots\dots\dots\dots\dots\dots\dots\dots\dots\dots\dots\dots\dots\dots d_m$
Foreign Exchange	$f_{11} \dots\dots\dots\dots\dots\dots\dots\dots\dots\dots\dots\dots\dots\dots\dots\dots\dots\dots\dots f_m$
Income Transfer t_1	**F**
.	$t_{11} \dots\dots\dots\dots\dots\dots\dots\dots\dots\dots\dots\dots\dots\dots\dots\dots\dots\dots\dots t_{1m}$
.	
Income Transfer t_k	$t_{k1} \dots\dots\dots\dots\dots\dots\dots\dots\dots\dots\dots\dots\dots\dots\dots\dots\dots\dots t_{km}$

Figure 4.2   Extended SIO table: direct coefficients

additional tax revenue associated with changes in foreign exchange. The structure of an extended SIO table similar to those used in the Lithuanian, Latvian and Ethiopian studies is illustrated in Figure 4.2.

Using the same example as for the conventional SIO table, the extended SIO table is set out in Table 4.3.

The extended T matrix and associated conversion factors are shown in Table 4.4 using a domestic price numeraire. This allows ready identification of the income transfers associated with expenditure on any sector or labour category. Of particular significance in identifying income transfers to relatively poor people is the additional income to unskilled workers (Yul) associated with the direct and indirect expenditure on unskilled labour in each sector. Table 4.4 provides a breakdown in terms of various transfer payments, average domestic consumption (DC) and foreign exchange (FE). The only iteration then required is the relationship between the value of FE and DC which can be established endogenously by modifying the value of FE until convergence for the value of DC at 1.0 is reached. Alternatively the breakdowns can be used with an exogenously estimated value for the SER, an approach that from a purist point of view might be regarded as inconsistent but in practice would probably not make a great deal of difference. The difference between the value of the SER and 1.0 would be regarded as an income transfer associated with the additional income derived from taxes on traded goods. A simplified example of how the results of the extended SIO table can be used to derive the distribution analysis for a project is provided in the Appendix.

Examples of the use of this approach to derive indirect income effects include the reworking of a World Bank funded district heating

Table 4.3   Extended semi-input–output table direct coefficients

Sector/Labour Category		A	M	C	U	T	S	UL	SL
Agriculture	A	−0.001	0.011	0.532	1.035	0.873	0.013	0.363	0.020
Manufactured Products	M		0.002	0.073	0.148		0.014	0.105	0.220
Construction	C		0.001		0.033		0.001	0.084	0.030
Utilities	U								0.010
Transport	T	−0.030	0.067	0.038	0.024	0.046	0.005		0.140
Services	S	−0.007	0.023	0.009	0.011	0.020	0.070	0.167	0.580
Unskilled Labour	UL	−0.006	0.001	0.090	0.080	0.135	0.005		
Skilled Labour	SL	−0.001	0.001	0.097	0.140		0.016		
Primary Factor/Transfer									
Domestic Consumption	AC	0.494	0.115	0.101	0.139	0.036	0.786		
Foreign Exchange	FE	0.574	0.614	0.024	0.156				
Taxes and Subsidies	Tx	−0.023	0.145			−0.116			
Operating Surplus (Public)	Pub	0.011	0.007	0.012	−0.773		0.045		
Operating Surplus (Private)	Pri	−0.011	0.013	0.024	0.007	0.006	0.045		
Income to Unskilled Labour	Yul							0.281	

Table 4.4 Extended SIO table T matrix and conversion factors

Primary Factor/Transfer		A	M	C	U	T	S	UL	SL
Domestic Consumption	DC	0.476	0.159	0.319	0.498	0.304	0.867	0.361	0.604
Foreign Exchange	FE	0.552	0.667	0.495	1.034	0.628	0.028	0.317	0.287
Taxes and Subsidies	T	−0.024	0.148	0.092	0.181	0.020	0.005	0.015	0.042
Operating Surplus (Public)	Pub	0.010	0.008	0.023	−0.781	0.013	0.049	0.015	0.025
Operating Surplus (Private)	Pri	−0.012	0.016	0.042	0.039	0.028	0.050	0.009	0.038
Income to Unskilled Labour	Yul	−0.002	0.001	0.029	0.029	0.007	0.002	0.283	0.004
		DC	FE	T	Pub	Pri	Yul		
Seed Values		1.00	1.09	0.00	0.00	0.00	0.00		
		A	M	C	U	T	S	UL	SL
Conversion Factors		1.08	0.88	0.86	1.62	0.99	0.90	0.71	0.92
Domestic Consumption		0.528	0.069	0.025	0.009	0.043	0.326		
Domestic Consumption		1.00							

rehabilitation project in Latvia, which used the Latvian SIO study (Potts, 1999) and a semi-fictitious case study based on some Tanzanian tea projects and a modified version of the Ethiopian SIO table (Potts, 2003). Both cases have some limitations. In the Latvian case the original study did not include any analysis of the direct distributional impacts of the project by consumer income group, so the distribution analysis was only able to trace the indirect effects, in particular those deriving from income losses to unskilled workers resulting from job losses and a positive net fiscal impact arising from savings to public sector institutions. The latter (Tanzanian) case had the advantage that it demonstrated the full potential of the method in terms of generating information on both direct and indirect distributional impact and it illustrated the potential value of agricultural census data in the conduct of such studies since the income shares to farmers were derived from the Tanzanian agricultural census. However, it clearly suffers from the limitations of relying on semi-fictitious data from multiple sources that allowed any practical data problems to be assumed away.

The extended SIO system makes it easier to examine the impact of projects on key macroeconomic variables, in particular on fiscal impact (Taxes and Subsidies and Operating Surplus (Public) and the premium on Foreign Exchange in Table 4.4) and the trade balance (Foreign Exchange). This is potentially useful, particularly for large projects in relatively small countries, especially if the values are estimated on an annual basis rather than as present values. In such cases it is possible to get some idea not just of the scale of the impact but also of its timing. To do this a set of sector breakdowns similar to that set out in the first part of Table 4.4 can be multiplied by the appropriate market price values in a project to derive a table consisting entirely of the annual values of changes in primary factors (Potts, 1999: 591). The shadow price adjustments to the primary factor values represent the indirect income distribution effects of the project.

IS SEMI-INPUT–OUTPUT ANALYSIS STILL RELEVANT IN A RAPIDLY CHANGING GLOBALISED WORLD?

It can be argued that the case for using shadow prices is undermined by the extensive liberalisation of trade and deregulation of prices that has taken place and the rapid pace of changes in technology. The former processes reduce the extent to which the market price of traded goods is likely to differ from the shadow price and the extent to which the prices of non-traded goods differ from the long-run marginal cost of production. The latter process has implications for the reliability of conversion factors calculated under changing technical conditions. Can the estimates produced by SIO studies ever be sufficiently reliable to be usable? The response rests on two propositions.

First of all the use of shadow prices can be justified where there are market imperfections. This is recognised to be the case even in the European Union. The most recent guide of the Directorate General for the Regions (European Commission, 2008) recommends the use of a system of shadow pricing to take account of factors like regional unemployment as well as market imperfections in the markets for goods and services. Although liberalisation has reduced the extent of the difference between market prices and economic values, it has not removed them entirely.

Secondly, it can be argued that the use of semi-input–output methods provides the most appropriate way of estimating a systematic set of shadow prices using a model that, once established, can be modified according to changing circumstances. Furthermore, such a model in its extended form can provide valuable information on indirect distributional outcomes and impacts on macroeconomic variables that are highly relevant given the twin objectives of poverty reduction and macroeconomic stability. The model is therefore fit for purpose and potentially very useful.

The major problems in practice are that most countries do not ensure that the estimates, once made, are periodically updated and the full potential for using SIO studies to generate information on project effects has not been effectively exploited. This would require the establishment of expertise along with a commitment both to make effective use of that expertise and not to allow it to wither away. While many SIO studies have been accompanied by human resource capacity building, such capacity has rarely, if ever, been maintained or properly utilised, with the predictable result that studies become so out of date that eventually the model is unusable and a completely new study is required. It therefore appears that a potentially highly valuable tool has not been provided with the attention and resources it needs to deliver the output of which it is capable.

NOTES

1. An alternative procedure could be to include average domestic consumption in the '*F*' matrix, in which case this would also have to be solved by iteration.
2. This was the case in the SIO study conducted for Ethiopia (MEDaC, 1998) where prices charged by the water and electricity sectors did not cover full economic costs and where the value of full economic costs varied considerably with the discount rate because of the capital intensity of dam-based water and electricity supplies.

3. The same Ethiopian study was commissioned as an update of a study that was conducted ten years previously with fewer sectors and in a very different economic environment. Not surprisingly some of the updated estimates were very different.

4. In the Ethiopian study estimates were derived for an average conversion factor (the weighted average for all sectors) and for a standard conversion factor (the weighted average for all traded sectors, arguably equivalent to the reciprocal of a standard SER estimate). The resulting estimates were within 1 per cent of each other.

APPENDIX   APPLYING SIO PARAMETERS TO PROJECTS: AN EXAMPLE

The following example presents a simplified set of costs and benefits for a hypothetical agro-industrial project to illustrate the potential practical uses of economic parameters derived from SIO studies, the information generated and associated limitations. In order to simplify the example no attempt has been made to conduct a full financial analysis, and working capital has been ignored. As a result the set of costs and benefits associated with the 'net benefit to the factory' are all assumed to accrue to the factory owners whereas in reality some of this return would accrue to lending institutions, some to the government in tax and some to debtors and creditors. In order to demonstrate the potential use of the analysis for examining distributional issues it has been assumed that the project involves the purchase of agricultural raw materials from a farming community that includes small owner-occupier farmers, landlords and sharecropping tenants. The project is assumed to have an economic life of ten operating years with no salvage value and no capital replacements.

Table 4A.1 sets out the costs and benefits to farmers. It is assumed that the construction of the new factory will cause farmers to switch from an existing less profitable crop to the new crop and that the net benefits from land farmed by tenant farmers are shared between the tenants and the landlords on a sharecropping basis. Although the crop is shared between tenant and landlord the labour is provided by the tenant so the share of the landlord in the net benefits is larger. In the case of the small owner-occupier farmers the entire net benefit goes to the farmer. It is assumed that no capital costs are involved for the farmers so the farmers gain a net benefit in every year from the commencement of production. In the first year only 50 per cent of production is assumed because the factory takes more than one year to build.

Table 4A.2 sets out the costs and benefits to the factory, which is assumed to start operation in Year 2 but only operates for part of that year. The costs are classified in the same way as in the SIO Tables 4.1 and 4.3, and the processed output is assumed to be an import substitute. In line with normal practice the shadow price for the output is assumed to be project specific but the SIO data are used in its estimation. The factory achieves a positive NPV at the assumed discount rate of 8 per cent and an IRR of 14 per cent so it appears to be profitable to the owners.

Table 4A.3 shows the overall costs and benefits of the project at constant market prices, including both farmers and the factory. Since there are no investment costs to the farmers and the new crop is more profitable than the existing crop, the NPV of the project increases and the IRR rises to 20 per cent. The project appears to be very viable.

Table 4A.1   Annual statement of costs and benefits to farmers ($'000 constant market prices)

Year	1	2	3	4	5	6	7	8	9	10	11
Revenue – New Crop		1800	3600	3600	3600	3600	3600	3600	3600	3600	3600
Less Revenue – Old Crop		–900	–1800	–1800	–1800	–1800	–1800	–1800	–1800	–1800	–1800
Incremental Revenue Costs		900	1800	1800	1800	1800	1800	1800	1800	1800	1800
Rural Labour – New Crop		400	800	800	800	800	800	800	800	800	800
Manufactured Inputs – New Crop		800	1600	1600	1600	1600	1600	1600	1600	1600	1600
Less Rural Labour – Old Crop		–300	–600	–600	–600	–600	–600	–600	–600	–600	–600
Less Manufactured Inputs – Old Crop		–200	–400	–400	–400	–400	–400	–400	–400	–400	–400
Incremental Costs											
Rural Labour		100	200	200	200	200	200	200	200	200	200
Manufactured Inputs		600	1200	1200	1200	1200	1200	1200	1200	1200	1200
Net Incremental Benefit to Farmers		200	400	400	400	400	400	400	400	400	400
Share to Landlords		70	140	140	140	140	140	140	140	140	140
Share to Tenants		50	100	100	100	100	100	100	100	100	100
Share to Owner-Occupiers		80	160	160	160	160	160	160	160	160	160

Table 4A.2 Annual statement of costs and benefits to factory ($'000 constant market prices)

Year	1	2	3	4	5	6	7	8	9	10	11
Construction	2000										
Machinery	4000	2000									
Total Investment Costs	6000	2000									
Unskilled Labour		300	600	600	600	600	600	600	600	600	600
Skilled Labour		200	400	400	400	400	400	400	400	400	400
Purchase of Crop		1800	3600	3600	3600	3600	3600	3600	3600	3600	3600
Crop Transport		300	600	600	600	600	600	600	600	600	600
Manufactured Inputs		350	700	700	700	700	700	700	700	700	700
Utilities		150	300	300	300	300	300	300	300	300	300
Services		100	200	200	200	200	200	200	200	200	200
Total Operating Costs		3200	6400	6400	6400	6400	6400	6400	6400	6400	6400
Sales Revenue		4000	8000	8000	8000	8000	8000	8000	8000	8000	8000
Net Benefit to Factory	−6000	−1200	1600	1600	1600	1600	1600	1600	1600	1600	1600

NPV at 8% = 1985

IRR = 14%

Table 4A.3   Annual statement of resource costs and benefits ($'000 constant market prices)

Year	1	2	3	4	5	6	7	8	9	10	11
Construction	2000										
Machinery	4000	2000									
Unskilled Labour		300	600	600	600	600	600	600	600	600	600
Skilled Labour		200	400	400	400	400	400	400	400	400	400
Forgone Crop		900	1800	1800	1800	1800	1800	1800	1800	1800	1800
Additional Rural Labour		100	200	200	200	200	200	200	200	200	200
Additional Manufactured Farm Inputs		600	1200	1200	1200	1200	1200	1200	1200	1200	1200
Crop Transport		300	600	600	600	600	600	600	600	600	600
Manufactured Inputs		350	700	700	700	700	700	700	700	700	700
Utilities		150	300	300	300	300	300	300	300	300	300
Services		100	200	200	200	200	200	200	200	200	200
Sales Revenue		4000	8000	8000	8000	8000	8000	8000	8000	8000	8000
Net Benefits at Market Prices	−6000	−1000	2000	2000	2000	2000	2000	2000	2000	2000	2000

NPV at 8% = 4299

IRR = 20%

93

Table 4A.4 shows the application of the conversion factors estimated by the conventional SIO process using a world price numeraire. The conversion factor for manufactured products is assumed to apply to all manufactured inputs for both farmers and factory. The conversion factor for agriculture is assumed to apply to the forgone crop and to agricultural labour costs on the grounds that labour costs are based on an estimate of the opportunity cost of rural labour at market prices but the main output of rural workers is agricultural products. The results show that the project now has a negative NPV at the given discount rate and an IRR of 6 per cent. While it is clear from the size of the conversion factor for utilities that one of the reasons has to do with underpricing of utilities, Table 4A.4 does not give enough information for a detailed analysis of the reasons for the reversal of the result and the distributional implications.

Table 4A.5 sets out the unit breakdowns for the various categories of costs and benefits using the information derived from the extended SIO table (Table 4.4). Setting the table out in this way allows the use of the Microsoft Excel =SUMPRODUCT function to facilitate the estimates in Table 4A.6. The conversion factors are also indicated, this time using a domestic consumption numeraire, but they are not actually used.

Table 4A.6 shows the breakdown of the market price costs and benefits into changes in domestic consumption, foreign exchange and various transfer payments including additional income to unskilled workers. Shadow price adjustments are then made by taking the negative value of the transfer payments to remove them and adding the foreign exchange premium indicated in Table 4.4 (i.e. 1.09 – 1.00) multiplied by the foreign exchange effect.[1] The results are equivalent to Table 4A.4 with the NPV larger due to the change in the numeraire. However, the table gives a wealth of useful information. The project is clearly a net foreign exchange earner but it has a strong negative impact on the government in terms of forgone taxes and increased losses of public utility companies. By dividing the present value of changes in domestic consumption by the present value of changes in foreign exchange the domestic resource cost of foreign exchange can be calculated at 1.13, greater than the SER, indicating that the project is relatively inefficient in earning foreign exchange.

Table 4A.7 summarises the distribution effects of the project on the various stakeholders and investigates the poverty impact. It is assumed that sharecropping tenants and small farmers are poor, as are unskilled workers. The results indicate that the government makes a substantial loss and that more than 50 per cent of the positive benefits accrue to the non-poor. The project therefore cannot be justified on the grounds of poverty impact and clearly has a strongly negative fiscal impact. It can be seen that using the parameters defined through the extended SIO approach

Table 4A.4 Annual statement of resource costs and benefits at shadow prices, conventional SIO, world price numeraire ($'000)

Year	CF	1	2	3	4	5	6	7	8	9	10	11
Construction	0.79	1578										
Machinery	0.81	3252	1626									
Unskilled Labour	0.65		195	389	389	389	389	389	389	389	389	389
Skilled Labour	0.84		169	337	337	337	337	337	337	337	337	337
Forgone Crop	0.99		891	1782	1782	1782	1782	1782	1782	1782	1782	1782
Additional Rural Labour	0.99		99	198	198	198	198	198	198	198	198	198
Additional Manufactured Farm Inputs	0.81		488	976	976	976	976	976	976	976	976	976
Crop Transport	0.91		272	545	545	545	545	545	545	545	545	545
Manufactured Inputs	0.81		285	569	569	569	569	569	569	569	569	569
Utilities	1.49		224	448	448	448	448	448	448	448	448	448
Services	0.83		83	165	165	165	165	165	165	165	165	165
Sales Revenue	0.79		3174	6348	6348	6348	6348	6348	6348	6348	6348	6348
Net Benefits at Shadow Prices		−4831	−1157	939	939	939	939	939	939	939	939	939

NPV at 8% = −435
IRR = 6.3%

Table 4A.5 Breakdowns and conversion factors, domestic consumption numeraire

	Category	CF	DC (%)	FE (%)	Tx (%)	Pub (%)	Pri (%)	Yul (%)
Construction	C	0.86	31.9	49.5	9.2	2.3	4.2	2.9
Machinery	M	0.88	15.9	66.7	14.8	0.8	1.6	0.1
Unskilled Labour	UL	0.71	36.1	31.7	1.5	1.5	0.9	28.3
Skilled Labour	SL	0.92	60.4	28.7	4.2	2.5	3.8	0.4
Forgone Crop	A	1.08	47.6	55.2	-2.4	1.0	-1.2	-0.2
Additional Rural Labour	A	1.08	47.6	55.2	-2.4	1.0	-1.2	-0.2
Additional Manufactured Farm Inputs	M	0.88	15.9	66.7	14.8	0.8	1.6	0.1
Crop Transport	T	0.99	30.4	62.8	2.0	1.3	2.8	0.7
Manufactured Inputs	M	0.88	15.9	66.7	14.8	0.8	1.6	0.1
Utilities	U	1.62	49.8	103.4	18.1	-78.1	3.9	2.9
Services	S	0.90	86.7	2.8	0.5	4.9	5.0	0.2
Sales Revenue	Proj Spec	0.86	4.4	75.3	19.3	0.4	0.6	0.2

Table 4A.6 Breakdown of resource costs and benefits and net benefits at shadow prices ($'000 domestic consumption numeraire)

Year	1	2	3	4	5	6	7	8	9	10	11
Domestic Consumption	-1275	-1251	-1865	-1865	-1865	-1865	-1865	-1865	-1865	-1865	-1865
Foreign Exchange	-3657	-6	2655	2655	2655	2655	2655	2655	2655	2655	2655
Taxes and Subsidies	-778	311	1216	1216	1216	1216	1216	1216	1216	1216	1216
Operating Surplus (Public Sector)	-79	80	194	194	194	194	194	194	194	194	194
Operating Surplus (Private)	-149	-42	-18	-18	-18	-18	-18	-18	-18	-18	-18
Income to Unskilled Labour	-61	-93	-183	-183	-183	-183	-183	-183	-183	-183	-183
Net Benefits at Market Prices	-6000	-1000	2000	2000	2000	2000	2000	2000	2000	2000	2000
Shadow Price Adjustments											
Government											
Foreign Exchange Premium	-318	-1	231	231	231	231	231	231	231	231	231
Taxes and Subsidies	778	-311	-1216	-1216	-1216	-1216	-1216	-1216	-1216	-1216	-1216
Operating Surplus (Public Sector)	79	-80	-194	-194	-194	-194	-194	-194	-194	-194	-194
Operating Surplus (Private)	149	42	18	18	18	18	18	18	18	18	18
Income to Unskilled Labour	61	93	183	183	183	183	183	183	183	183	183
Net Benefits at Shadow Prices	-5251	-1257	1021	1021	1021	1021	1021	1021	1021	1021	1021

NPV at 8%   -473
IRR =   6.3%
DRC of FE   1.13

Table 4A.7 Distribution of resource costs and benefits ($'000 domestic consumption numeraire)

Year	1	2	3	4	5	6	7	8	9	10	11
Direct Benefits											
Landlords	0	70	140	140	140	140	140	140	140	140	140
Tenants	0	50	100	100	100	100	100	100	100	100	100
Small Farmers	0	80	160	160	160	160	160	160	160	160	160
Factory Owners	−6000	−1200	1600	1600	1600	1600	1600	1600	1600	1600	1600
Indirect Benefits											
Government	539	−392	−1179	−1179	−1179	−1179	−1179	−1179	−1179	−1179	−1179
Private Sector	149	42	18	18	18	18	18	18	18	18	18
Unskilled Workers	61	93	183	183	183	183	183	183	183	183	183
Net Benefits at Shadow Prices	−5251	−1257	1021	1021	1021	1021	1021	1021	1021	1021	1021

Present Values at 8%	
Landlords	810
Tenants	578
Small Farmers	925
Factory Owners	1985
Government	−6153
Private Sector	268
Unskilled Workers	1114
Total NPV	−473
Poor	2618
Non-Poor	3062

can potentially provide a lot of useful information on the indirect effects of projects and can make a significant contribution to more informed decisions

Note

1. In order to maintain full consistency between the various tables the value of the SER actually used was taken to four decimal places (1.0869). Of course such a level of precision is spurious in practical use and is only adopted to ensure full consistency of the figures.

5.   Projects and the MDGs: estimating poverty impact

Manabu Fujimura

Well before the adoption of the Millennium Development Goals (MDGs) by the United Nations in 2000, the development community had been looking into how to harness development programmes and projects toward benefiting the poor (see for example World Bank, 1990). In the literature on project economics, since its heyday in the 1970s various efforts have been made to extend project analysis to incorporate distributional and poverty impacts. This chapter reviews such efforts on both analytical and operational fronts. It first discusses general issues involved in distribution and poverty impact analysis, then reviews experiences at multilateral development banks including recent case studies at the Asian Development Bank. The chapter concludes with some lessons learned.

ISSUES

To Target or Not to Target?

The development community seems to have reached a consensus that growth is a necessary but not sufficient condition for poverty reduction and 'pro-poor' growth is preferred to growth maximisation. However, it is not entirely clear what exactly constitutes the sufficient condition and how things should be done differently from the past. While many governments and donors fund targeted interventions for poverty reduction, it is not easy to demonstrate that in general targeted interventions bring greater benefits to the poor than non-targeted interventions. Some may argue that non-targeted infrastructure projects are superior to targeted social sector projects in having far-reaching poverty reduction effects, provided that the policy and institutional environment is right. Such sentiment may be stronger among economists who witnessed the experience of East Asian economies. On the other hand, a number of empirical studies (for example

World Bank, 2000) appear to show that high inequality may be bad for growth, raising the possibility of a virtuous circle in which targeted interventions to improve the health and education status of the poor increase their productivity and contribute to higher growth. While this issue is often debated in a macroeconomic context and in a rather ambiguous timeframe and institutional environment, project analysis is tasked to pin down and delineate benefits and costs accruing to the poor and those accruing to the non-poor.

Absolute or Relative Poverty Reduction

A strong interpretation of pro-poor growth would be that the poor's share in national income must rise with growth. As we will see below, this criterion has been applied to the cut-off rule of poverty-targeted interventions at multilateral development banks. They required that the share of poor beneficiaries in total net benefits be above the national average ratio. This is implicitly associated with a relative concept of poverty reduction as opposed to an absolute one which would simply require that the poor's income increase absolutely with growth regardless of the change in income distribution. In principle, which criterion, or compromise, is preferred would be a matter of social choice. In practice, however, targeted interventions are often assigned the strong role of shifting income shares toward the poor. Since classification of projects (targeted or non-targeted) itself tends to be eclectic in practice, as we shall see later, project analysis might simply set out a benefit–cost profile between the poor and non-poor and leave the cut-off criterion on what is an acceptable share of benefits going to the poor to decision-making entities.

What Poverty Measure to Use?

Any poverty impact estimation must first define poverty and a measure of some threshold level with which to distinguish the poor from the non-poor. Underlying the popular use of a poverty line is the proposition that income or expenditure represents living standards through command over economic resources. Some may argue that poverty is multi-dimensional and advocate the use of non-income social indicators such as health and education status or their composite index. Others may argue that an income or expenditure measure is highly correlated with social indicators and the former can adequately approximate the latter. Project analysts must be able to use either type of poverty measure depending on the policy makers' objective and data availability.

Identification and Delivery Errors

Provided that a poverty line is chosen to distinguish the poor from the non-poor, collecting accurate data on income or expenditure at the project level is often difficult. Poverty mapping techniques, which combine data from household surveys with those from population censuses that collect detailed location-based data on households, have yet to be widely applied. Many countries still use approximate indicators for identifying the poor: for example various basic needs measures or rough estimates of average income at a village level. When income estimates are unreliable, other indirect indicators such as house material, land area, ownership of livestock and consumer durables are used. In addition to technical difficulties in identifying the poor beneficiaries, there is a great deal of uncertainty about the extent to which project services actually reach the intended beneficiaries: the issue of under-coverage and leakage. Numerous evaluation studies document leakages from various poverty-targeted programmes, be they regional targeting, individual targeting or self-targeting, due to weak governance and other reasons.[1] Similar problems are likely to occur during the implementation of development projects. Project analysis therefore must properly take account of the possibility of these errors in estimating poverty impact.

Distributional Weights

Favouring the poor as a beneficiary group in project analysis means assigning higher weights to benefits and costs they receive than to those received by the non-poor. The seminal work by Little and Mirrlees (1974) devoted one chapter to discuss different weights that might be applied between income groups, between consumption and investment benefits, and between benefits accruing to the public and private sectors.[2] In practice, however, 'the weights were hardly ever used except in an experimental manner in a few cases' (Little and Mirrlees, 1994: 207). The dominant practice simply lays out the distribution of net benefits to various beneficiary groups without assigning different weights – namely, giving an equal weight of 1.0 to all groups. One can defend current practice by arguing that equal weighting enables isolation of an efficiency test (that is, the 'potential compensation test') for project selection, putting aside the distributional effects of a project. As long as project analysis provides consistent information based on the efficiency criterion, it can function as a screening device to check against inefficient projects, while the efficiency test need not be the final decision-making rule. Ranking alternative projects according to an efficiency improvement would provide valuable information because decision makers can know the extent to which they might choose to trade off efficiency against distributional considerations.[3] Such social choice procedure should be made transparent.

EXPERIENCES AT MULTILATERAL DEVELOPMENT BANKS

Inter-American Development Bank (IDB)

'Low-income' targeting at the IDB was formally operationalised as early as the late 1970s (see Powers and Howard, 1979; Londero, 1996a). Its board's mandate at that time aimed to lend 50 per cent of its resources to benefit low-income people whose income was below US$2 per day at 1985 purchasing power parity (PPP) prices. For this purpose, a methodology for estimating benefit incidence for low-income groups was developed and applied to all project loans in the 1980s.

The IDB applied three alternative indicators.

1. First, where project benefits could not be expressed in monetary terms, the ratio of the number of low-income beneficiaries to the number of total beneficiaries was used. An obvious limitation of this indicator is that it cannot capture the benefits received by the target group relative to the total project net benefits.
2. Second, where benefits could be valued, the share of the net benefits accruing to the low-income beneficiaries in the total project net benefits was used. This is equivalent to the poverty impact ratio defined in the guidelines at the Asian Development Bank (ADB, 1997). However, the IDB encountered a serious problem in the treatment of government income. Their original methodology (Powers and Howard, 1979) suggested a rule of thumb of 0.5 as the share of government income ultimately benefiting the poor. However, detailed studies to identify the distributional consequences of public sector income in a number of countries failed to produce convincing results (Powers, 1989: 57–8).
3. In response to this difficulty, a third indicator was used: the share of the net benefits accruing to low-income beneficiaries in the total project net benefits minus net government income. This gives the share of benefits to the poor as a proportion of net private sector benefits.

At least one of the above indicators was systematically applied in project analysis with a view to establishing the overall poverty impact of

IDB lending. The results reported in Powers (1989) show an aggregate indicator of just below 50 per cent in the 1980s with significant sector variations. Infrastructure sectors such as energy and transportation on average showed the lowest indicators. It is not clear whether this is due to the fact that these sectors genuinely have the weakest poverty impact or whether it is more difficult to trace the full distribution effects in these sectors.

The IDB renewed its low-income targeting under the Directive issued in 1994. One of their operational targets was that at least 40 per cent of the total loan amount and 50 per cent of the total number of loans should be allocated to either 'social equity interventions (SEQ)' or 'poverty-targeted investment (PTI)'. All loans in social sectors (projects or programmes) were automatically categorised as SEQ while, to qualify as a PTI, a project had to satisfy one of the following criteria (IDB, 2001):

a. Sector automatic classification: projects were automatically classified as PTI when they were in the following subsectors: pre-school, primary education, early childhood development, primary health care, nutrition, urban development of marginalised areas, smallholder agricultural production, microenterprises, social investment funds, and emergency employment operations.
b. Geographic classification: projects were classified as PTI when their benefits were targeted to regions, cities, neighbourhoods, or areas identified as poor within each country. Proxy income measures such as unsatisfied basic needs, below country-average social indicators, or other household characteristics that are strongly correlated with poverty could be used to classify such areas, but generally if the indicators were below the country average, the project would be classified as PTI.
c. Headcount classification: projects could be classified as PTI when more than 50 per cent of the potential beneficiaries were likely to be poor according to the selected PTI poverty line for each country.

Apparently in response to this Directive, the amount of the IDB's social sector lending (health, education, urban development, water and sanitation) doubled from 20 per cent in the 1960–93 period to 40 per cent in the 1994–2000 period. More than half of the social sector lending (in real terms) over this period took place after 1990 with a pronounced increase in health and education lending (IDB, 2001). The automatic PTI qualification given to social sector projects could have worked both ways: on the one hand it allowed project staff time to concentrate on designing the targeting mechanism; on the other hand it could have worked as a disincentive for rigorous poverty impact estimation. While the lending target for low-income people continued through the 1990s, it is not clear whether the consequent lending shift in fact brought greater net benefits to the target group. A practical reason for the shift to the apparent eclectic criteria for PTI may have been an increased use of broader programmes such as institutional reforms that are not easily amenable to rigorous cost–benefit analysis.

World Bank

While, as mentioned above, in the 1970s the World Bank experimented with the development of a social weighting system to allow recalculation of project benefits and costs, this was never operationalised apart from some studies of a research nature. In the late 1990s a separate body of literature emerged on benefit incidence analysis (for example, van de Walle, 1998). This involved identifying the beneficiaries of broad categories of government expenditure – such as primary and secondary education – and disaggregating these by income class, such as quintile or decile. However, this work was not directly linked with project analysis and has largely been used for policy discussions on the distributive impact of different expenditure categories, such as primary, secondary or tertiary education or preventative versus curative health expenditure, and does not appear to have been applied in a project context. Moreover, a simple benefit assumption was used, that benefits to the categories of recipient equalled the financial cost met by the government rather than a theoretically more accurate measure of benefits based on willingness to pay.

In the 1990s the World Bank set out the 'programme of targeted interventions (PTI)' under which at least one of two criteria had to be met: (a) the project has a specific mechanism for targeting the poor; or (b) the proportion of the poor among project beneficiaries is significantly larger than their proportion in the overall population (which is equivalent to using the IDB indicator from the 1970s). To qualify as a PTI, project components which meet either of these criteria must account for at least 25 per cent of the total loan amount (World Bank, 2001a). As a result, the share of PTI projects in total project lending increased from 24.7 per cent in FY1992 to 49.6 per cent in FY1999 (World Bank, 2001b). Accordingly, the share of lending to the main social sectors (education, health, nutrition and population, and social protection) increased fourfold from 5 per cent in the early 1980s to 20 per cent in the late 1990s, while that for agriculture, industry and power declined from 55 per cent to 23 per cent over the same period.

This obviously reflected the managerial preference of targeted over non-targeted projects. However, there are reasons to be cautious about the implications of such a trend. A review of project appraisal and progress reports by the World Bank's evaluation department found that the criteria for PTI were too broad to be operationally useful, and in many instances PTI status appeared to be assigned almost routinely to every basic health and primary education project.[4] The World Bank abandoned the PTI system in 2001.

Asian Development Bank (ADB)

Being a late entrant into poverty targeting and the application of distribution and poverty impact analysis of projects, ADB can perhaps offer the latest experience in this area. ADB adopted its poverty reduction strategy in the late 1990s (ADB, 1999) and set out a category of targeted projects as either 'poverty interventions' or 'core poverty interventions'. Poverty interventions were aimed to benefit the poor *disproportionately* – equivalent to PTI adopted by IDB and the World Bank. Core poverty interventions were a subset of poverty interventions and were targeted specifically at indigenous and ethnic minority people. At least 40 per cent of ADB's total public sector lending was aimed to be allocated to these targeted projects.

Later in 2004, the categorisation of targeted projects was changed to three subgroups: 'household-targeted', 'geographically-targeted' and 'MDG-targeted' projects (ADB, 2006). For the household-targeted projects, the proportion of the poor among project beneficiaries must be significantly larger than their proportion in the overall population and in no cases less than 20 per cent. The geographically-targeted projects were those located in geographic areas with a significantly higher poverty incidence than the national average and had to address constraints that were responsible for poverty in the project area. The MDG-targeted projects were those with a direct impact on the non-income dimensions of poverty.

ADB's *Guidelines for the Economic Analysis of Projects* (ADB, 1997) offer a basic methodology for distribution and poverty impact analysis to assess whether the above 'poverty interventions' or 'household-targeted' projects would indeed benefit the poor as intended. The methodology is similar to the one developed at IDB earlier and its wider application was explored in Fujimura and Weiss (2000) and ADB (2001).[5] A step-wise procedure to distributional analysis can be summarised as follows:

1. Set out the annual financial data on the project showing inflows and outflows from the perspective of the project owners. This is sometimes termed a 'return to equity' calculation. Strictly this analysis can be

done accurately only after the project financing plan is finalised (since only then will the loan–equity split be known).

2. Discount each annual inflow and outflow to derive present values for each category (taxes, profits, loan principal and interest, and so forth) and a net present value (NPV). This is a financial NPV showing the income change for project owners. For example, when subsidised loans are provided to finance the project, there will be a net gain to the government and net loss to the financiers. For discounting, normally the ADB-standard rate of 12 per cent, an assumed 'economic' opportunity cost of capital, is used because ultimately the project analysis is concerned with economic viability. Obviously, a financial viability test should follow the usual practice of using the financial opportunity cost of capital faced by the project entity as a discount rate, the proxy of which is usually the weighted average cost of capital (WACC).

3. Identify sources and structures of the difference between financial and economic values of each project input/output, identify the conversion factor for each to allow shadow pricing and then express all project inputs and outputs in economic values. The conversion is simpler if the difference between financial and economic values is assumed constant over the project life, which allows the use of constant conversion factors. But changing conversion factors over time could be handled by doing annual calculations on the items concerned and discounting values for each individual year to the present. On the choice of a numeraire, normally for distribution analysis, it is simpler to use the domestic price numeraire (recommended in UNIDO, 1972, 1980) as it means that total income from the financial and economic calculations will be in the same price units. If the world price numeraire is used for the economic calculations, all financial data in steps 1 and 2 must be converted to world prices by multiplying by the standard conversion factor.

4. Allocate any difference between the financial and economic NPV to relevant groups. This, plus the financial NPV going to project owners and others, gives the economic NPV of the project. The net benefits to different groups must sum to the economic NPV of the project (see below for further explanation). When there is no financial revenue for the project entity, as in the case of road rehabilitation projects for example, the economic NPV still needs to be distributed between different groups.

5. Estimate for each identified group affected by the project the proportion of economic NPV that will go to those below the poverty line. Groups involved will vary between the different types of project, but would at least typically include consumers, workers, producers,

government and the rest of the economy. For estimating the net
benefit for the government, what is required is an estimate of the
counterfactual: that is, what proportion of government expenditure
diverted from other uses by the project would have otherwise ben-
efited the poor.

6.   Finally, sum all economic NPV going to the poor and divide by the
total project economic NPV. This gives a 'poverty impact ratio (PIR)'
of the project under consideration. This indicator might be used
against the project criterion that might require disproportionate net
benefits going to the poor relative to the share of the poor in national
income.

The logic involved in step 4 above (distribution analysis) can be understood by drawing on the identity: $NPV_{econ} = NPV_{fin} + (NPV_{econ} - NPV_{fin})$
where the subscripts *econ* and *fin* refer to economic and financial flows,
respectively. Some simple examples for the allocation of $(NPV_{econ} - NPV_{fin})$
are: subsidies to project inputs as a net gain to input suppliers and a net
loss to government (or the rest of the economy); employment of surplus
labour in the project area as a net gain to workers and a net loss to the
project owners by the difference between the actual payroll and its economic value; and safe drinking water at a lower cost than the existing one
as a net gain to consumers and a net loss to the existing producers.[6]

Of the parameters to be estimated in step 5 above, two are the most
fundamental. One is benefit incidence – the extent to which it is possible
to distinguish between the poor and non-poor among direct beneficiaries.
The other is the problem of establishing the indirect impact of the gains/
losses that accrue to the government and the rest of the economy.

Estimation of how the poor among direct beneficiaries are affected
by a project in question can be complex. In most cases identifying the
poor among project beneficiary groups would require extra effort at the
project design stage. When existing household survey data are available
at regional or district level, these can be combined with census data to
infer the poverty profiles of the project-influencing area using a poverty
mapping technique. When such data are not available, an alternative
would be to conduct a project-specific household survey. Given the difficulties in accurately capturing household income in a one-off survey (for
example where there is significant subsistence activity and multiple family
jobs) or household expenditure (for example where recall bias is present),
it may be appropriate and more cost effective to seek proxy indicators
of poverty such as lack of clean water or adequate shelter or access to
primary education. Benefit incidence is also affected by the form of service
delivery. In particular, user charges would discourage access by the poor,

raising the possibility of a trade-off between poverty impact (at least of a direct nature) and project sustainability. Analysis of demand elasticity of the poor is needed. The issue of under-coverage and leakage must also be addressed. Pre-investment socioeconomic assessments should yield adequate information on these points.[7]

Since governments are major participants in public sector projects even where they have no direct equity commitment, a critical parameter in poverty impact analysis is the extent to which marginal government expenditure and taxation accrue to the poor, namely, an estimate of marginal benefit or tax incidence on the poor with respect to additional government expenditure or revenue. This is particularly important where poverty-targeted projects receive subsidies. Normally, however, such information is not available and in itself is a subject that requires intensive research. Unless such knowledge is available for the country for which project analysis is being done, some simplifying procedure would be needed to overcome the problem. For example, for simplicity one could assume, admittedly with no rigorous theoretical underpinning, that the way the government spends additional funds raised by a project or collects funds necessary for subsidising a project will not alter the distribution of income, so that the poor will share in the benefits created by any additional government income in direct proportion to their share in gross domestic product (GDP). Then the poor's share in GDP can be calculated using the poverty line, poverty headcount and poverty gap indexes, and used as a proxy for the share of the poor in the benefits created by the expenditure of additional government income.[8]

CASE STUDIES

ADB's practice in the distribution and poverty impact analysis outlined above has to some extent repeated what was experienced at IDB earlier, namely, a gradual loss in zeal after trials and errors, and a shift of poverty focus away from the project context to the macro and sector context. ADB (2006: 77) reflects, 'experience to date. . . has been mixed due to considerable differences in the way the methodology has been interpreted and applied'. Nevertheless, a review of the recent project documents reveals that the practice did survive, and in certain subsectors, such as railways, the use of distribution analysis seems to be standardised, although the extent of rigour and thoroughness varies. Here six case studies are summarised based on publicly available documents on ADB projects that were approved between 2003 and 2008. Only the relevant economic analysis for each case is presented, while other important aspects of project analysis (such as the project rationale, demand analysis, least-cost analysis, financial sustainability, institutions, sensitivity and risk) are omitted.[9]

Vietnam: Northern Power Transmission Expansion Sector Project

The project represents a five-year time slice (2006–10) of Electricity of Vietnam's (EVN) transmission expansion programme, comprising individual subprojects. It covers the northern part of Vietnam, which is relatively poor. The project will enable power to be supplied to the planned industrial zones in the region, facilitating employment and income-generating opportunities for the poor and ethnic minorities. The 'without' scenario assumes that no investment will be made in the north beyond 2007 but allows a possibility of meeting demand until 2010 with the spare capacity in the south. The 'with' case assumes that at the end of the time slice, any incremental sales after 2015 would require further investments, so the analysis does not include benefits after 2015. Non-incremental benefits are based on the saved cost by either substitution from less efficient energy sources (for residential consumers) or self-generation (for non-residential or commercial consumers). Incremental benefits are estimated using consumer surveys conducted by EVN in 2003. Capital and operating costs are adjusted from their border prices to domestic prices with conversion factors of 1.08 and 1.10, respectively.

Table 5.1 shows a summary result of the benefit–cost distribution among the major stakeholder groups. All groups stand to gain from the project, while residential consumers and the government (and the general economy) are the larger gainers. Despite the profits tax, the electricity company maintains positive financial benefits even at the 12 per cent discount rate.[10] The analysis stopped short of extending to a poverty impact analysis, presumably because the project is non-targeted and faced the difficulty of estimating the benefit incidence for the general economy. Nonetheless, it would have been useful to explore what was the proportion of poor beneficiaries, at least among residential consumers.

China: Pali–Lijiang Railway Project

The project is a railway, 167 kilometres in length, located in the north-western part of Yunnan province, a relatively poor part of China. It will connect Kunming, Shanghai and Beijing through three of the 16 east–west and north–south railway corridors. It also promotes regional integration for the Greater Mekong Subregion (GMS). Freight traffic for the route was forecast by commodity (such as coal, petroleum products, iron and steel, cement, timber) for two categories of traffic: traffic diverted from

Table 5.1 *Distribution analysis for Vietnam: Northern Power Transmission Expansion Project (billion dong)*

Item	Fin NPV	Econ NPV	ENPV – FNPV	EVN	Residential consumers	Non-res. consumers	Govt/ Economy
Benefits							
Revenue from residents	38 232	38 232	0				
Revenue from non-residents	107 137	107 137	0				
Surplus: residents		56 281	56 281		56 281		
Surplus: non-residents		2 313	2 313			2 313	
Costs							
Capital	−70 618	−76 312	−5 694				−5 694
O&M	−17 996	−19 935	−1 939				−1 939
Purchases from IPPs	−2 855	−2 855	0				
Profit tax	−50 906	0	50 906				50 906
Net benefits	2 994			2 994			
Gains and losses		104 861	101 867	2 994	56 281	2 313	43 273

Notes: NPV = net present value; EVN = Electricity of Vietnam; Economy = the rest of the economy; O&M = operations and maintenance; IPP = independent power producer.

Source: Modified from the loan document available at ADB website.

other modes (mainly roads); and traffic generated by the project railway. The economic benefits consist of: (i) operating cost savings in freight and passenger traffic diverted from roads; (ii) operating cost savings in diverted passenger traffic estimated by the difference between cost by railway and bus; (iii) time savings in passenger traffic diverted from buses based on value of time estimated from the net income of local residents; (iv) net economic value for additional production due to the project railway; and (v) net economic value of generated tourist days valued at the average tourist expenditure. The project costs are separated into tradables, non-tradables, labour and land. A shadow exchange rate factor of 1.013 was used to convert border prices into domestic price values. A shadow wage rate factor of 0.67 was applied to unskilled labour.

Table 5.2 shows a summary result of the benefit–cost distribution among the major stakeholder groups. All groups except the railway operator stand to gain, while the government and the general economy is the largest gainer, mainly as a result of the induced production activities. While the railway operator incurs an economic loss at the 12 per cent discount rate, it maintains positive financial net benefits at the estimated WACC of 4.5 per cent (financial internal rate of return is estimated to be 6.7 per cent). The analysis here also stops short of extending to a poverty impact analysis. Again it would have been useful to explore the proportion of poor beneficiaries, at least among direct users of the railway.

Nepal: Road Connectivity Sector I Project

The project constructs and upgrades ten feeder roads with a total distance of 490 kilometres in 17 districts. It will improve access of remotely located people to social facilities and employment opportunities in major towns. Economic analysis was carried out for three sample roads, which represent about 46 per cent of the project roads by length. Traffic volume by vehicle type was measured at various locations and normalised by seasonal factors to obtain annual average daily traffic for the base year of 2005. Traffic growth was estimated based on forecast GDP growth and an income elasticity of transport demand. The economic benefits were quantified in terms of vehicle operating cost savings and time savings under the 'with' scenario compared with the 'without' scenario. The economic costs were derived by applying a shadow exchange rate factor of 1.1 to tradable inputs and a shadow wage rate factor of 0.7 to unskilled labour.

Table 5.3 shows a summary result for the benefit–cost distribution among the major stakeholder groups and in this case the poverty impact. While direct users of the road (passengers, freight users, vehicle owners) and workers gain, the government (and the general economy) loses greatly

Table 5.2 Distribution analysis for China: Pali–Lijiang Railway Project (million Chinese yuan)

Item	Fin NPV	Econ NPV	ENPV – FNPV	Railway operator	Shippers	Passengers	Labour	Govt/ Economy
Benefits								
Freight revenue	1576	1576	0					
Passenger revenue	1353	1353	0					
Cost saving for freight		1877	1877		1877			
Cost saving for passengers		1009	1009			1009		
Generated production		5074	5074					5074
Generated tourism		448	448					448
Costs								
Capital and O&M	−3202	−3682	−480					−480
Labour	−489	−328	161				161	
Tax	−219	0	219					219
Net benefits	−981	7327	8308					
Gains and losses				−981	1877	1009	161	5261

Source: Modified from the loan document available at the ADB website.

Table 5.3 Distribution and poverty impact analysis for Nepal: Road Connectivity Sector I Project (million Nepal rupees)

Item	Fin NPV	Econ NPV	ENPV – FNPV	Passenger users	Freight users	Vehicle owners	Labour	Govt/Economy
Benefits								
Road user benefits		2245	2245	416	559	1229		41
Costs								
Capital	−987	−1188	−201					−201
O&M	−23	−25	−2					−2
Labour	−503	−352	151				151	
Net benefits	−1513	680	2193					
Gains and losses				416	559	1229	151	−1675
Proportion of the poor				0.5	0.5	0	0.8	0.15
Benefits to the poor				208	280	0	121	−121
Poverty impact ratio					488/680 = 0.717			
Net benefit to the poor per project cost					488/1513 = 0.323			

Notes:
The net loss to the Government/Economy (−1675) is calculated as: − 1513 + 41 − 201 − 2.
The original loan document used the world price numeraire in valuing project costs, but here they were converted to the domestic price numeraire for consistency with this chapter.

Source: Modified from the loan document available at the ADB website.

114

because it incurs all project costs while there are no user charges. While the project is financed as a grant and the operation and maintenance (O&M) cost is estimated to be low relative to the capital cost, it is not entirely clear how the project services will be maintained in the long run as the project document does not provide a fiscal sustainability analysis. On the other hand, the project is pro-poor in that half of the direct user benefits accrue to the poor, making the poverty impact ratio high – although the 'efficiency of poverty impact' (project net economic benefits to the poor divided by project cost) is not very high.

China: Jilin Urban Environmental Improvement Project

The project is an initiative of the Jilin provincial government and is composed of three components: (i) improved and expanded water supply, wastewater services and solid waste management in the city of Changchun; (ii) improved and expanded water supply and wastewater facilities in the city of Yanji; and (iii) improved air quality in Yanji through a more efficient central heating system. Through improved service delivery by the six local providers, the project is expected to benefit 3.6 million urban residents (3.2 million in Changchun and 0.4 million in Yanji). Economic benefits of all the components are estimated by the contingent valuation method which uses surveys to elicit willingness to pay for the project services. Economic costs of tradable components were converted to domestic price units using a shadow exchange rate factor of 1.013 and those of unskilled labour were derived using a shadow wage rate of 0.8.

Table 5.4 shows a summary result for the benefit–cost distribution among the major stakeholder groups and the poverty impact. Direct consumers gain greatly relative to the other groups. While the service providers incur a small economic loss at the 12 per cent discount rate, the project has positive financial net benefits at the estimated WACC of 3.5 per cent (the base-case financial internal rate of return is estimated to be 9.0 per cent) as cost recovery mechanisms through various tariffs are designed under the project. In terms of poverty impact, due to the relatively low poverty incidence among the direct beneficiaries in the urban areas affected, the project is unlikely to be targeted sharply. The efficiency of poverty impact is not very high – although accurate judgement is difficult in the absence of information on alternative targeted interventions in the same geographical area.

Indonesia: Vocational Education Strengthening Project

In Indonesia demand for senior secondary education exceeds supply as education up to the secondary level is rapidly becoming the minimum

Table 5.4 Distribution and poverty impact analysis for China: Jilin Urban Environmental Improvement Project (million Chinese yuan)

Item	Fin NPV	Econ NPV	ENPV – FNPV	Service providers	Consumers	Labour	Govt/ Economy
Benefits	4001	7235	3234		3234		
Costs							
Capital	−1680	−1703	−23				−23
O&M	−2117	−2154	−37				−37
Labour	−58	−48	10			10	
Profit tax	−200	0	200				200
Net benefits	−54	3330	3384				
Gains and losses				−54	3234	10	140
Proportion of the poor				0	0.12	0.15	0.17
Benefits to the poor				0	388	2	20
Poverty impact ratio					410/3330 = 0.123		
Net benefit to the poor per project cost					410/3855 = 0.106		

Source: Modified from the loan document available at the ADB website.

standard for formal sector employment. Labour statistics indicate that vocational school graduates outperform general school graduates in the labour market. Under such circumstances, the project will expand some model vocational schools to create large schools with enrolments of around 1500 students where courses on offer will be diversified with stronger industry linkages and with stronger teaching and mentoring teams than in existing secondary schools. This is a national level project and will develop 90 public model schools (at least one model school cluster per province) and strengthen curriculum linkage with industries. The project's economic viability is assessed by judging whether the wage differentials due to the project would be adequate to achieve a threshold economic rate of return of 12 per cent. The project will lead to 367 000 male and female working graduates generating 3.7 million work-years over 16 years. Under the general scenario in which the graduates from the project schools join the labour force with the assumed unemployment rate taken from the 2006 National Labour Force Survey, the wage differential required to achieve the 12 per cent economic rate of return is estimated to be Rp52 800 per month per working graduate. This is calculated to be 6.9 per cent of the current median wage and is equivalent to an additional paid 30 minutes per workday. It is considered feasible for the project to make this difference.

While estimating net benefits accruing to the poor is difficult for education projects, mainly because of the difficulty of attributing a specific segment of education to lifetime earning differential, an indicative headcount assessment is possible. It turns out that in senior secondary education including vocational schools, location plays a large role in determining participation by different income groups, with urban students having better access to schools than rural students (Table 5.5). The table indicates that in comparison with general schooling, vocational schools serve lower-income groups in the bottom quintiles slightly better, indicating some pro-poor potential from the project. However, no formal analysis of benefit incidence is conducted as part of the appraisal partly because of the geographically non-targeted nature of this particular project. For more geographically targeted education projects, headcount poverty impact assessment would be possible at least.

Bangladesh: Second Urban Primary Health Care Project

The project covers eleven cities and municipalities in Bangladesh and contracts out primary health care services to NGOs through partnership agreements. This approach proved effective under the preceding primary health care project. The current project requires that at least 30 per cent

Table 5.5   Distribution of senior secondary students by income quintile, gender and location (%)

	Q1	Q2	Q3	Q4	Q5	Total
VS urban	11.3	14.4	14.8	13.2	9.1	62.8
VS rural	3.7	5.0	7.4	9.5	11.6	37.2
VS male	8.8	12.1	13.6	13.8	12.8	61.1
VS female	6.2	7.3	8.6	8.9	7.9	38.9
VS total	15.0	19.4	22.2	22.7	20.7	100.0
GS total	12.7	17.3	19.9	23.5	26.6	100.0

Notes: Q = quintile; GS = general senior secondary school; VS = vocational senior secondary school.

Source: Loan document available at ADB website.

of the preventive and curative services are provided free for the poor, while user fees are charged to people who can afford them. An attempt was made to estimate DALYs (disability adjusted life years) to assess the cost-effectiveness of the project based on the reduction in infant, under-five and maternal mortality and child malnutrition rates (see Chapter 6 in this volume). In total, the project will reduce 2.3 million DALYs or 16 per cent of the estimated DALYs under the 'without' scenario over the next 20 years. The cost per DALY saved is estimated to be $35, which is comparable with the preceding project and is within the acceptable range listed in ADB's health sector policy.

To assess economic viability and poverty impact, two streams of benefits were considered: resource cost saving for the existing patients due to the improved access and quality of primary health care, and productivity gain from the prevention and early treatment of diseases. The former is based on the saved out-of-pocket expenses on outpatient visits, treatments and prescriptions, which are taken as $0.5–1.0 per person per year in the areas covered by the project. The productivity gain was calculated based on the estimated lifetime earning of workers due to the time saved by surviving and escaping sickness. Time saved from reduced under-five and maternal mortality and child malnutrition rates is estimated to be about 16 days per year. Time saved from reduced sick days is estimated to be about four days per year. The value of one day is estimated at $0.2 considering that the majority of the beneficiaries are poor people, women and children with limited earning opportunities. Table 5.6 is reconstructed from the explanation in the text. It shows how the poverty impact analysis might have been carried out. As the project document omits further details such

*Table 5.6   Poverty impact analysis for Bangladesh: Second Urban
Primary Health Care Project (US$ million)*

	Econ NPV	Service providers	Users	Govt/ Economy
Benefits				
Resource cost saving				
Productivity gain	139.4		139.4	
Costs	−74.6	−4.0		−70.6
Net benefits	64.8			
Gains and losses		−4.0	139.4	−70.6
Proportion of the poor		0	0.3	0.1
Benefits to the poor		0	41.8	−7.1
Poverty impact ratio		34.7/64.8 = 0.535		
Net benefits to the poor per project economic cost		34.7/74.6 = 0.465		

Source: Constructed and modified from the loan document available at ADB website.

as the estimated number of beneficiaries and the assumed life expectancy, it is not clear how the total resource cost saving and total productivity gain were derived. Considering the uncertain reliability of the assumptions used in benefit valuation here, this is only one indication of how health projects could be subjected to poverty impact analysis. A more conservative approach to poverty impact would be to compare DALYs saved for the poor as a proportion of DALYs saved for all project beneficiaries.

LESSONS LEARNED

Advantages

There are several advantages of carrying out distribution and poverty impact analysis as illustrated above. First, it can remedy the deficiency of a headcount approach, which simply counts the poor beneficiaries among the total project beneficiaries. The headcount approach is simple but is a blunt measure of poverty impact – similar to the problem with the use of a poverty headcount index as opposed to a poverty gap ratio. The headcount approach is also deficient in neglecting those affected negatively by the project. In many projects that are net users of public funds, people outside the project influence area are losers and their losses must also be distributed between the poor and non-poor in poverty impact analysis.

Furthermore, the headcount approach tells nothing about the 'efficiency of delivering poverty reduction impact'. While some targeted projects may provide tangible benefits to the identified beneficiaries, the question remains whether their delivery mechanism is cost effective. As illustrated in the case studies above, the poverty impact analysis can check the efficiency of poverty reduction by calculating the net benefits going to the poor per unit project cost.[11]

Second, disaggregating benefits and costs across different stakeholders ensures that the economic and financial analyses are done in a consistent manner: the differences between financial and economic values arising from a project will be equal to a series of distributional impacts that must be identified and quantified. Therefore the extent of incompleteness in the project economic analysis will be reduced. It forces a more thorough cost–benefit analysis than is conventionally carried out. For example, in the analysis of agricultural projects, focusing on distribution and poverty impact forces separate consideration of different farm sizes when preparing farm-income statements, which in turn may lead to a more detailed analysis of the rate of adoption of technology, contributing to better accounting for differences in expected productivity increases among farmers (Londero, 1995).

Third, the estimation of net benefits accruing to different stakeholders will help clarify who are the major gainers and losers, and sharpen the judgement of project sustainability both from a financial and a political economy perspective. It can show, for example, the extent to which different designs of tariff structure in public utility projects allocate net benefits to particular income groups, which can better inform policy choices.

Limitations

In practice, there are numerous limitations and difficulties associated with distribution and poverty impact analysis. First, while distribution analysis in principle requires no additional information beyond that required for a good conventional financial and economic analysis, imperfect practice due to resource constraints often means that additional resources will be required to do what is considered a good distribution analysis. Financial NPV is estimated from a financial analysis and its derivation should identify income flows to various groups, while economic NPV is a natural extension of such financial analysis. However, if appraisal is done crudely (for example, financing arrangements are not included), or economic NPV only contains a single economic price such as a shadow exchange rate, then the distribution information that can be obtained will be only crude. In other words, distribution analysis can be no more sophisticated than the conventional financial and economic calculations on a project.

Second, there is a broad range of project types and the method outlined above is not always applicable. At one end of the range are projects in sectors such as power and irrigation, where economic analysis techniques are regularly applied in a relatively rigorous way and where the use of distribution and poverty analysis can be a natural extension of current work. At the other end of the range are projects in social sectors for which economic benefits or rate of return are rarely estimated. Here the headcount approach may be the best that could be done: for example, beneficiaries may be in terms of numbers of poor patients or poor pupils and cost effectiveness in terms of cost per patient or pupil. We have already seen the limited nature of poverty assessment for the education and health projects discussed here. On the other hand, the risk of targeting and delivery errors should be assessed carefully for social sector projects.

Third, it is well known that indirect and dynamic project effects can have distribution consequences that may be at least as significant as direct effects. The counterfactual problem, which is inherent to any policy analysis, is magnified the more dynamic effects are to be taken into account. The cost–benefit literature includes some extension of project analysis to dynamic models in which key parameters including shadow prices and discount rates need not be constant over time. The same argument would apply to the parameters specific to poverty impact analysis such as the proportion of project benefits accruing to the poor out of additional government income, which is assumed constant in the current practice. However, it seems to take a heroic effort to make dynamic models operational in the practice of project appraisal, while to some extent dynamic models are useful for policy-level analysis as the resources involved in such modelling could be warranted at the policy level (Fujimura and Weiss, 2000).

Promises

All in all, it is feasible to estimate the poverty impact of projects; it can be a natural extension of a reasonably competently conducted economic analysis, and it is more reliable than the available alternatives such as the headcount approach or approaches based on assertions about particular sectors being 'pro-poor'.

To the extent possible, project-specific surveys should be carried out to characterise the main constraints to increased income and improved access and to enable estimation of poor beneficiaries and the extent to which they will benefit from a project. When a resource constraint does not allow project-specific surveys, complementary information could be sought at the sector level, including cross-country studies of the same sector or similar projects. Careful assessment of poverty at the sector level can also inform the context for project implementation, including the macroeconomic, public expenditure, and institutional contexts. Public expenditure incidence analysis can be used as a rough indicator for the benefit distribution of government net benefits between the poor and non-poor. Institutional analysis can also be used to refine knowledge on the channels and mechanisms through which project benefits are likely to reach the poor. For example, in power or water supply projects, if theft by poor households is widespread, it could be countered by offering free connection and water bill discounts so that new user charge income more than offsets loss due to leakage, and the coverage of the poor households can be expanded in a monitorable way. In education and health projects, teachers and health workers could be trained and employed exclusively from ethnic minorities in order to serve their own people who might otherwise not have access to the services due to language and cultural barriers. In all types of projects, workfare mechanisms can be employed to implement project components that require only unskilled work.

NOTES

1. Weiss (2005) examines these issues in detail in the context of Asia.
2. Squire and Van der Tak (1975) refined these aspects and developed formulae to derive the weights. MacArthur (1978) and UNIDO (1980) provided detailed case studies on the use of distributional weights. Ray (1984) extended the analysis and advocated a systematic use of distributional weights in project analysis.
3. See Harberger (1978) for this line of argument.
4. See Evans (2000) for details.
5. See also Gajewski and Luppino (2004) and Gajewski et al. (2004).
6. Jenkins (1999) provides a detailed discussion on these points.
7. See ADB (2001: 18–20, 45–66) for a fuller discussion.
8. See ADB (2001: 20–21, 137–40) for a fuller discussion. In the case studies discussed, government income and the residual income to the rest of the economy are treated as the same, and the constant share of the poor in benefits from marginal government expenditure is applied to both categories.
9. Outside Asia, Potts (2003) provides a case study of distribution analysis applied to a semi-fictitious Tanzanian project.
10. At the estimated WACC of 6.9 per cent, the project would yield greater financial benefits than indicated in the distribution analysis.
11. In this regard, Mosley (2001) and Potts (2001) offer an interesting debate as to how far one could attempt to estimate a 'poverty elasticity of aid expenditure'.

6. Projects and risk

John Weiss and Keith Ward

Uncertainty about future project values is present in all projects and in practice is addressed with differing degrees of rigour. The theory underlying these adjustments has been known for a long time. In an uncertain world where decision takers are unconcerned about the level of risk (risk-neutrality) expected future effects must be estimated based on their probability of occurrence and a measure of project worth calculated at a discount rate that is unadjusted for risk. This is the standard assumption applied in the appraisal of many public sector projects. Alternatively, where risk is perceived as a cost by decision takers (risk-aversion), there are two possible approaches. In one approach, future expected effects are adjusted for risk by conversion to a certainty equivalent value.[1] If this is done the normal unadjusted discount rate can be applied. In the other approach future effects are valued at their expected future value but the discount rate is adjusted upwards to incorporate risk. In other words, where decision takers place a cost on risk, either net benefits are adjusted downwards or the discount rate is raised.

Theoretically the procedure of adjusting the discount rate upwards by a fixed margin to address risk is likely to be misleading since it will only be correct where uncertainty increases through time. In practice a majority of public sector appraisals adopt the expected value (or probability-weighted) approach to risk, which has been greatly simplified by the advent of computer software packages. However, there are a number of possible amendments that can be introduced following several contributions to the theoretical literature, which this chapter highlights.

This chapter focuses on three adjustments for addressing an uncertain future that have been added to the toolkit of project analysis in recent years. These are:

- a probability weighted risk analysis;
- an assessment of the benefits of waiting to reduce uncertainty through the estimation of an option value;
- the application of a declining discount rate.

RISK ANALYSIS

The standard distinction in the theoretical literature is between risk, defined as measurable uncertainty in the form of a probability distribution for all future project values, and uncertainty, defined as a lack of knowledge of the relevant probabilities. In practice it will be rare that exact probabilities will be known (although climatic models for example can apply time series of data to predict the likelihood of rainfall with some precision) and risk analysis involves assigning estimates of probabilities based on computer simulations of many trial runs. The classic statement of this approach, Pouliquen (1970), was written before the advent of computer software packages made the application of probability-based project analysis readily accessible.[2] What is involved is the random variation of all important project variables within specified functional forms for the underlying probability distribution for each variable (so-called Monte Carlo simulations). For example, a normal distribution might be specified and once a mean or 'best guess' and the standard deviation are estimated, values for a project item can be allowed to vary within the distribution. Since particular items may vary together (for example selling price and output will be negatively related in most projects) it will be important to build co-variance into the model.[3]

However, despite the overcoming of computational limitations to the application of such techniques, there are major practical considerations in relation to data and the extent to which a situation can reasonably be defined as risk (as opposed to uncertainty) through the construction of a meaningful probability distribution of outcomes. The actual situation with data availability is likely to vary enormously both between projects and also across different sources of variability within any one project environment. At one extreme, large volumes of reliable cross-sectional or time series data may be available from historical sources for the variable concerned (for example, for rainfall, for commodity prices, for traffic flows). At the other extreme there may only be a few data points (for example, just three specified as most likely, minimum possible and maximum possible values), which are expectations of experts involved in preparing the project. Other possibilities lying within these extremes might be based on modelling forecasts for parameters such as trade flows, commodity prices or household demand.

It is important to note that risk analysis can be undertaken with modest amounts of data since simplifying assumptions can be adopted. At the very least 'best guesses' for most likely, maximum and minimum values can be used to apply triangular distributions for key variables.

Table 6.1 summarises some of the key principles and steps to be followed in practical situations.

Table 6.1   Principles to apply in handling data

Principles to apply
1 Those key variables for which future values are unknown and which are likely to affect project returns should be identified.
2 The general nature and origin of the data set which is used for modelling those variables' values should be fully explained.
3 If the data is derived from subjective sources, the method by which it was elicited should be explained.
4 The form of the probability distributions assigned to the key variables should be explained (for example whether these distributions are triangular, uniform, normal, logarithmic, or exponential).
5 The goodness of fit of the distribution to the data set should be made clear (if fitted with risk software), and the appropriate statistical measures cited.
6 Any correlation thought to exist between the key variables used in the risk analysis should be made explicit and justified.

Source: Adapted from ADB (2002, Table 1).

Using probability estimates from various sources risk analysis allows the calculation of an expected measure of project worth, such as a probability weighted NPV or IRR, in other words the sum of all possible outcomes weighted by the estimated probability of their occurrence. In addition and importantly the variance of this return and the probability of project failure are also derived. Thus the result of risk analysis is to identify projects (or alternative designs of the same project) which have two essential characteristics – that is, the expected value of their economic return (as measured by their expected NPV, or IRR etc.) and their degree of risk (as measured by their variability in general) – captured by the distribution's measures of dispersion, such as variance and coefficient of variation, and also by the probability of the return falling below some unacceptable level, such as a cut-off IRR.[4] This quantitative measure of risk adds to the information available to the decision maker, although in itself it does not necessarily provide any guide as to whether any individual project is acceptable (or even as to which project among several possible ones actually should be undertaken). However, where conducted at an early stage of a project's life, risk analysis allows for project redesign to reduce the level of risk, whether for example through engineering redesign or organisational changes, such as concluding a long-term supply contract for key raw materials.

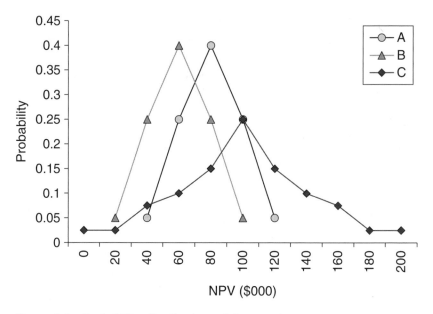

Figure 6.1   Probability distributions of three projects

The discussion of the 'acceptability' of particular levels of risk is usually presented in terms of choice among competing projects.[5] Figure 6.1 shows three project alternatives (A, B and C). Project B is inefficient, in the sense that whilst its variability is the same as project A's, so it does not offer greater stability in income, its expected value for the NPV is lower. On the other hand, project C has a higher expected value of its NPV than project A but it also has a greater variability of returns (including the possibility that its return will be zero).

Project B can be ruled out immediately but the choice between A and C depends on the trade-off between greater potential returns – reflected in the higher expected NPV – and greater variability of these returns, implying greater risk.

A decision on which project to select requires that the expected higher returns of project C be weighed against the increased degree of risk of the project, so optimal project choice in such circumstances will be determined by reference to the decision makers' risk-aversion, or the rate at which they are prepared to trade off expected returns against their variability.

Figure 6.2 shows how individuals are thought to be risk-averse; the line joins points of equal utility (giving an indifference curve) from combinations of expected income (measured in $000) and variability of income (measured by annual income variance). It is drawn to illustrate that greater

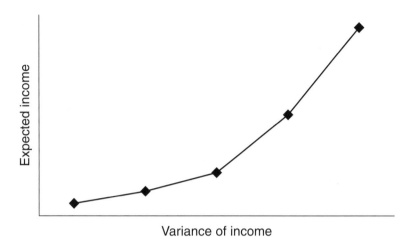

Figure 6.2   Risk-aversion: line of equal utility

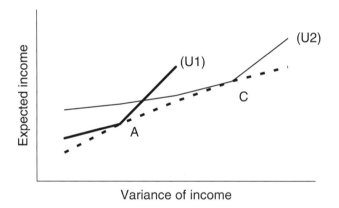

Figure 6.3   Project choice and risk-aversion

variability in income must be compensated by an increasingly larger expected income. In theory the optimal combination of expected returns and their variability will depend on the trade-off of decision makers.

Figure 6.3 combines the expected returns–variance frontier for projects A and C with two alternative indifference curves of a decision maker. With individual utility function (U1) project A will be chosen (lower expected NPV, lower risk) while with U2 the choice will be project C (higher expected return, higher risk).

In practice decisions are often taken on the basis of expected values of NPV or IRR but in some circumstances the risk involved (as measured for example by the probability of project failure) is taken into account. The standard view taken towards public sector investment is that governments with large project portfolios can afford to ignore the riskiness of investments as long as the expected values are acceptable, in other words governments should be risk-neutral. This is because, with a large number of investments, the costs of any individual project failure can be absorbed readily within the portfolio as a whole.[6] Exceptions to this argument arise only for very specific cases:

- where projects are very large relative to the overall portfolio or the economy as a whole;
- where project returns are large and pro-cyclical (such that bad performance of a project is correlated with a bad out-turn for the economy as a whole);
- where a project has a major impact on particular groups (for example in one poor region) such that the impact on those affected is severe.

For example, for large projects, particularly in small countries, since we know from *ex post* evaluation studies that there is always a failure rate, a simple rule of thumb is not to accept a project whose probability of failure is greater than the historic failure rate for the portfolio.[7]

More broadly the primary role of the analysis of the risks faced by projects lies not in enabling choice among competing projects but in the information this provides about the proposed project and its particular environment – such that consideration can be given as to how the project may be redesigned to reduce risks to an acceptable level. Ideally, the same level of expected benefits may be found to be achievable with less risk, or – if risk reduction also reduces expected net benefits (either by increasing costs or reducing benefits) – then the extent of that trade-off can be made clear to decision makers and stakeholders. Table 6.2 suggests some general principles which can be applied to risk analysis for the purpose of project design.

The results of a risk analysis are not only of use in designing the components of a project to allow for risk mitigation. They can also be used to inform the processes of implementation management and financial planning. In particular, identification of the most risky parameters can help determine the most important items for risk monitoring and risk response planning. This in turn can affect financial planning in relation to sharing risks with other parties or transferring risks through insurance or contracts.

Table 6.2   Principles in applying risk analysis in project design

Principles to apply
1 Identify any risks facing the proposed project as soon as possible.
2 Construct a 'risk matrix' for the proposed project, ranking risks according to their relative likelihood of occurrence and their expected scale of impact.
3 Identify 'key' variables (for example, quantities, unit costs, output mixes, output prices, uptake/adoption rates, price and income elasticities of demand) which are sources of risk and determinants of project returns.
4 Decide which of these variables may be subject to quantitative description.
5 Identify data sources for each variable whether forecasts or 'best guesses'.
6 Construct probability distributions of key variables.
7 Perform simplified probabilistic analysis (that is, Monte Carlo simulation using computer software) to generate a cumulative distribution function of expected IRR/NPV, or minimum/maximum expected values of the IRR and NPV.
8 On the basis of results, decide whether the risk of IRR<discount rate or NPV<0 is acceptable.
9 *If extent of risk is regarded as 'acceptable'*, redesign may not be necessary.
10 *If extent of risk is regarded as 'not acceptable'*, either redesign or abandon the project.

Source: Adapted from ADB (2002, Table 6).

OPTION VALUES

Formal risk analysis uses future project values on the basis of prob-abilities. However, an important theoretical development related to uncer-tainty highlights the value of waiting (Dixit and Pindyck, 1994).[8] There is a clear theoretical case that under uncertainty, where a project decision is irreversible and waiting can increase learning and information on likely outcomes (thus leading to a more informed decision), the cost of not waiting should be taken into account in project analysis. As many project decisions are irreversible (roads and power plants, once built, cannot be moved and forest land, once cleared for development, cannot be easily replanted) in principle this is an important issue and relates to the familiar problem of optimal timing decisions for projects.

The original project analysis of timing decisions compared the future values of benefits and costs, where projects commenced in different years, but all future values were discounted back to the same base year. Thus the optimal timing choice would be based on the highest NPV with all present values in terms of a common year t. Thus where there are three alternative start dates, year t, year $t+1$ and year $t+2$, all benefits and costs will be discounted back to year t, no matter which year the project commences. The key manual from the 1970s discussed timing as an example of mutually exclusive alternatives, arguing that 'Postponing a project can be advantageous only in circumstances where the potential benefit and cost stream will increase independently of when a project is begun. . .the project should be begun in that year when the present worth is greatest' (Gittinger, 1972: 118–19). This analysis projects future benefits and costs as if they are known with certainty and critically makes no allowance for the fact that the process of delaying a project may improve information on project outcomes.

However, where irreversibility holds, the option of waiting to see how things develop (for example if road traffic or power demand grows as predicted) is ruled out, which is a potential lost benefit. This can be illustrated algebraically for a simple two-period case, with investment in one year and benefits arising in the next. Where the conventional timing approach is taken for a choice between three starting years (0, 1 and 2) we must compare the NPV for the three alternatives where:

$$NPV_0 = B_1/(1 + i) - K$$

$$NPV_1 = B_2/(1 + i)^2 - K/(1 + i)$$

$$NPV_3 = B_3/(1 + i)^3 - K/(1 + i)^2$$

where B refers to benefits; the subscripts refer to years in which they arise; K is capital cost; and i is the discount rate.

However, this approach makes no allowance for risk and the fact that delaying can improve information. These aspects can be incorporated simply where investment K in year 0 generates either a high benefit B_A or a low benefit B_B in the following year with probabilities of p_A and $(1 - p_A)$. Using risk analysis the standard decision criterion is to invest if the economic NPV is positive where:

$$NPV = (p_A.B_A + (1 - p_A).B_B)/(1 + i) - K$$

Waiting a year allows K to be invested at i for one year in liquid assets and for a decision to go ahead to be taken one year later only if the higher benefit figure occurs in year 1. If the lower benefit figure accrues, the investment need not go ahead and the funds can be invested elsewhere at *i*. Since they will grow at the discount rate they will not increase in value. Initial costs *K* have fallen by waiting as they were invested in year 0 at *i* per cent. Thus with a delay of one year, if the higher benefit occurs, the net present value is:

$$NPV_1 = p_A B_A/(1 + i) - K/(1 + i)$$

and with the lower benefit the investment will not take place. Similarly if there is delay of two years:

$$NPV_2 = p_A B_A/(1 + i)^2 - K/(1 + i)^2$$

The difference between the NPV figures ($NPV_1 - NPV$) and ($NPV_2 - NPV$) is the value of the option to wait. Although rarely done, as Dixit and Pindyck (1994) argue in relation to financial appraisal, the value of the option should be treated as part of the opportunity cost of investment funds and added to the initial investment cost of a project under consideration. This should guarantee the correct timing decision, since only if the value of waiting is negative (so the delayed project has a lower NPV than the original one) will the decision to invest immediately be the best choice.[9]

Much of the option value discussion occurs in the context of the environment on whether to conserve or develop environmental assets. However, it has a considerably broader application in the context of uncertainty affecting all large irreversible projects.

UNCERTAINTY AND THE DISCOUNT RATE

Uncertainty underlies an important theoretical development in the academic literature, relating to the discount rate. The seminal theoretical pieces are Weitzman (1998 and 2001), which show that once we introduce an uncertain future into calculations, theoretically the social time preference discount rate should decline even if the key parameters in the standard formula remain constant (a 'hyperbolic' discount rate). Chapter 3 in this volume also addresses this issue.

The social time preference (STP) discount rate is the value society places on present as opposed to future consumption and is based on comparisons of utility across points in time or different generations. For example, the UK Treasury Green Book (HM Treasury, 2003) follows the formula:

$$STP = p + ng$$

where p is the utility discount rate (based on pure time preference and catastrophic risk); n is the elasticity of marginal utility with respect to consumption; and g is average per capita consumption growth.

It uses a combination of pure time preference and catastrophic risk to imply a rate of p of 1.5 per cent annually. A past growth of per capita consumption of around 2 per cent annually has been calculated for the period 1950–98 and this is projected into the future as a value for g. The elasticity parameter n is set at 1.0 based on the use of this value in several other studies. Putting these values into the formula gives an STP equal to 3.5 per cent. This is in fact rather higher than other estimates principally because of the figure of 1.5 per cent for p. However, as noted below, a novel feature of the Treasury estimates for the UK is that long-run project effects (taken as arising after 30 years) are to be discounted at slightly lower rates.

The discount rate (DR) implies an annual discount factor (DF) which is the value placed on a monetary unit received in the future. Hence for a DR of r the discount factor for year t is:

$$DF = 1/(1 + r)^t$$

In turn this relation implies that the discount rate can be found for a given DF by rearranging so that:

$$r = (1/DF^{1/t}) - 1$$

The introduction of uncertainty means that theoretically probability-weighted future values are required for discount factors. Thus for each year in an uncertain future monetary values need to be adjusted by a weighted average of a set of possible future DFs with the weights given by the probability of any particular value being the correct one (which can be termed a certainty equivalent DF). Hence the certainty equivalent discount factor (CEDF) is:

$$CEDF = p_1.DF_1 + p_2.DF_2. \ldots \ldots p_n.DF_n$$

where there are n possible cases with a probability of p and $p_1 + p_2 + \ldots$ $p_n = 1.0$.

The CEDF will imply a certainty equivalent discount rate r_c where, as above,

$$r_c = (1/CEDF^{1/t}) - 1$$

Table 6.3   Illustrations of a hyperbolic discount rate

Discount rate	Discount factor year 10	Discount factor year 30
2%	$1/(1.02)^{10} = 0.8203$	$1/(1.02)^{30} = 0.5521$
6%	$1/(1.06)^{10} = 0.5584$	$1/(1.06)^{30} = 0.1741$
CEDF	0.6894	0.3631
Certainty equivalent discount rate (r_c)	$(1/(0.6894)^{1/10}) - 1 = 0.0379$	$(1/(0.3631)^{1/30}) - 1 = 0.0343$

If we take as an illustration a scenario with two possible discount rates, 2 per cent and 6 per cent, each with an equal probability of being correct, then in Table 6.3 we can illustrate how a declining certainty equivalent discount rate can arise.

From the application of the formulae for CEDF and r_c we find that there is a slight decline in the implied discount rate between years 10 and 30 from 0.038 to 0.034. This decline, which is only shown here for the two years, will be continuous over time. Mathematically, as the time horizon lengthens the certainty equivalent discount rate will tend towards the lowest of the possible values of the discount rate. It is an argument like this that justifies the declining discount rate after year 30 used presently by the UK Treasury, presumably on the grounds that uncertainty only becomes significant 30 years ahead, as market interest rates may adequately reflect shorter-run risks.

Although in practice placing probabilities on different possible rates is fraught with difficulty and modest rates of decline in the discount rate, particularly 30 years or more into the future, will have only a limited impact on project calculations, the theoretical point that, even with constant values for the basic parameters in the discount rate formula under uncertainty, the discount rate must decline is an important new conclusion and one that is relevant for long-lived projects (for example relating to long-term environmental effects).[10] It has already been applied in UK public sector project appraisal although in practice, given the values involved, it is not clear that the use of a declining discount rate has actually been influential in altering decisions.

CONCLUSIONS

Risk analysis can now be applied readily as part of the standard apparatus of project appraisal. This means that probability weighted expected values and estimates of the risk of failure (the probability of a negative NPV) can be derived for every project. It is important to use this information in thinking through key features of a project rather than simply putting it as another technical appendix in a feasibility report. A pragmatic approach to the use of risk analysis is warranted; each project is unique, and the sources of uncertainty and risk faced will be similarly unique to its own individual circumstances. The extent to which risk can be quantitatively dealt with will also vary. Nevertheless, similar types of projects are likely to face similar analytical issues, and similar types of risk analysis techniques will therefore be appropriate to use across a number of projects. As a general rule,

- the greater the extent to which risk can be identified and quantified within the scope of project analysis, the stronger will be the overall project design (assuming mitigating measures are put in place once the scale and impacts of known risk are clear) and the smaller will be the likelihood of project failure;
- the more that risk analysis can be used to investigate the specific financial, environmental and institutional aspects of project design the greater will be the likelihood of the sustainability of project effects over time.

The key point about risk analysis is the focus it generates on ways of reducing project risk by redesign, delay or ultimately project rejection.

The other aspects of risk dealt with here – the option of waiting and the use of a moderately declining discount rate – provide further refinements to the basic probability weighted analysis. They may have little relevance for some types of project but for others (particularly those where timing is a key issue) they offer further important insights. Certain types of project will be both long-lived and irreversible and here the use of option value analysis in particular becomes relevant.

NOTES

1. A certainty equivalent is that 'level of sure income that gives an individual the same level of satisfaction as a lottery with the same expected utility' (Brent, 2006: 216). Brent (2006, Chapter 7) has a good textbook discussion of approaches to measuring the certainty equivalent income.
2. Other early discussions are Clarke and Low (1993) and Savvides (1994).
3. ADB (2002) describes the application of the @Risk software. It stresses a variety of distributions can be tried, including a triangular, uniform and discrete, as well as a normal distribution. The approach is illustrated in the context of ADB projects. The following sections draw heavily on ADB (2002).
4. Another measure that is sometimes given is the mean value of the negative NPV values.

It is not just the probability of a loss that matters but also the size of the potential loss in relation to the funding of the project.

5. The discussion here draws heavily on ADB (2002).
6. This is the Arrow–Lind theorem after Arrow and Lind (1970).
7. Weiss (1996) used this argument to recommend a 25 per cent probability of failure as a cut-off, on the basis of evidence from development agency *ex post* evaluations.
8. The initial theoretical formulation comes from Arrow and Fisher (1974) in the context of the environment, and recent discussions of option value have focused on environmental issues like reaction to global warming (Pearce et al., 2006).
9. The original formulation comes from Arrow and Fisher (1974); see Pearce et al. (2006: 146–53).
10. Theoretically declining discount rates raise the question of whether time inconsistent decisions may be taken, although in practice this is unlikely to be a serious issue. A more extended discussion of the issues surrounding the choice of discount rate can be found in Chapter 7 in this volume.

7. Discounting: does it ensure intergenerational equity?

Erhun Kula

INTRODUCTION

The social rate of discount is one of the most important parameters in economics since it is required in a number of situations. First, it is required for determining the optimal rate of saving or how much a utility-enhancing society should save out of the income that it generates (Ramsey, 1928). Second, it is needed to determine the depletion rate of non-renewable resources, such as fossil fuel deposits. This is sometimes referred to as the cake-eating model (Hotelling, 1931; Solow, 1974). Third, it is required for the calculation of the social opportunity cost of public resources used for a multitude of purposes (Marglin, 1963). Last but not least, in cost–benefit analysis, it is needed for the appraisal of public sector projects. For example, a project may qualify by yielding a positive net present value at a 5 per cent discount rate, but the same project may fail at a 6 per cent rate.

There are a number of important issues in the discounting debate such as the distinction between private and social rates of discount, determining the correct magnitude of the social rate, taking account of the interests of both present and future generations and, last but not least, determining the theoretical foundation for the social rate. There have been many contributions and a number of different viewpoints expressed on these issues.

It can be argued that in a world of perfect competition a single interest rate can equate the marginal time preference rate of savers with the marginal rate of return on capital, with the aid of a set of heroic assumptions, including those on environmental issues. Preference patterns of consumers include the desired distribution of income over time. By borrowing and lending at the market rate of interest they arrange their expenditure to maximise their satisfaction over the entire period for which their plan extends, as judged by their present preferences. Firms invest up to a point where the rate of return on marginal investments is equal to the interest rate. Consumers' plans to save are brought into equality with producers' plans to invest and the ruling rate of interest both reflects the time preference of consumers and the returns which can be earned on capital projects. In this world the optimal rate of investment and saving is achieved and there should be no divergence between the private and social rates of discount.

The choice of a discount rate is even more important for developing countries striving with extremely scarce capital resources to catch up with the developed countries. In this endeavour investment projects are at the cutting edge of economic development and so carrying out robust cost–benefit analysis on proposed development projects is crucial, otherwise the process may lead to inefficient or even totally wasteful expenditures and a loss of scarce capital funds. Environmental issues which are closely linked with discounting provide a further challenge for project planners in developing countries.

The next section considers the theoretical foundation of the social rate of discount. It is followed by a discussion of the intergenerational dimensions of the discounting debate which looks at different methods of discounting that have been proposed to achieve intergenerational justice and environmental sustainability. This section makes it clear that standard discounting is no longer the only possible approach. The following section considers environmental issues in the discounting debate which are now gaining prominence. The experience of the UK is mentioned as a country that has developed a clear position on the determination of the discount rate.

FOUNDATION OF THE SOCIAL RATE OF DISCOUNT

What is the foundation of the social discount rate in cost–benefit analysis? There is much debate in the academic literature about this issue, (e.g. Arrow, 1966; Feldstein, 1964; Mishan, 1988; Kula, 1998). There are, basically, four approaches: the market rate of interest; the government borrowing rate; the social opportunity cost rate; and the social time preference rate.

The Market Rate of Interest

Many economists, including Fisher (1930) and Hicks (1965), who contributed to the discounting debate at the early stages of cost–benefit analysis, believed that the ideal discount rate to be used in public sector capital projects was the one that would achieve a social welfare maximising rate of capital formation, which involves some temporary sacrifice of present consumption. The value of the sacrificed consumption then becomes the key to the selection of a discount rate, as it comes closest to representing the marginal opportunity cost of extra capital formation. The interest rate determined by the capital market provides a starting point for discount rate selection.

However, it was pointed out that there are a number of shortcomings associated with the market rate. First, volatility has been a notable feature of all markets, including money markets (James and Lee, 1971). Second, imperfections can exist in financial markets as well as in goods markets. For example, financial markets in some developed countries are dominated by a few institutions which, on occasion, may collude with each other to create imperfections to their advantage. According to Eckstein (1961) capital markets are highly imperfect. They are rife with rationing, ignorance, differential tax treatments and reluctance to finance some investment projects, especially those with long gestation periods, and they have slow adjustment processes. All of these factors undermine the normative significance of market rates. These problems are even more acute in developing countries. On the positive side, market rates, however imperfect or numerous, do exist but this alone cannot justify their use. Therefore, these days most governments do not recommend the use of market rates in cost–benefit analysis.

The Government Borrowing Rate

In the past the use of the long-term borrowing rate was thought to be appropriate for the appraisal of public sector projects for a number of reasons. First, since public sector projects are essentially risk free, largely due to a large portfolio where risk can be spread across a range of projects, what we need for cost–benefit analysis is the risk-free rate. Interest rates on long-term government bonds are thought to be representative of the most risk-free rates. Second, the government borrowing rate represents the cost of capital used in the construction of public capital projects.

During the 1930s, in the United States, when cost–benefit analysis was used to evaluate large-scale land-based projects, the discount rates employed by various appraisal agencies were closely in line with the long-term government borrowing rate. The quotation below from the President's Water Resources Council makes this clear:

> The interest rate to be used in plan formulation and evaluation of discounting future benefits and compounding costs, or otherwise converting benefits and costs to a common time basis shall be based upon the average rate of interest payable by the Treasury on interest bearing marketable securities of the United States outstanding at the end of the fiscal year preceding such

computation which, upon original issue, had terms to maturity of 15 years or more. (President's Water Resources Council, 1962: 12)

However, the alleged merits of the long-term government borrowing rate have always been subject to dispute. The market value of government bonds and the rate of interest implied are subject to risks, with interest returns affected by fluctuations in the base rate of interest in response to changing macroeconomic conditions. Also it is not correct to assume that the borrowing rate represents the cost of capital used to finance projects. In reality governments raise a relatively small proportion of their revenue by borrowing, as the bulk of the funding comes from taxation.

The Social Opportunity Cost Rate

Some economists, such as Hirshleifer et al. (1960), Krutilla and Eckstein (1958) and Kuhn (1962), contended that since capital funds are limited, a public sector project will displace other projects in the economy. Therefore in economic appraisal of projects the appropriate rate of interest must be the one that reflects the opportunity cost of capital. Generally, the next best alternatives are thought to be in the private sector and the objective behind this approach is to avoid displacing good capital projects in the private sector.

However, it is commonly agreed that the rate of return in the private sector cannot be used to measure social profitability. First, in private rate of return calculations, by definition, external costs such as noise, pollution and congestion which are not internalised will not be taken into consideration. Second, profits and hence the rate of return to capital may be quite high in the private sector, not as a result of efficient operation, but as a result of restrictive conditions such as monopoly, cartel and oligopoly, all of which work against the public interest. Most economists believe that private profits and resulting rates of return on capital require a substantial social adjustment before they can be used in public sector project evaluation.

In addition, Eckstein (1961), Marglin (1963), Feldstein (1964) and Henderson (1965) questioned why we should assume that public projects always displace private investment rather than private consumption. It may well be the case that funds used to construct public projects partly displace both private investment and private consumption.

There seem to be two methods available for identifying the social opportunity cost rate: the rate of return on a comparable project in the private sector and the reciprocal of the capital output ratio. These yield widely diverging rates. It was pointed out by Tinbergen (1956) that, for a long period of time, values for the capital output ratio of about 3 had been observed in some countries. A capital output ratio of 3 would imply a yield of about 33 per cent, whereas ordinary investors get a few per cent on their liquid capital. Obviously, the two methods, that is the output–capital ratio and earnings on private capital, yield very different figures. On this point Henderson (1965) commented that 'it is a rather sad commentary on the state of economics that different sets of authors should be advocating such widely divergent criteria for measuring benefits, with little apparent meeting of minds simply because they happen to have approached the question from different directions'. However, it is worth mentioning that the capital–output ratio is an average value whereas the social opportunity cost is a figure at the margin which is bound to be below the average whenever there are declining returns (Potts, 2002).

In considering the gap between private and social rates of return some economists believe that the latter is a much more reliable indicator. For example, Feldstein (1964) argues that, in a fully employed economy, investment projects increase the productivity of labour and hence the wage rate improves. This increment is a cost to private investors who calculate the rate of return net of factors other than capital. From the communal viewpoint the increased income of the wage earners is a gain and thus the social rate is likely to be greater than the private efficiency of capital. Little and Mirrlees (1974) contended that where structural unemployment prevails, the shadow price of labour may very low, especially for the unskilled. In other words, wages are not an economic cost to public projects if labour is drawn from the unemployment pool. If such an argument is accepted, incremental output, in the main, must be attributed to capital, broadly defined so as to include land.

In addition to theoretical issues there have been some questions over the use of the social opportunity cost rate in practice. For example, the World Bank and the Asian Development Bank tend to use discount rates of 10–12 per cent for projects with monetary benefits on the basis of little or no empirical evidence; see for instance Belli et al. (2001: 238–44) and Asian Development Bank (1997, Ch. 11). Worse still, the British government in the past recommended the British rate of 10 per cent to developing countries where there was no centrally determined discount rate. 'Current experience suggests that a discount rate of 10 per cent applied to costs and benefits in constant prices is a useful guide over a wide range of countries' (Ministry of Overseas Development, 1977). Clearly, economic conditions in each country, including the marginal productivity of capital, are different and in principle one rate should not be applied to investment projects across a wide range of countries.

The Social Time Preference Rate

Another school of thought believes that the correct rate of discount for public projects is the social time preference rate (STPR), sometimes called the subjective communal discount rate, or the consumption rate of interest (CRI) (Feldstein, 1972; Evans and Sezer, 2003). The rationale for this argument is quite simple: the purpose behind investment decisions is to increase future consumption, which involves a sacrifice of present consumption. Therefore, what we need to do is to ascertain the net consumption stream of an investment project and then use the STPR or the CRI.

What are the constituent elements of a social time preference rate? There seem to be three factors: diminishing marginal utility of consumption, pure time preference and risk.

With regard to the first factor, it can be argued that in most societies the standard of living enjoyed by individuals is rising over time. As the income of a person increases steadily, the satisfaction gained also increases, but at a slower rate. That is, each addition to his or her income yields a successively smaller increase in the person's economic welfare. Therefore, $1.00 now should mean more to the individual than $1.00 some years later, if the person involved is getting richer.

As for the second item, more than a hundred years ago William Jevons (1871) argued that in order to secure maximum benefit in life, all future incidents should have the same impact on us as those in the present, regardless of their remoteness in time. But the human mind is not constructed in this way and thus a future utility is almost always less compelling than a present one. Arthur Pigou (1929) suggested that our telescopic faculty is defective, causing us to see future pains and pleasures on a diminishing scale. As the years to which satisfactions are allocated become more remote, they will be represented by a scale of magnitude which is continuously diminishing.

The third reason given for the existence of time preference rate is risk, which can be split into two parts: the risk of not being alive in the future when a consumption benefit is anticipated, and the risk of saving/investment being lost due to various other factors. Irving Fisher (1930) argued that, since we are all mortal, it is reasonable for us to exhibit a greater preference for consumption today rather than tomorrow, as we may not survive to enjoy it then. Otto Eckstein and Paul Henderson realised the feasibility of calculating a pure time discount rate based upon survival probabilities in which the utility to be enjoyed at each future moment ought to be multiplied by the probability of being alive at that time. Since this probability falls with the remoteness of the period, a rational time discount rate will emerge. For derivation of this rate see Kula (1984 and 2008), Evans (2004), Evans and Sezer (2003 and 2005).

As for the second component parameter of risk, although the individual who expects a consumption benefit at a future point in time may survive, his or her expectation may not materialise due to many other factors. For example, savings deposited with a bank may be lost if the bank goes out of business, and dividends and capital gains expected from the purchase of a share certificate may not materialise if the firm runs into problems. Hicks (1965) argued that every investment is a gamble and thus the expected return must reflect compensation for risk-taking, which varies from person to person, and from business to business.[1]

The formula used to measure the social time preference rate is:

$$S = eg + m$$

which is a simplified version of:

$$S = (1 + g)^e (1 + m) - 1$$

where S = social time preference rate; g = growth rate of income/consumption; e = elasticity of diminishing marginal utility of income/consumption; and m = pure time discount rate.

Fisherian Synthesis

If we leave the market rate of interest and the long-term government borrowing rate aside, as theoretically flawed, there will be two approaches left: *the social opportunity cost* of capital and *the social time preference rate*. The time preference of individuals and the productivity of capital funds were first brought into equilibrium via the market for loanable funds by Irving Fisher (1907) in his book *The Rate of Interest*, subtitled *As Determined by Impatience to Spend Income and Opportunity to Invest*. Previously, funds for consumption and production were analysed separately and in isolation. The Fisherian Figure 7.1, adjusted for social conditions, provides the basis for modern social discount rate theory.

A community's consumption in year zero, C_0, is measured along the horizontal axis and consumption in year 1, C_1, along the vertical. The opportunity cost rate relates to the slope of the transformation schedule, or physical investment line; the time preference rate refers to the gradient of the indifference curve at an appropriate point. If the community decides to have zero consumption in Year 1 we may represent the situation by point P along the horizontal axis indicating that society is using

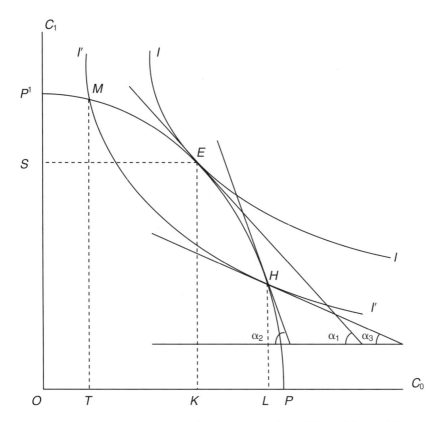

Figure 7.1   Communal time preference rate and equilibrium/disequilibrium

up the entire consumable/investable funds in year zero. Conversely, if the community decides to consume the entire endowment in year 1 the situation would be P^1 along the vertical axis. PP^1 shows the overall investment possibility frontier which is bowed out, indicating diminishing returns to capital projects. That is, a movement from P to P^1 implies that, *ceteris paribus*, the marginal productivity of capital diminishes as more of it is used. The slope at any point along the transformation schedule measures the marginal *social productivity* of capital. Feldstein drew attention to the fact that a closed economy can redistribute consumption through time only along the production possibility frontier, not by international trade.

The communal indifference map is aggregated by registering the pref- erences of all individuals who exist at a given point in time. It should be mentioned that there are some aggregation problems especially regarding the social indifference map. Arrow (1963: 15) looked at the possibility of a meaningful aggregation of individual preferences into a social preference function and found it impossible, the so-called impossibility theorem. However, Tullock (1967) contended that although no decision process will meet Arrow's criteria perfectly, the majority voting process normally leads to a determinate outcome which may be satisfactory. This common decision process meets Arrow's conditions to a very high degree of approximation and this permits us to reconcile the theoretical impossibility with the practical success of democracy.

When we superimpose the communal indifference map on the communal transformation frontier, one contour will be tangent to it. This happens at E, where the slope of the transformation schedule is equal to the slope of the social indifference curve, shown by angle α_1.

But when we are at a point like H there is a difference between the social time preference rate and the social opportunity cost rate, the latter being greater than the former, as indicated by α_2 and α_3. Conversely, when we are at a point like M the social time preference rate would be greater than the social opportunity cost rate, that is the slope of the indifference curve, $I'I'$, is greater than the gradient of the transformation schedule, PP^1.

It must be clear that there is a direct link between the saving/investment ratio and the social rate of discount. At the optimal equilibrium the saving ratio is KP/OP where the social time preference rate is the same as the social opportunity cost rate. At H the saving/investment ratio, LP/OP, is far below the optimal rate. At M, however, we have the opposite case in which the community is investing more than the optimum level and the actual saving ratio, TP/OP, is greater than the optimum saving ratio KP/OP.

In developing countries this problem is likely to be more pronounced. With a small amount of capital funds available for investment projects the rate of return may be expected to be high. That is, we will be at a fairly low point along the transformation schedule, close to P. Notice that at this level the slope of the transformation curve is quite steep, indicating high returns on investment projects hence a greater gap between the social time preference and social opportunity cost rates. Furthermore, regarding Arrow's aggregation problem about establishing a social preference function, a number of the issues mentioned by Arrow, such as information problems and the existence of authoritarian governments, might be more prevalent in developing countries than in developed countries. Tullock's belief that democracy in practice will succeed in ironing out theoretical problems would be more difficult in many poor nations that suffer from undemocratic and authoritarian regimes.

THE INTERGENERATIONAL DIMENSION IN DISCOUNTING

It is now commonly accepted that governments are, or should be, the custodians of future generations in their social, economic and environmental policies. In the undertaking of public projects it is normally claimed that they should be beneficial to present as well as future generations. Large-scale projects in areas such as infrastructure, energy provision, land use, and environmental improvement are normally analysed using cost–benefit methods to make sure that they are beneficial to all generations.

Many communal projects involve a considerable transfer of natural as well as man-made resources between generations, and in this way raise moral questions. Forestry is a good example. In the United Kingdom the average gestation period for hardwood species is high. Hardwood trees such as oak, beech and ash require long periods (about 100 years) to reach commercially desirable maturity. Figures in many other parts of Europe are even higher. These long periods make it obvious that afforestation redistributes income between generations. When felling takes place now, the present generations reap the benefits of an investment which was established by earlier generations some time ago. When we plant trees now, the benefits that will arise from them will be captured, in the main, by future generations.

Some other projects, such as nuclear power, are unusual in the sense that they have consequences many years into the future. Certain nuclear residues created by nuclear power generation units remain active for tens of thousands, or even millions, of years. They must be safely insulated from the human environment for the period that they pose a serious threat to living organisms. If mishandled, such wastes could undermine, seriously, the health, safety and civil liberties of countless generations yet to be born. How do economists handle such projects that impose substantial costs and benefits on many generations? In the economics literature this issue by and large is dealt with within the discounting debate. There are a number of issues involved here regarding the magnitude of the discount rate and also the method of discounting.

Isolation Paradox and the 'Low' Discount Rate

The interdependence of welfare between generations and the implications for the discount rate appeared in the writing of Landauer (1947) and Baumol (1952). In a later article Baumol (1968) elaborated that present members of society would be willing to make a sacrifice to benefit future generations only as part of a collective decision process. Individuals left to their own devices, and in isolation, would not make the sacrifice. This argument has an important bearing on the magnitude of the social rate of discount for project appraisal in the sense that it may suggest a lower communal rate than the individual rate.

Dealing with the same issue other economists such as Marglin (1962, 1963) and Sen (1967) argued that private investment decisions in which benefits appear only after the investor's death are undertaken because of the existence of a market which makes it possible to change the returns which occur after the investor's death into consumption benefits before the investor's death. But why do governments require citizens to sacrifice current consumption in order to undertake investments which will not yield benefits until those called upon to make the sacrifice are all dead, despite the fact that there is no market by which one generation can enforce compensation on the next? Is it because there is a difference between the way individuals view their saving versus consumption decisions collectively and individually?

One possible explanation is that individuals have dual and inconsistent time preference maps; one map representing the selfish side of our character and the other the responsible citizen's. Let us set up a simple model with a number of assumptions: time is divided into two periods, present and future. As all members of the present community die at the end of the present, and their places are taken by individuals who come into existence fully grown at the beginning of the future period, the same investment opportunities are open to all individuals. The utility function of one individual is:

$$U = f(C_i, C_f, C_p - C_i) \qquad (7.1)$$

where U_i is the utility function of the ith individual, C_f is the consumption of future individuals, and $C_p - C_i$ is the consumption of the ith individual's contemporaries. Differentiating equation (7.1) we get:

$$dU_i = \frac{\partial U_i}{\partial C_i}dC_i + \frac{\partial U_i}{\partial C_f}dC_f + \frac{\partial U_i}{\partial(C_p - C_i)}(dC_p - dC_i) \qquad (7.2)$$

where:

$$\frac{\partial U_i}{\partial C_i} = 1; \frac{\partial U_i}{\partial C_f} = \partial; \frac{\partial U_i}{\partial(C_p - C_i)} = \beta > 0 \qquad (7.3)$$

That is, the marginal utility of each item in the utility function is positive. The marginal utility of the ith individual's consumption is unity, that of future generations is α and that of his/her contemporaries is β. Assume now that the marginal rate of transformation between present and future is r^*. That is, at the margin $1 of present sacrifice adds r^* to the consumption level of the next generation. The individual is willing to invest $1 as long as:

$$dU_i \geq \alpha r^* - 1. \tag{7.4}$$

But instead of him/her investing, if somebody else invests, he/she will still get satisfaction because the utility of future generations will increase to the same extent, but the loss in his/her eyes would only be β instead of 1. Therefore the *i*th person will be pleased if somebody else invests so long as:

$$dU_i \geq \partial r^* - \beta \tag{7.5}$$

A third person is also guided by equation (7.5). This means that nobody wants to invest personally, though each would like to see others invest. Each individual would be willing to invest provided others do so, for in this case the gain from the investment of others would outweigh the loss on one's own investment. If there are *n* individuals in the community, investment will take place if the following holds:

$$dU_i \geq n\partial r^* - 1 - \beta(n - 1) \tag{7.6}$$

where $n\alpha r^*$ is the utility gain to the *i*th person via the benefit of the future generation benefit; 1 is the utility lost to the individual for his/her sacrifice; and $\beta(n - 1)$ is the utility loss to the individuals due to their contemporaries' sacrifice. Each is made better off as long as:

$$n\alpha r^* \geq 1 + \beta(n - 1) \tag{7.7}$$

If the numerical values for the parameters were:

$$\alpha = 0.1; \beta = 0.15; r^* = 2$$

we would need at least 17 people ($n = 17$) to participate in a joint action.

This model is extremely sensitive to the assumed value of the parameters. A less altruistic value of, say, $\alpha = 0.074$, with other parameters being the same, leads to a different result. No matter how large *n* is, there would be no collective investment because equation (7.7) will not hold. Instead, the sacrifice should be made in relation to contemporaries rather than posterity. So the argument depends on the care value that present generations put on the position of future generations. If they assume that future generations will be better off than themselves then a collective disinvestment rather than collective investment would be more convincing. However, in view of growing environmental problems many believe that future generations are unlikely to be better off than present ones in real terms.

The isolation paradox, if it exists, has a bearing on the social rate of discount. A social indifference map obtained with caring individuals in a collective decision will contain flat indifference curves, meaning a relatively lower social discount rate, say 4 per cent instead of 5 per cent.

Modified Discounting Method

This method contends that the ordinary discounting method, on which attention has so far been focused, discriminates in a systematic way against future members of our society. It does this by assuming that society is like a single individual who has an eternal, or very long, life.

In order to see this clearly, let us construct, for illustrative purposes, a model by assuming a one-person society in which the life expectancy is, say, 40 years. When the living member dies at the age of 40, he/she is replaced immediately by a newcomer who also has 40 years to live, ad infinitum.

Imagine a public sector project – nuclear waste storage for instance – which requires $1 maintenance cost once every 40 years over a long period of time, say 1 million years, which is the timescale accepted by the UK's nuclear waste disposal company, NIREX (Kula, 1998: 109). Consider that the current individual, Person 1, is just born and the project's cost will appear at the end of the year. Forty years later there will be Person 2 who will also incur $1 cost one year after birth, and so on. Let us say that the discount rate, s, is 10 per cent, and then the discounted values by way of conventional criteria become as shown in Table 7.1.

The discrimination against future individuals must now be blindingly obvious when one remembers that all take an identical length of time to

Table 7.1   Treatment given to future generations in ordinary discounting at a 10 per cent discount rate

Person 1	:	$1/(1.1)$	=	0.9091
Person 2	:	$1/(1.1)^{40}$	=	0.0221
Person 3	:	$1/(1.1)^{80}$	=	0.0051
	:			
Person 250	:	$1/(1.1)^{10\,000}$	=	0.0000

incur their cost of $1; that is, one year. Also, each individual bears his/her own cost.

For the modified discounting method, discounting is conducted from the viewpoint of the affected individuals. In this, we calculate a net discounted value for the maintenance cost for each individual, whether alive now or yet to be born, who will be affected by the project. The method is an individualistic one as it traces the consequences of communal projects to the persons affected, a situation that prevails in many other areas of economics. For example, we obtain a market demand curve by adding up, horizontally, the individual demand curves. Likewise, the social welfare function is constructed by adding up individual welfare functions. In modified discounting, although each individual is governed by ordinary discounting, the society is ruled by modified discounting.

For practical purposes, the modified factors are calculated by Kula (1984, 1998) and Yaffey (1997) by putting the population into single age groups to establish cohorts to represent generations. In this way discounting has been conducted from the vantage point of each generation, whether alive now or yet to be born. As a communal project lives on, generations that die are taken out of the discounting equation, whereas generations born are included. One of the most interesting aspects of the new method is that unlike the ordinary criterion it does not wipe out the distant consequences of communal projects.

The formula for the modified factors can be obtained by making a number of simplifying assumptions. First, the size of the community and the life expectancy of the individuals are constant throughout. The population is put into single age groups to establish cohorts, which also represent generations. Defining generations in this manner will not only be convenient for computational purposes but will also fit in well with discrete time analysis which conducts discounting, mostly, on a yearly basis.

Then imagine a long-term communal project which provides a $1 net benefit every year over its lifetime. It is also convenient to assume that the $1 net benefit is divided equally among the community between individuals who are alive at the time. Recipients consume their share immediately as the money becomes available. Here a 73-year life expectancy is assumed as an average for males and females. Then the modified factors can be calculated in two stages by using:

$$MDF = \frac{1}{n}\left[\frac{1}{(1+s)^t}(n+1-t) + \sum_{i=1}^{t-1}\frac{1}{(1+s)^i}\right] \qquad (7.8)$$

when $t \leq n$ and

Table 7.2   Treatment given to future generations in ordinary and modified discounting methods at a 5 per cent discount rate

Years	Ordinary discount factors	Modified discount factors
0	1.00	1.00
20	0.38	0.44
40	0.21	0.30
60	0.05	0.27
80	0.02	0.27
100	0.00	0.27
200	0.00	0.27
1000	0.00	0.27

$$MDF = \frac{1}{n}\sum_{i=1}^{n}\frac{1}{(1+s)^t} \qquad (7.9)$$

when $t > n$, where n = life expectancy 73, constant, which also represents population cohorts; t = the age of the communal project which may go from now to eternity; s = the social time preference rate.

Yaffey (1997) tested the sensitivity of the above model to changes in life expectancy and the size and the growth rate of population, and found that they made little difference. A comparison of ordinary and modified discount factors for 5 per cent discount rate is as shown in Table 7.2.

The use of modified discounting on long-term projects will yield a result that is very different from the one obtained by the use of the standard method. For example, Kula (1998) argues that the devastating effect of ordinary discounting on the future costs of nuclear projects is beyond dispute. Realising the unacceptable consequences of ordinary discounting on distant costs created by the nuclear industry, some writers such as Logan et al. (1978), Cummings et al. (1981), and Burness et al. (1982) recommended further study on the philosophy of discounting, especially for cases concerning future generations.

UK Government Model of Declining Discount Rate

In 2003 HM Treasury published its long-awaited *Green Book* (a cost–benefit analysis manual for British civil servants) in which it is recommended that the discount rate is used to convert all costs and benefits to present values, so that they can be compared.[2] The recommended discount rate is 3.5 per cent.

This is based on the formula for the social time preference rate $S = eg + m$, given earlier; however, the parameters used appear to be on the low

Table 7.3   Current British discount rate for public sector projects

Years	0–30	31–75	76–125	126–200	201–300	301+
Discount rate (%)	3.5	3.0	2.5	2.0	1.5	1.0

side. Empirical evidence suggests that the STPR for the British economy is likely to be over 4 per cent (Evans and Sezer, 2003), even without assumed catastrophe risk (see HM Treasury, 2003: 97). With that type of risk the figure could be over 5 per cent.

In *The Green Book* (HM Treasury, 2003) it is assumed that $e = 1$ although empirical research suggests that the best value for e is 1.6 (Evans and Sezer, 2004, 2005; Evans, 2005). Regarding the growth rate of per capita income, the Treasury, by considering the works of Maddison (2001), Gollier (2002) and Weitzman (2001), employed a figure of 2 per cent, although the growth rate of per capita income over the last 15 years has been higher, at about 2.5 per cent. In fact Smith (2006) reports that the Bank of England and the Treasury work on the basis that the economy's long-term growth trend is 2.75 per cent. By taking a rather conservative figure of 2.5 per cent with $e = 1.6$, the social time preference rate without a pure time discount rate becomes 4 per cent (*eg*). With the Treasury's own pure time preference rate (*m*) of 1.5 per cent, the overall figure is 5.5 per cent, which is 2 percentage points higher than the recommended current figure for the official discount rate.

However, aside from the level of the official rate, the novel recommendation is that it should decline over time as shown in Table 7.3.

One reason that the UK government adopted a declining discount rate was the plight of future generations who will be at the receiving end of our decisions, good or bad. A high and constant discount rate will practically wipe out the adverse future consequences of many investment projects. In OXERA (2002), which underpins the current British method, it is contended that: 'the arguments for a declining rate are founded upon intergenerational equity and come closest to dealing directly with concerns that constant discounting simply represents the current generations' selfish refusal to consider the welfare of future generations.'

According to the Treasury another reason for the declining rate is risk and uncertainty. *The Green Book* (Annex 6) states that 'the main rationale for declining long-term discount rates results from uncertainty about the future. This uncertainty can be shown to cause a declining discount rate over time.'[3] This indeed is a surprising argument. In practice as well as in many theoretical debates uncertainty has been dealt with by way of *increasing* the discount rate, not decreasing it. Potts (2002) contends that

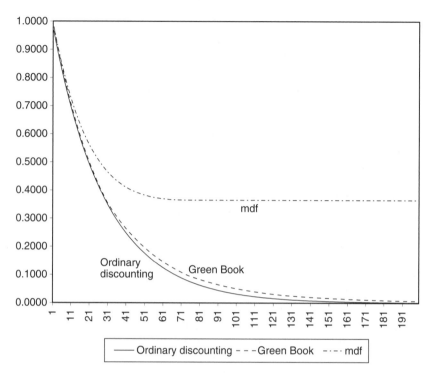

*Figure 7.2   Behaviour of the discount factor schedule in ordinary
            discounting, Green Book discounting and modified discounting
            (mdf) at 3.5 per cent discount rate*

the use of a *higher* discount rate as a means of taking uncertainty into
account is a very common practice, though a mistaken one from a social
point of view. Lumby and Jones (1994) also suggest that commercial firms
often use a higher discount rate to deal with uncertainty. Mishan (1988)
asserts that while there may be a case for adding something to a riskless
discount rate, the idea that uncertainty compounds itself over the future
is debatable. Likewise, the assumption that uncertainty reduces itself systematically over the future is equally problematic.

It appears that the declining long-term discount rate has no theoretical
foundation. Furthermore, the time segments identified above and corresponding discount rates appear to be arbitrary and thus it is possible to
argue for different intervals of various lengths. But the real problem with
the declining rate is that it makes no real difference in the appraisal of
long-term projects and in this way the British government's new method
becomes self-defeating. Figure 7.2 compares the behaviour of the discount

factor following three different discounting criteria: the modified discount factor, the standard discount factor and the British government's model of a declining rate. It is clear that it is only under the modified discounting approach that a 3.5 per cent discount rate translates into a discount factor that will allow long-term future costs to have any significant effect in the present.[4]

THE ENVIRONMENT AND DISCOUNTING

In earlier years environmental issues in cost–benefit analysis were not treated robustly, but the situation changed radically and it is now accepted by almost everybody that issues such as deterioration in the quality of the environment are crucial for both developing as well as developed countries, because they are closely connected with human well-being. The idea that in developing countries environmental control is a luxury that can wait for other decades is a myth. The truth is that environmental problems are most acute in the developing world and the survival of the poor often depends upon the quality of the environment they live in. Clean water is not a luxury, but is essential for survival. Deforestation and the resulting desertification in sub-Saharan Africa are not merely a discomfort to the people but a threat to their lives. Pearce (1991) reported that in Burkina Faso damage to crops, livestock and fuel-wood due to land degradation amounted to 8.8 per cent of the GNP in 1988 and the situation has not improved since then. In Ethiopia, the adverse effects of deforestation on crops and fuel-wood supplies were estimated to be 8–9 per cent of the GNP (Pearce et al., 1990).

In India since 1950 a substantial increase in agricultural productivity has been achieved as a result of the 'green revolution' in which many farmers were encouraged to replace their traditional farming methods with new ones such as deep ploughing, irrigation and inorganic fertilisers, which led to soil erosion and water contamination. Cost–benefit analysis of the new farming methods neglected these environmental costs (Douthwaite, 1992). Cost–benefit analysis today strives to capture most, if not all, environmental costs associated with investment projects by using various environmental valuation methods.

Although some economists have been writing for many years about the importance of discounting in environmental matters, the issue became more prominent after the publication of the Stern Report on climate change in which the role of discounting was emphasised (Stern, 2007). This report, in the main, recommends the use of a low discount rate in cost–benefit analysis so that future environmental consequences of investment decisions, especially those contributing to climate change, can be brought effectively into the net present value calculations. There is an even more radical section in the Report that states 'if conventional consumption is growing but the environment is deteriorating then the discount rate for consumption would be negative' (Section 2A.3, and p. 52).

A negative discount rate is not acceptable for it has no foundation in economics or other behavioural sciences such as psychology. A negative discount rate implies that adverse environmental effects would be preferred sooner rather than later, which contradicts well established attitudes. Economists such as Jevons, Pigou and Fisher argued a long time ago that it is well-acknowledged human behaviour that individuals prefer to postpone adverse effects rather than receiving them earlier on; see also Bohm-Bawerk (1887) and Rae (1905).

What about zero discounting on environmental or other projects? One of the earliest, and the clearest, references to the nature of discounting was made by Alfred Marshall at the end of the nineteenth century.

> If people regard future benefits equally desirable with similar and equal benefits at the present time, they would probably endeavour to distribute their pleasures evenly throughout their lives. They would therefore generally be willing to give up a present pleasure for the sake of an equal pleasure in the future, provided they could be certain of having it. But in fact human nature is so constituted that in estimating the 'present value' of a future benefit most people make a second deduction from its future value, in the form of what we may call 'discounting', that increases with the period for which the pleasure is deferred. Marshall (1899)

That is, the use of both discounting and present value in this excerpt from nineteenth-century economics illustrates clearly that the roots of modern economics were by that time already established.

The argument of Marshall clearly rules out not only a negative discount rate but also the zero discount rate. Without new and convincing evidence that either zero or negative discount rates are used by some communities under certain circumstances, say, regarding the deterioration of the global climate, then a case for it cannot be made. Anything other than that would be tantamount to distorting the reality. So we are left with a positive discount rate. Then what figure should be assigned to it?

Stern's recommendation for a 'low' discount rate can be criticised on the basis of arbitrariness as well as the potential acceptance of inefficient projects. Pearce et al. (1990), long before the Stern Review, contended that the burden of accounting for future generations should not fall on the discount rate. Lowering rates across the board was rejected because it would lead to more projects passing the cost–benefit rule, thereby increasing the demand for resources and environmental services. One way out may be to include within any portfolio of investments one or more shadow projects whose aim is to compensate for environmental damage from the other projects in the portfolio. This approach of requiring shadow projects appears to be an alternative to either not undertaking a project with adverse environmental impacts or ameliorating these adverse impacts through redesigning the project.

Pearce et al. emphasised that a low discount rate for environmental projects could run into further problems of deciding what is an environmental project and what is not, as most projects will impact upon the environment. If the scale of environmental impact is used to classify projects as environmental or not environmental, there will be a cut-off point, which will be an arbitrary feature of the procedure.

The *Financial Times*, in an interview with Stern, commented: 'The most forceful criticism was about the study's use of a very low discount rate, which is used to translate the probable costs and benefits of climate change decades ahead into a value for today.' Stern's answer was that to use a higher discount rate such as those more commonly used in economic modelling of future costs and benefits would not properly reflect the costs of climate change to future generations (*Financial Times*, 2007).

Forestry scientists have known about the devastating effect of a high discount rate on afforestation projects for many years (Faustman, 1849). Price has, over the years, argued in favour of the use of a low discount rate in cost–benefit analysis (or even not discounting at all) (Price, 1984, 1993, 1996a). He also pointed out that a high discount rate does not work in the sustainability context. 'Destructive exponential growth in the use of natural resources, and long-term pollution are apparent concomitants of a compound interest rate. Yet benefits like improved environmental quality are intrinsically not investible at a compound interest rate' (Price, 1993). Furthermore, he also favours using different rates of discount for different projects by arguing that it is not true that differential discount rates introduce distortions in the treatment of different projects. On the contrary, differential rates reflect real differences and remove the distortions which would be perpetuated by treating uniformly those things which are affected differently by the passing of time. A response to these viewpoints would be: how does one derive usable rules from a variety of circumstances?

In addition to distorting reality by artificially lowering the appropriate discount rate it is difficult to see what good these arguments can bring about either to protect the environment or to look after the interests of future generations. Consider the current UK government rate of 3.5 per cent, which is already low and gets lower and lower as time goes by. In

125 years from now it becomes 2 per cent, in 300 years it is 1 per cent. Then consider the behaviour of the Green Book discount factor curve in Figure 7.2. The curve is very close to the horizontal axis even with extremely low discount rates, and thus future consequences are almost wiped out! Clearly low discount rates do not address the issue of the effect of conventional discounting on consideration of the very long-term future.

Some economists are concerned about the choice of a 'high' discount rate in project appraisal in developing countries. Many infrastructure projects are long lived but they are essential for development. The excessive effect of a high discount rate kills off distant benefits, undermining development endeavours. Economists such as Livingstone and Tribe (1995) and Cline (1993) argued that for certain categories of projects with long-term effects, a different and much lower social rate of discount than that conventionally adopted should be used. Potts (1994) argued that high real interest rates in the 1980s and associated high discount rates undermined the viability of investment in perennial crops. Sectors such as forestry, transportation, power and environmental improvement also fall into this category. Intergenerational issues become prominent in this dispute once again. In some cases, such as global warming, current generations are likely to enjoy the benefits of many projects, but later generations incur the costs, which could be substantial. Alternatively for development projects designed to circumvent adverse environmental effects, current generations will bear the costs and later generations will enjoy the benefits.

Not everybody is convinced by differential rates of discount as they point out that it is essential to use a uniform rate of discount for all projects. Other ways of incorporating or avoiding long-term effects and externalities could be used, including the application of special taxes and subsidies to alter investor behaviour (Pearce and Turner, 1990; Birdsall and Steer, 1993; Pearce et al., 1990). Furthermore, with appropriate rates of discount, good rates of return to investment projects should occur, ensuring the creation of income which then can be used in the future to repair environmental or other damage.

On the issue of global warming, while Cline and others contest that lowering the discount rate would be appropriate, say, on grounds of uncertainty, Birdsall and Steer (1993) find this inappropriate.

> Lowering the discount rate is an imperfect and often misleading tool for capturing uncertainty and dealing with large irreversible impacts – as economists like Partha Dasgupta, Stiglitz and Krutilla have pointed out. In the case of uncertainty, a lower discount rate simply increases the weight we put on risks in the distant future compared to the near future.

This argument is also relevant for the UK government's declining rate, which was justified on grounds of risk and uncertainty. Of course, uncertainty can go both ways: unknown technological breakthroughs could greatly decrease the benefits of current investments to reduce later global warming. It is best to take on board such risks and uncertainties directly through the use of appropriate values for future project effects (Birdsall and Steer, 1993).

Dual Discounting for Projects Involving Global Warming

Recently there has been a further development in the economic appraisal of projects that are impacting (negatively or positively) on the greenhouse effect of atmospheric pollution. Kula (2011) argues that some parameters in the social time preference rate based on the growth of income should not apply to environmental benefits of investment projects, such as carbon sequestration of forests, because these are in a different category of attributes that cannot readily be converted to monetary terms and compared with other project effects. The fact is that environmental assets and benefits resulting from them are actually undermined by economic growth. As far back as the nineteenth century Marshall (1899) argued that natural capital is different from the man-made capital as it provides *an annuity fixed by nature*. We now fully realise that natural capital can be degraded and depleted so that the annuity corresponding to the services of the environment can be eroded. This can be hidden for a while by liquidating natural capital and not recognising that we are in fact running down the asset that gives rise to the annuity. In reality what is happening is that the marginal productivity of ecosystems is diminishing, reducing the rate of return to agriculture and fishing in particular.

Kula (2011) asserts that neither economic growth nor the diminishing marginal utility of consumption of ecosystem goods or services should have any place in the social time preference discount rate for environmental impact, whilst environmental resources are becoming scarcer. Economic growth as we have experienced so far actually undermines the natural environment, which provides utility just like other goods and services. In this argument environmental impacts in cost–benefit analysis would be identified and discounted separately. Discounting environmental impacts separately and at a lower rate would be an important step in enabling cost–benefit analysis to move to a dual focus on both efficiency and sustainability.

This argument can be applied to the UK government discount rate. The largest part of the current rate of 3.5 per cent relates to the relationship between economic growth (taken as 2 per cent) and the diminishing marginal utility of consumption (unity), and it is this which should be suppressed when discounting environmental impacts. Only the other parts, that is 0.5 per cent for catastrophe risk and 1 per cent for a pure time discount rate, should apply, giving a full rate of 1.5 per cent. This is the rate that should apply to environmental effects. For the other costs and benefits the full discount rate of 3.5 per cent may be applicable. As an example of a dual stream of discounting, Kula (2011) considers an afforestation project in the United Kingdom which includes timber and carbon sequestration benefits. For the former he uses a 3.5 per cent discount rate and for the latter 1.5 per cent. Overall this treatment boosts the economic viability of this project.

Dual discounting has also been proposed by other writers. For example, Yang (2002) suggests that while the private sector can be guided by a conventional discount rate, environmental investments, especially in the public sector, may be guided by a much lower environmental rate. Similarly, Tol (2003) argues for dual rates of discount for long-term environmental problems such as global warming on the grounds of shifting time preference. According to Guo et al. (2006), when the social cost of carbon is estimated in forestry the figures should be discounted at a lower rate than the conventional one.

CONCLUSION

The magnitude of the social discount rate and the method of discounting are immensely important in cost–benefit analysis. In many cases they are make or break items and thus in all countries government policies in relation to discounting must be based on sound principles.

As we have seen, the first substantive theory on the discount rate was established by Irving Fisher (1907), who argued that both the time preference rate and the opportunity cost rate should play a role in any policy. In his book Fisher restricted his discussion to a comparative static analysis which contained two time periods. In later years this was criticised strongly by Samuelson (1967), who argued that Fisher never faced up to an infinite period model. In Samuelson's discounting model, which contains an infinite time horizon, society is treated as if it were a single entity with an eternal life without due regard to the mortality of individuals who in fact make up any community (see also Ramsey, 1928). I am inclined to believe that Fisher confined his analysis to a two-period case as he did not wish to make the unrealistic immortal individuals assumption.

It is now a topical debate to look at discounting from the viewpoint not only of present generations but also of future ones because almost all long-term investment projects impact upon the latter either positively or negatively. In this respect three different models have been considered here: a low discount rate due to the isolation paradox, the UK government's declining discount rate, and the modified discounting approach. This last approach considers that in order to eliminate the intergenerational bias introduced by conventional discounting, in essence, the discounting process should be restarted for each generation, the amount of discounting of a benefit, or cost, depending on how many years the particular members of each generation have had to wait to enjoy, or endure, it. In this way all generations are treated in the same way. The UK government *Green Book* argues strongly that future generations are as important as the present one, but in practice, by using conventional or declining rates of discount, the opposite is true (see Figure 7.2).

Economists now include discounting in the global warming debate (Stern, 2007). A recent development on this issue is dual discounting, which basically uses a different discount rate for environmental costs and benefits emanating from investment projects. For all other items a higher rate (say 3.5 per cent in the UK) can be used in the usual or the modified form. This aims to take on board both efficiency and sustainability.

Global warming and other environmental issues have raised further questions in relation to discounting with the recommendation of a lower rate for environmental effects. The environmental problem created by the nuclear industry of the disposal of large quantities of highly radioactive and long-lived waste is one of the most topical examples of how the choice of discount rate and method can make a major difference to the analysis of policy options.[5]

It is clear that in some countries government practices are changing, most visibly in the United Kingdom. The European Union has also changed its practice recently by having two-tier discount rates, one for the established member countries and the other for new members. Developing countries could learn something from the experience of other countries when they decide on their policies on both the discount rate and discounting method. We have seen that opportunity cost-based discounting is logically flawed and tends to give very high rates that are potentially damaging for investment choice because of the excessive relative weight given to early costs and benefits. Social time preference-based rates tend to be lower and they may be preferable to opportunity cost-based rates, but they still suffer from the tendency to reduce the weight on costs and benefits in the distant future to very close to zero. The multiple rates approach for different periods adopted by the UK can be regarded as an unsatisfactory compromise that also fails to address the distant future issue and rests on debatable logic. The dual rate for environmental costs and benefits approach has some theoretical basis and does address some issues, but it does not fully address the long-term future issue and there are issues about defining the distinction between environmental and non-environmental goods. The modified discounting approach does address the distant future issue but so far it has only been used to a limited extent in some countries. The debate on discounting is far from closed.

NOTES

1. For a detailed discussion of the parameters of the social time preference rate see Kula (2008).
2. Prior to this the British government relied heavily on the concept of the social opportunity cost rate in which profitability in the private sector was used as a benchmark. For example, in a 1967 White Paper, *Nationalised Industries: A Review of Economic and Financial Objectives* (Cmnd 3437), it was recommended that publicly owned industries should use a *test rate of discount* of 8 per cent in their appraisal of important projects. It was also emphasised that this figure was broadly consistent with the average rate of return, in real terms, earned on a low-risk project in the private sector. The reliance on the social opportunity cost rate continued until 2003.
3. See Chapter 6 of this volume for an argument along these lines.
4. The discount factor (DF) for year *n* under ordinary discounting is $DF = 1/(1 + i)^n$ where *i* is the discount rate.
5. For example an OECD committee (OECD, 1980) contended that widely used economic principles are totally useless in the cost–benefit analysis of very long-term projects such as in the nuclear industry by noting that the impact of the difference between zero and even a very modest discount rate can be enormous.

8. Environmental valuation

P.B. Anand

WHY DO WE NEED ENVIRONMENTAL VALUATION?

The aim of this chapter is to provide an overview of issues related to environmental assessment in project appraisal. As entire books have been written on this very subject, trying to capture all of the relevant issues in the space of a single chapter is an impossible task.[1] The chapter has the modest aim of providing an overview of environmental valuation in the context of cost–benefit analysis or investment appraisal of projects.

It is now widely recognised that if environmental impacts are not taken into account, costs can be significantly underestimated and project decisions can be biased.[2] Just as the London smog of 1952 led to air pollution control regulation, a second wave of environmental regulations emerged after major industrial disasters such as the Bhopal Gas Disaster in the Union Carbide plant in December 1984 and the Chernobyl nuclear reactor accident in April 1986, which contributed to raising public awareness of environmental risks. As a result, there is now some evidence to suggest that investors take the environmental performance of firms into account and that oil spills or other such industrial accidents do affect how a company's stock is valued by investors (Yamaguchi, 2008; Capelle-Blancard and Laguna, 2010). In fact, institutional investors such as pension funds and ethical (or socially responsible) funds have begun to exert significant influence on firms that contribute to harmful environmental impacts (Kreander et al., 2005). A survey by Standard Life (2010) indicated that when investors were asked to rank among 42 different items or aspects to consider when choosing an ethical fund, the top three issues chosen were: the clearing of tropical rainforests, making of chemicals without adequate attention to environmental impacts, and human rights. Thus, it is clear that investors respond to environmental performance by firms and that this has an impact on the way firms consider environmental issues. Increased awareness has also led to more stringent environmental regulations.

The various services provided by nature are broadly considered in terms of three or four categories, namely: resources or materials (R), where the environment provides raw materials or inputs to production or consumption; sink or assimilation (S), where the environment receives effluents and emissions from production and consumption; amenities and vistas (A), where the environment makes a place special because of how it is.[3] Some of the cultural and identity aspects of the environment can be included under this third category. A fourth aspect may be considered as 'existence' or 'ecosystem services' (E).

As an illustration of the multiplicity of environmental services, consider coral reefs. Such reefs provide the necessary condition for a wide variety of fish to breed. As a result, the fisheries in the area of seas surrounding the coral reefs may be a direct result of the reefs. This is the R component of coral reefs. The rich diversity of species in and around coral reefs attracts tourists who want to enjoy the amenity value (A). Coral reefs may also help in controlling erosion and sedimentation in the beaches nearby and this is an example of the S aspect. However, coral reefs themselves may be very valuable to us, not because of any of the immediate or direct and indirect benefits they bring to us but for the crucial role they play in maintaining biodiversity, and for this reason we may value them. This is the E aspect of their value. Studies by the World Resources Institute are in progress to estimate the economic values of coral reefs. In a study already completed, Burke et al. (2008) reported that in the case of Tobago the direct and indirect benefit of coral reefs to fisheries is estimated to be US$0.8 to US$1.3 million. The direct and indirect impact due to tourism is estimated to be US$101 to US$130 million, and shoreline protection due to coral reefs is estimated be worth US$18 to US$33 million. For comparison, the authors suggest that the island's GDP is around US$286 million.

An important study by Costanza et al. (1997) identified up to 17 ecosystem functions including gas regulation, climate regulation, water regulation, soil formation, nutrient recycling, recreation and cultural aspects (see Table 8.1). In that study, based on a synthesis of over 100 published studies, Costanza et al. estimate the value of global ecosystem services, most of which are not marketed, to be in the range of US$16 to 54 trillion per annum with an average of US$33 trillion or approximately 1.8 times the then global GNP.

That landmark study highlighted that although many of the environmental goods and services are 'difficult to value' as markets may not exist for some or most aspects of such goods and services, it is possible to estimate such values and these are not trivial. The standard economic argument for valuation is to say that non-valuation of impacts on environmental goods and services would result in excessive consumption, distort

Table 8.1 *Four categories of ecosystem functions and their correspondence with 17 functions identified by Costanza et al. (1997)*

Categories of ecosystem functions	Correspondence with 17 ecosystem services [and values in US$ trillion] as identified by Costanza et al. (1997)	Value in trillion US$ (and share of global value)
R Resources/ materials	Soil formation [0.05] Water supply [1.69] Pollination [0.12] Food production [1.38] Raw materials [0.72]	3.96 (12.2%)
S Sink/ assimilation	Nutrient recycling [17.08] Waste treatment [2.28] Erosion control and sediment retention [0.57] Biological control [0.41]	20.34 (62.5%)
A Amenities and vistas	Recreation [0.8] Cultural [3.0]	3.8 (11.7%)
E Existence or ecosystem services	Gas regulation (1.34) Climate regulation (0.68) Disturbance regulation (1.78) Water regulation (1.12) Genetic resources (0.08) Habitat, refugia (0.12)	4.44 (13.6%)

Source: Author's estimates based on Costanza et al. (1997).

the allocation of expenditures and systematically disadvantage those in future generations. The purpose of environmental assessment in project appraisal is to anticipate and assess potential and actual environmental impacts of the investment and operations of a project and the resultant loss of well-being.

The concept of valuing raises several ethical or normative issues: who is doing the valuing, what is to be valued, how far should non-consumptive or existence values be incorporated, is the act of valuing essentially *anthropocentric* (that is, centred on human beings) and hence, is it biased in favour of aspects of environmental services that are of direct use to humans? Related to these issues are questions such as whether environmental assessments should recognise only the impacts which are of consequence to human well-being or whether impacts must be considered irrespective of consequences. Further, it is possible to ask whether such an exercise should recognise the universalism of life claims – that is, claims of both present and future generations of human beings. Others could raise objections on the grounds that universalism requires that along with the rights of present and future generations of humans, rights of other living organisms must also be recognised. However, this can result in a break-down of reason as soon as the existence of one living organism erodes the right to life of its prey. A compassionate or non-violent ethic such as that in Buddhist and Jainist writings elevates a stewardship role to not merely the absence of violence by humans against other beings (achieved for example by preventive action such as covering one's mouth with a cloth to avoid involuntary killing of invisible micro-organisms) but a positive requirement to do something to protect and nurture such organisms wher-ever possible. Thus, it is important to recognise that the utilitarian ethical framework which underpins economic valuation is simply one among several alternative ethical frameworks. We shall return to these ethical issues in the final section of the chapter.

ENVIRONMENTAL VALUATION WITHIN PROJECT APPRAISAL

Environmental valuation has several distinct aspects. Environmental impact assessment (EIA) is concerned with identifying and measuring the impact of an activity on the environment. The focus of EIA is to establish clearly, with a scientific basis, how an activity is likely to impact on the environment. Initially, the purpose of EIA was to identify impacts on the biophysical environment. Over a period of time, in recognition of the dif-ficulties in deciding where the boundaries are between where the biophysi-cal domain ends and where the cultural, social and economic environment begins, EIA studies began to embrace these dimensions as well. Measuring the impacts of an activity or project can involve significant scientific and technical work including measuring and modelling, and thus can be quite expensive. Therefore, it makes sense to develop some subjective criteria to determine when incurring such expenses is justified.

At early stages in project identification and preparation of feasibility reports, potential environmental impacts can be flagged up even without detailed environmental impact studies. During the project design phase, when comparing alternatives, it would be useful also to include poten-tial environmental impacts of the alternatives as part of the assessment process.

When a final design is being considered in terms of investment appraisal, detailed environmental impact assessment is essential. However, not all investment projects may involve significant environmental impacts.

Consider, for example, a project to promote literacy or a project aimed at improving hygiene awareness amongst school children. In such projects, there will be both positive and negative environmental impacts. (For example, are any leaflets or educational material being published? If so, where, and using what methods? Will there be an increase in chemical pollution during the production process?) However, in these two examples, it is highly likely that positive environmental impacts outweigh negative impacts.

Organisations such as the World Bank and Asian Development Bank consider projects in terms of categories and then require environmental assessment in the case of some projects and exempt others. For example, operational policy 4.01 of the World Bank considers various categories: category A projects are those with significant and irreversible adverse environmental impacts and hence a comprehensive environmental assessment is required for project appraisal; category B projects are those with potential adverse environmental impacts – in most cases mitigation measures are considered feasible and are included in the project; category C projects are those with minimal or no adverse environmental impacts.

Identifying an impact is just the first step. Suppose that a project impacts on 40 acres of land and results in additional water pollution to the tune of 40 tonnes per day of various chemicals in a local river. What does this mean to an analyst appraising the project? Information on physical impacts in itself is of limited use unless it can be translated into how it affects the well-being of affected citizens. Environmental valuation helps to convert the information in physical magnitudes of impact into monetary measures, which can then be used in investment appraisal.

EXTERNALITIES

In an ideal world, individuals (and firms) acting as moral agents take into account the consequences of their actions for themselves and others. However, in the real world, our capacity to act as complete moral agents may be hampered by self-interest, ignorance, uncertainty or simple callousness. When the actions of an individual (or a firm) impact on other individuals (or firms) and there has been no compensation exchanged between the parties concerned, such impacts are externalities. Many actions involve externalities – social norms at a given point in time may dictate what is acceptable and what is not acceptable. The role of regulation in this is complex and evolves over time. Between the extremes of 'do nothing' or 'impose an outright ban' there exists a grey area where we need to exercise reason weighing the costs and benefits of actions.

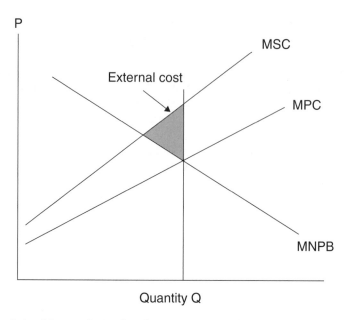

Figure 8.1   Marginal social and private costs in the case of an externality

Unmitigated environmental impacts of a project are the classic textbook case of externalities, where decisions taken by one person or organisation in relation to a project activity affect other persons or organisations without any compensation. If an externality is not internalised, then there will remain a difference between marginal social costs (MSC) and marginal private costs (MPC). The individual or organisation concerned will compare marginal net private benefits (MNPB) with the marginal private costs and will choose a magnitude of activity (that is, a magnitude of pollution) where marginal benefits equal marginal costs. However, as can be seen from Figure 8.1, this results in setting the magnitude of activity in excess of what is socially desirable.

One theoretical solution to the problem of externalities is the so-called Pigovian tax – to impose a tax on the polluter of an amount equal to the difference between marginal social and private costs. Thus, the difference between marginal social and private costs disappears, and the individual or organisation will then choose a quantity of activity up to a point where marginal private benefits equal marginal social costs. However, imposing a Pigovian tax is not straightforward in practice – there must be a regulator, the regulator must know both the social and private cost profiles for each firm, then set a marginal rate of taxes just equal to the divergence between social and private costs and maintain this dynamic given technical progress and market structure for pollution abatement technologies. Though this idea has been developed and applied mainly in relation to pollution taxes (and hence the 'polluter pays principle'), the basic idea about internalising an externality using the concept of divergence between marginal private cost and marginal social cost remains relevant to most classes or categories of externalities. An alternative solution to internalising the externalities was proposed by Ronald Coase. In this solution, the main problem is identified as lack of ownership of common resources, such as clean air or an unpolluted water resource such as a lake. Clarifying property rights produces the same effect of collapsing the divergence between marginal social and private costs and thus internalising the externality concerned. The concept of tradable emission permits has been developed from this perspective.

This discussion points a way to connect an EIA study and its consequences. As an EIA study of a project identifies potential impacts, the logical next step is to find ways to 'internalise' these externalities by way of mitigation measures. Some of these measures may be changes in design specifications such as 'height of the chimney' or 'location of the dam' and others may require activities throughout the life of the project such as 'install and operate a wastewater treatment plant' or 'install and operate a water sprinkling mechanism to reduce airborne particulate emissions' (for example in the case of quarrying, open-cast mining or storage of excavated earth or fly ash). These activities or necessary changes will need to be included as part of project costs in the revised financial and economic analysis.

The purpose of *ex ante* EIA is thus twofold: (a) to identify 'reversible' impacts of the project and to internalise such externalities by way of mitigation measures; and (b) to identify impacts or externalities that have not been mitigated and thus result in a loss of social welfare. The rest of the chapter discusses various methods that can be used for valuing environmental impacts especially when these have not been mitigated.

MICROECONOMIC MODEL OF CONSUMER

The economic value of a good exchanged in the market is the Marshall–Dupuit consumer surplus estimated from the demand curves. Thus, the various ecosystem services or functions of the environment affected by a project activity can be considered under three types:

- those that are traded in markets (food production, raw materials such as timber or minerals);

- those that are not themselves traded but form part of other com- modities that are exchanged in markets (such as recreational use, amenity, flood protection, gas regulation);
- those that are neither traded directly nor as part of other commodi- ties (such as climate regulation, habitat protection).

Environmental valuation methods initially focused on the first two types of environmental goods and more recently have aimed to address the third type.

When valuing, what the analyst is trying to estimate is often considered as the 'total economic value' (TEV). This includes various components, namely:

- *Direct use value*: where the magnitude of value is directly related to the use to which the environmental good or service can be put. Thus, direct use value is closely related to consumptive or extractive use of the resource or good concerned. In the case of a piece of land, this can be estimated as the present value of a stream of income that can be generated by the most direct or 'next best' use. Suppose an acre of land in a given region can be used only to grow a certain crop; the projected annual yield and market price for the crop can give us an estimate of the direct use value. There is, however, a judgement involved in assessing the next best use.
- *Indirect use value*: where the magnitude of value is related to experi- ence rather than consumptive or extractive use. If a piece of land offers a view of a national park or an aspect of nature, there can be an indirect use value.
- *Option value*: the value of keeping an option open, that is not making an irreversible decision. The estimation of option value depends on the probability of a high-value event occurring and the correspond- ing magnitude of the benefit. For instance, in the case of the plot of land mentioned above, even if this is presently some distance away from the peri-urban fringe, depending on the nature of urbanisation and infrastructure investment decisions there is a possibility that this piece of land may become quite attractive in terms of real estate in the future – say it can fetch £1 million in today's prices. However, the probability of such an event could be very small as the city may not grow, or it may grow but not in this direction, and so on. So let us say the probability that this particular plot would become a real estate 'gold mine' is 1 in 1 million (so there are 999 999 other similar plots which face the same prospect). Thus, the option value of keeping this option open is in essence £1 million times 0.000001, which is £1.

While this is just an illustration, option value can sometimes include cultural or identity issues which are extremely difficult to value.[4]

- *Bequest value*: in addition to the direct and indirect economic benefits that a plot of land offers, it brings with it some heritage and the potential to pass on that heritage to future generations.
- *Existence value*: as the name implies, this is the value of a piece of land not related to its economic benefits but for its existence itself. Sometimes this referred to as 'intrinsic value'.[5]

Total economic value is supposed to encompass all these aspects. However, for some of the environmental goods and services, some components or values of TEV may be more important or relevant. Plottu and Plottu (2007) argue that option and non-use values should be considered differently as compared to use values.

At the centre of most environmental valuation methods is the microeconomic model of individuals and their utility and consumer demand based on concepts developed by Marshall and Dupuit. Such an individual is assumed to have well-behaved preferences (that is preferences are complete, transitive and reflexive). Such an individual may trade their income (and other resources they possess) in order to produce a bundle of commodities they wish to consume. The consumer's well-being is reflected in their utility function – the consumer compares alternative consumption bundles and chooses the bundle that gives greater utility or well-being. Thus using the concept of demand functions, consumer surplus can be estimated as an indicator of change in well-being due to either price or quantity changes caused by the environmental impacts of a project.[6] Thus if a change in environmental quality affects consumer well-being, the aim of valuation in project analysis is to estimate this change in well-being through appropriate methods.

It should be noted that this approach to environmental valuation based on rational consumer choice, whilst now very widely used, has also been controversial. Environmental philosophers and other social scientists are critical of this approach of the rational choice–utility maximising model for various reasons. These criticisms can be grouped under four major categories.

1. A set of criticisms focuses on the utilitarian perspective at the centre of rational choice theory. We can call this 'utilitarianism' criticism. Such critics argue that people may value the environment for many reasons (including cultural, social, historical and metaphysical reasons) and not because of direct utility that they expect to gain from 'consuming' the environmental goods and services.

2. A second set of criticisms challenge the underlying assumptions of the rational choice model: whether consumers have all the information, whether preferences are stable, whether consumers maximise or simply use a satisficing calculus, whether consumers convert all information into one metric (commensurability) and how events over different time periods are compared (discounting and the inter-temporal choice issue). We can call these 'questioning the assumptions' criticisms.

3. The third set of criticisms are also related to the model of a consumer with examples including the 'citizen–consumer' dichotomy (Sagoff, 1988). That is whether individuals use the consumer choice model for certain goods and services, but behave as citizens when considering other issues such as environmental resources and sustainability.[7] Another example includes the question of whether consumers use different approaches when making decisions for private matters as opposed to social goods (see for instance, Rabin, 2006; Loewenstein et al., 2007; Hards, 2011; Fehr and Hoff, 2011).

4. A fourth set of criticisms suggest that instead of using a rational choice–consumer utility model, alternative mechanisms such as a referendum or citizen jury or participatory methods such as community-based social accounting approaches may be better suited to understanding how communities or groups of individuals value environmental resources. We can call this 'participation' or 'democratic process' criticism. Some critics suggest alternatives instead of using an individual-centred approach to valuation (see Sagoff, 1988; Orr, 2006; Spash, 2007).

While these debates have certainly informed environmental assessment approaches and methods, there is still merit in using the microeconomic model as a limited but useful approach, especially as an input to cost–benefit analysis and project appraisal. The other approaches usually produce information that may be valid but is difficult to incorporate as a quantitative input in cost–benefit or project analysis.

EXAMPLES OF PRACTICAL VALUATION METHODS

In this section, an attempt is made to briefly discuss a number of practical methods that can be used in environmental valuation. Various methods are discussed, in each case with some examples of applications in developing countries drawn from the literature. Some of the shortcomings of each method are also discussed.

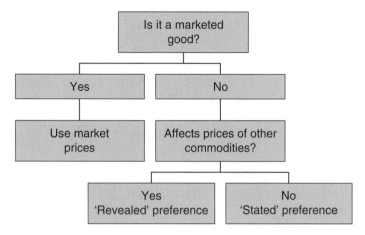

Figure 8.2   Decision tree in choosing valuation methods

The valuation methods that can be used depend on which aspect of the total economic value concerned is the most important. For whatever aspect, it will always be useful also to ask whether market prices already exist for the good concerned. If they do, then market prices can be used in estimating the environmental impact. If they do not exist, then it may be useful to ask whether the good or service in question affects the value of something else; then by observing decisions concerning this latter good, we may be able to draw some conclusions about the preferences for the original good in question – hence such approaches are termed *revealed preference* methods. Certain goods or services (aspects of the environment such as biodiversity or existence value) do not have markets and it is not easy to deduce revealed preferences for them by observing something else. In such cases, consumers (or a representative sample of such consumers) need to be asked directly about their willingness to pay. This decision tree is summarised in Figure 8.2.

The most obvious example of market price-based methods is the change in production method. Examples of revealed preference methods include the travel cost method of estimating recreation benefits and the hedonic price method of estimating amenity, as well as the contingent valuation method (CVM) and choice modelling (CM).

Change in Production Method

When an environmental impact directly affects the production of a good or service which has market prices, valuation can be quite straightforward. The three main issues are: first establishing a clear link between the environmental change and production activity, secondly comparing the impact of the change to the situation without the project, and thirdly deciding which prices to use to value this net effect. To take a simple example, suppose that a project results in increased water pollution (due to discharge of effluents) in a river. In such cases, the change in production method can be used to translate the impact of increased pollution on downstream fisheries. Long-term data on fish production in the river may be helpful to establish the 'without project' trend. Experience from other similar projects or models may be necessary to estimate the extent of the impact of increased pollution level on fish production. These models may be used to forecast fish production 'with the project'. The reduction or difference between 'without project' and 'with project' is the net impact of the project. If the impact constitutes only a small proportion of national production, it can be assumed that the reduction in fish production on this site will not result in changing prices. Thus, the magnitude of the loss of production can be converted into monetary terms using existing price data. However, if the magnitude of the impact on this site is likely to have a significant impact on national production (for example, in small countries such as the Caribbean islands or when the project is very large in magnitude as in multi-purpose dam projects, super thermal power stations or petro-chemical complexes), then the dynamics need to be analysed with the help of macroeconomic models to forecast the likely equilibrium price 'with project'. This price will then be used to estimate the value of the magnitude of the net reduction in fish production due to the project. If the change in production mainly affects firms, then we will need to estimate producer surplus using a combination of prices with and without the project.

A good example of this method is a study of changes in fish production in an evaluation of the impact of various projects associated with the Lesotho Highlands Development Project (LHDP). Turpie (nd) reports use of the change in production method to value fisheries in the Malibamatso, Matsoku, Senqu and Senqunyane rivers. Various surveys were used in the study including a survey of 1680 households. Based on these surveys, current production and prices were obtained and the project impact was valued in terms of the anticipated reduction in fish catch. Similar results are reported in Matete and Hassan (2006, Table 2).

Related to this type of approach are 'dose–response' methods. While the change in production method is mainly used to value the impact of a project on goods or services that are directly marketed (with prices), dose–response methods are mainly used to estimate the magnitude of project impact on the health of the population affected. An example of this is a study of the health impact of air pollution in Hong Kong by Brazer et al. (2006). In that study, the authors use extensive data on pollution in the Pearl River Delta region to make projections of pollution levels under different scenarios. Then they use Hong Kong-based epidemiological data to construct pollution–response functions. They then estimate averted mortality and averted morbidity (in terms of hospital admissions) for two scenarios, namely adopting World Health Organization (WHO) standards and the second scenario of bringing down pollution to Hong Kong standards. These are compared with the business-as-usual scenario. They then apply the value of statistical life from previous studies to estimate the value of the number of lives saved by reducing pollution to WHO standards. The value of averted morbidity is estimated using data from previous surveys of willingness to pay to avoid a day in hospital. Based on these approaches, they estimate that the value of health benefits from reducing air pollution in Hong Kong to WHO standards is approximately US$5.5 billion (with a range from US$2.4 to $8.5 billion). On an annual basis, they argue that this compares to about 12 per cent of government health expenditures.

The main advantage of change in production methods is that in most cases converting information on the magnitude of the impact into monetary values can be fairly straightforward. However, the main criticism is that they tend to focus only on environmental goods or services that already have a market price. Thus, many non-marketed aspects would remain omitted. Therefore, the change in production could significantly underestimate benefits from ecosystems which provide multiple benefits or services. As we saw in Table 8.1, resources or materials account for only 12 per cent of the total value of global ecosystem services. Another potential drawback of change in production methods is that certain environmental impacts may take a long time to feed into production processes or to impact on health, so change in production methods are likely to be better at dealing with more immediate and direct impacts than long-term and indirect impacts.

Revealed Preference Methods

As mentioned earlier, this class of methods is based on the principle that changes in environmental quality affect some other marketed goods, so that by establishing a connection between environmental quality and change in price, some evidence of how consumers value environmental quality can be deduced.

Defensive or preventive expenditures
While some environmental impacts themselves may not be valued, they may in turn require individuals or firms to undertake preventive or

mitigating actions. The cost of such actions can be used as a guide to the value of the negative impacts. For instance, in order to avert noise pollution from roads or airports, households adjacent to such roads or directly in the flight path of aircraft landing or taking off from an airport may have to incur additional expenditure in double or triple glazing their windows or having other insulation installed. This additional cost of such measures can give an indication of the negative externality imposed by the aircraft or road noise. During the May–August 2011 period, a consultation by Heathrow airport was in progress with regard to its noise mitigation measures due to the ending of the existing Cranford agreement preventing easterly take-offs from the northern runway over the village of Cranford. In this consultation, Heathrow airport was offering four types of assistance: residential daytime noise reduction, residential night-time noise reduction, community buildings noise reduction and financial help with moving costs to those who wanted to move. The value residents place on the loss of amenity or inconvenience due to aircraft noise is reflected in such offers by airport operators.

The replacement cost method or 'shadow project' methods are essentially based on the same principle. When a particular environmental resource is likely to be used up or damaged by a project, regulators or funders may require that the environment is restored to its original state or that the community is compensated in terms of the creation of an equivalent site elsewhere. For example, in the case of oil spills, one of the starting points for a discussion on damage estimation is usually the impact of an oil spill on local beaches. Among various methods that can be used, including the change in production approach, to estimate the value of loss to fisheries or the sea food industry, one is to calculate the cost of cleaning up beaches and restoring them to their original condition. For example, the British Petroleum (BP) Sustainability Review 2010 includes data pertaining to the consequences of the Deepwater Horizon accident in April 2010. Environmental expenditures to the tune of US$18.4 billion were made in 2010 compared to about US$2.4 billion in 2008 and 2009. In a previous oil spill of Exxon Valdez in Alaska, the replacement cost method was used to estimate damage caused to sea birds and mammals (Brown, 1992).

The main advantage of the replacement cost method is that it requires 'like-for-like' compensation or restoration after damage. However, there are many shortcomings. Baseline information must be available as a reference point for comparison.[8] Secondly, institutions are supposed to be working effectively and factors such as corruption are assumed not to exist. However, in reality, environmental regulations can present themselves as a rent-seeking opportunity. For example, when the cargo-ship MV Rak, carrying coal to Gujarat, sank near Mumbai in India in August 2011, the consequent oil spill damage raised debates about whether ships may be sunk deliberately by companies at certain locations with lax regulations to try to avoid the costs of decommissioning and any liability for damage. Thirdly, legal instruments must be in place to enable courts to enforce replacement cost methods, otherwise the exercise would remain a hypothetical tool rather than a useful policy instrument.

Travel cost method: forest recreation, tourism

The underlying premise of this approach is that resources are scarce and human beings will not expend resources to bother to travel to a recreational site unless the perceived benefits from visiting that site are at least equal to the total travel costs. Thus, travel cost provides a clue to the demand for recreational use of a site such as a forest or beach. To operationalise this method a survey of users of a recreational site is conducted. Data collected from such a survey will include information on the origin of the trip, mode of travel, journey time, frequency of visits, number of members in the party, data that will help in estimating capital and running costs of the vehicle used for the journey, and socio-economic details of the respondent. An inverse relationship is expected between travel cost and number of journeys.[9] To connect the sample to the relevant population, models need to be developed that can help estimate the number of trips from different zones. Such a trip generation function will include information on population, travel cost, distance and so on. Using this information, a relationship between travel cost and number of trips – a derived demand curve – is estimated. Travel cost includes both the actual cost incurred in terms of vehicle and fuel costs and travel time cost in terms of the actual time spent travelling. Though originally meant for estimating recreational values of day trips to forests over a period of time, the method has been developed to cover recreational benefits of the entire tourism industry in the case of small islands.[10]

Chen et al. (2004) used the travel cost method to estimate the value of recreational benefits for a beach in Xiamen Island in south-eastern China. For this purpose, they conducted an on-site survey in 1999. Their sample of 560 visitors were each interviewed and allocated to some 34 origin zones. There were two components: one was the travel cost to the island itself (which was zero for local residents) and the second was the travel cost within the island from the tourist's place of stay to the beach on the eastern side, where the survey was conducted. Since the beach surveyed is one of six other beaches on the island and many visitors visit the beach as part of multi-destination travel, the authors apportioned travel cost to the island based on the survey respondent's views about how to allocate the total cost to the beach. After estimating trip generation functions, one using education of respondent as an independent variable and another using income per capita as an independent variable, they estimated the total value of recreational benefits from the eastern beach on Xiamen island to be US$53.5 million in 1999 or a per visit, per visitor consumer surplus of US$16.9. They recommended the introduction of a user fee to recover the cost of maintaining the beach.

In a travel cost study of international wildlife tourism in Uganda, Andersson et al. (2005) estimated that recreational benefits from wildlife tourism could be increased by between US$30000 and US$220000 by considering the market to be a monopoly rather than aiming to achieve cost recovery. Another study, also from Uganda, by Buyinza et al. (2007) used two methods, one of travel cost and another of stated willingness to pay. Based on the travel cost method, the authors estimated the recreational benefit from the Bujagali Falls Recreation Park to be approximately US$370000.

Hosking (2010) used the travel cost method to estimate the recreation benefit of visiting seven estuaries in South Africa with and without improvement to freshwater flows. Change in consumer surplus was then attributed to the recreational benefits generated by the project. His team conducted surveys and used them to produce trip generation functions. For example, in the case of Heuningnes estuary, there were three zones; after estimating visits per 1000 of population they proceeded to estimate a regression equation where the visitation rate was the dependent variable and travel cost was the independent variable. Using this information and assuming various alternative entrance fee scenarios, they estimated the number of visits. Using this information, they estimated a recreational demand curve between travel cost (price) and number of visits (quantity).

There are numerous criticisms of the travel cost method. The main criticisms can be divided into two groups as epistemic and methodological. Epistemic criticisms include issues such as: the problem of tourists versus the local population, who may value a resource highly but whose valuation is not captured in the travel cost calculation because they may live close to the site; the problem of recreation benefits versus non-use or intrinsic values which are not captured in the travel cost surveys; the problem of intra-household inequalities (one or two persons may have made the decision that the entire family must visit the site); the problem of captive visitors (having come to an island or a distant location, there is nothing else to do but visit whatever is there, irrespective of the magnitude of recreation benefits). Methodological criticisms include the problem of truncation bias (only those who visited the site are sampled, and hence valuation by non-visitors is not taken into account); the problem of multiple destinations (and thus precise allocation of travel cost to different sites); the problem of having reliable data on vehicle capital costs and operating costs; and the problem of valuation of travel time and whether or not it should be included in calculating travel cost.

Hedonic price method (HPM)
Anyone who buys a laptop or a mobile phone or car will have implicitly conducted a hedonic price analysis when comparing two or more similar goods with different values of various attributes before reaching a decision. Hedonic pricing is based on the model of consumer choice set out in Lancaster (1966: 134) which relates goods and characteristics. The three main elements of this approach are that: (1) 'the good per se does not give utility to the consumer, it possesses characteristics and these characteristics give rise to utility'; (2) a good may have 'more than one characteristic and many characteristics will be shared by more than one good'; and (3) when goods are consumed in combination the whole may be different from the sum of the parts, that is, 'goods in combination may possess characteristics different from those pertaining to the goods separately'. The use of this characteristics approach to examine housing prices or prices of relevant goods has come to be known as the hedonic price method and by the late 1970s it had become a well-established method to understand the demand for environmental quality (see Maclennan, 1977; Freeman, 1979; Malpezzi, 2003). The essence of the method is to collect information on house prices and all the various attributes of houses that affect prices and to express prices as a function of the various observed characteristics to estimate the hedonic or implicit prices of such attributes.

Applications of the hedonic price method in Africa appear to be quite common in agricultural economics, for example to understand whether food prices are affected by quality (Dury and Meuriot, 2010) or whether different aspects such as age and body weight affect livestock prices (Akinleye et al., 2005).

In a study of house prices in Windhoek townships, Humavindu and Stage (2003) found that, apart from the usual housing attributes, environmental quality in terms of location close to a waste (garbage) dump has a significant negative impact on house prices. In their study, being close to a waste dump (less than 250 metres) reduced the house price by about 35000 Namibian dollars (NAD) compared to average house prices of 60000 NAD. Being close to Goreangab dam recreational site, on the other hand, increased house prices by as much as 22000 NAD. Though these results were statistically significant, we should interpret them with some caution because in this study, out of 479 observations, only 6 per cent appeared to be close to a waste dump and only 1 per cent close to the Goreangab dam site.

A similar result has been reported by Bello and Bello (2008) in a hedonic price analysis of house prices in two locations within Akure, the capital of Ondo state in Western Nigeria. The authors surveyed 100 houses in each location. Their regression analysis had property value as a dependent variable while independent variables included eight variables depicting housing characteristics (wall material, ceiling, roofing material, window, room size, and whether a kitchen, toilet and fencing were available); eight variables representing environmental quality (condition of access road, regularity of electricity supply, condition of drainage, hours of water supply, crime rate, number of government approved private schools, public schools, and distance from a waste dump); and five socio-economic characteristics. Access roads, electricity and distance from a waste dump were statistically significant and positively associated with house prices.

Wen et al. (2005) report a hedonic price study of house prices in Hangzhou city in China. In that study, seven variables related to the housing structure, seven variables related to neighbourhood characteristics (including environmental quality indicators) and three location characteristics were used. About 60 per cent of the house price was contributed by structural characteristics, 16.5 per cent by neighbourhood characteristics and 19.8 per cent by location characteristics. Distance to West Lake had a negative sign, as expected, and had a hedonic price of -3.6, meaning that a 1 kilometre increase in the distance from West Lake would result in house prices decreasing by 36 240 RMB. After floor area, distance from West Lake appears to have been the second most important variable among the 14 variables affecting house prices.

The main advantage of hedonic price analysis is that policy makers perceive it to be based on real information as opposed to hypothetical information. House price information by way of databases compiled by mortgage institutions tends to be readily available. However, there are a number of issues that could potentially affect the reliability of this analysis. First, it is most directly relevant to the environmental issues that affect house prices, and hence it tends to be more relevant to urban areas than rural contexts. Secondly, the underlying assumption is that there is a well-functioning market for housing transactions. In many countries, housing markets are imperfect and even where they do function, they may consist of several individual sub-markets, for example due to segregation, social exclusion, formation of ghettos, and social and historical factors related to identity which may lead to the concentration of one group or community of individuals in one part of the city. Each such sub-market may have very different drivers of house prices. In that case, unless hedonic analysis is done for each sub-market, city-wide hedonic price analysis could produce spurious results as upward and downward variations in the same factor or characteristic in different sub-markets could lead the researcher or analyst to draw incorrect conclusions. For example, in areas near a university, there may be demand for single-bedroom apartments or those with four or more bedrooms (so that a group of students could live together and share the kitchen and other amenities). In such cases, in regression analysis, a second bedroom may appear with a negative hedonic price, suggesting that somehow a house with two bedrooms is less valuable than a house with a single bedroom, while elsewhere, in other housing markets, an additional bedroom usually has a positive impact on house prices. Third, data may not be available in sufficient detail to permit this type of analysis. Where data are available, there may be doubts about their reliability. For instance, in many countries, registered house prices may not reflect actual market prices due to corruption, as a lower price may be declared to reduce the stamp duty payable.

In many cities in the developing world, rent control mechanisms or other forms of rigidities impose significant transaction costs which may not be captured fully in house prices. Sometimes, land values in large cities are so high that there is little variation caused by other characteristics of houses including environmental quality indicators. In such cases, factors external to housing or neighbourhood characteristics may have a significant influence on house prices in an entire location or area within a city, which may not be captured by hedonic analysis, for example speculation on the plausible location of a new international airport or route by which a metro railway is likely to be built in the near future.

Also, certain environmental quality parameters such as urban air pollution or noise may not show adequate variation to be captured by house prices. For example, the pollution level in an entire neighbourhood or city (such as Beijing or Shanghai) may be high and not be differentiated by residential zones. In other cases, such as proximity to a polluted river or waste dump, residents may have no option but to live in such locations.

Stated Preference Methods

Contingent valuation method
Contingent valuation is one of the most popular amongst environmental valuation methods and is also the most controversial. In a contingent valuation analysis a survey is conducted in which a scenario is constructed whereby an environmental good, resource or situation which is currently not traded in the market is proposed to be traded, or whereby a payment is required in relation to an environmental good or service. An appropriate payment vehicle is described. Then the survey respondents are asked to express their willingness to pay (WTP). In early applications in an

open-ended question, the respondent is simply asked 'how much are you willing to pay for X?' and the response is then considered as the WTP. However, many studies have indicated that such open-ended questions are not incentive-compatible – that is there is no incentive for the respondent to reveal their true WTP. Various experiments showed that responses to open-ended questions can become significantly biased by the language used in the survey, by the way the surveyor is dressed or by other trivial factors which should not affect WTP. Alternatives included a bidding game in which the respondent is asked a series of closed questions until a 'tipping point' is reached.[11] Another alternative is a single closed question such as 'if this will cost you X dollars per month, would you be willing to pay?' (Bishop and Heberlein, 1979). Subsequently, it has been shown that if two dichotomous choice questions are used instead of one, the statistical efficiency of responses in estimating WTP improves (Hanemann et al., 1991).

From the early attempts in the 1960s, the number of such studies steadily increased such that in the 1980s two influential studies were published on the 'state of the art' of the method (Cummings et al., 1986; Mitchell and Carson, 1989). However, the method really 'took off' after the 1989 Exxon Valdez oil spill near Prince William Sound in Alaska. In 1992, as part of the proceedings, the District Court in Alaska commissioned a study of 'passive non-use values' using the contingent valuation method (Carson et al., 1992). At about the same time, a number of critics published various findings questioning the validity and reliability of contingent valuation (Hausman, 1993).

This controversy led to the formation of a 'blue ribbon panel' co-chaired by two Nobel laureates, Kenneth Arrow and Robert Solow. After hearing the arguments for and against, the panel concluded that contingent valuation can be a useful tool provided various measures are taken to ensure that results are internally consistent and meet various theoretical and methodological requirements (Arrow et al., 1993). The measures recommended by the Arrow–Solow Panel report include the use of a referendum format (dichotomous choice question); reminding respondents about an income constraint; making the payment vehicle as realistic as possible; designing experiments with care; and including appropriate tests for scope sensitivity and tests for internal consistency including alternative methods to deduce WTP information in addition to contingent valuation alone. Though the 'passive non-use values' study contributed to the Alaska Court's decision to raise the overall damages payable to US$5 billion, subsequent appeals resulted in a Supreme Court decision in 2008 which reduced the overall damages payable to around US$500 million. That judgment also set the standard that punitive damages in maritime accidents should be no greater than actual damages.

Among the main criticisms of the method are studies which indicated that respondents seemed to be insensitive to the scale or scope of the good being valued – an example being a study in which there was little variation in WTP for protecting 2000 birds or 20000 birds or 200000 birds (Desvousges et al., 2010). This phenomenon is sometimes referred to as 'part–whole' bias (see Bateman et al., 1997; Whitehead et al., 1998). A similar issue has also been termed an 'embedding effect' by Kahneman and Knetsch (1992), whereby WTP in two or more settings does not differ significantly even where we would conclude from economic theory that the responses should be significantly different. The issue was considered in an NOAA panel report (Arrow et al., 1993) and subsequent discussions (see Diamond and Hausman, 1994; Carson, 1997; Bateman et al., 2002). Notwithstanding the various criticisms, the number of contingent valuation studies has been steadily increasing because it is perceived that they offer a practical means of eliciting household response to environmental concerns.

Zhongmin et al. (2003) report a contingent valuation study on the valuation of ecosystem services of the Ejina region in the Hei river basin in Gansu province, China. In that study, they conducted a survey of 700 households: 324 households in urban areas drawn by random digit dialling of telephone numbers and 376 households in rural areas drawn by a random selection from a sample frame of all households. The payment scenario was of a referendum whereby if a majority of households vote in favour of restoring the Ejina ecosystem to the level of the early 1980s, the programme will be implemented, and if a majority of households vote against it, the project to restore it will not take place. If the respondent chooses to vote in favour of restoring then they are asked to indicate their willingness to pay by circling an appropriate number from a ladder with amounts per annum starting from 0 and going up to 300 RMB. This was followed by an open-ended question about a single lump sum payment in the form of a capital contribution. Ninety-two per cent of sample households were willing to pay some amount. Median WTP was just under 20 RMB per annum, with those in the main valley having a higher median WTP than those living in surrounding regions. The regression results suggested that WTP was positively correlated with urban residence, education and income. It is not clear how the authors tested for and avoided collinearity, for example between education and income.

In a study of contingent valuation in South Africa, Turpie (2003) presented information collected from a sample of some 814 income-earning (that is, non-poor) households in Western Cape province. The survey elicited WTP for national biodiversity conservation at the broadest level and for actions to prevent climate change. After respondents gave their overall

WTP for biodiversity conservation, they were asked to allocate their WTP to seven areas related to seven major biomes in South Africa. One of the main findings of this study was that WTP was positively associated with the level of knowledge about local biodiversity areas and interest in biodiversity conservation.

One of the main criticisms of contingent valuation studies is that of construct validity (how what is said in the survey relates to reality) and of the need to avoid hypothetical bias or freeriding whereby respondents may answer questions in a survey and indicate WTP even though in a real situation they would not be willing to pay. For this reason, many such studies try to include some measure of actual WTP and compare this with stated WTP. Two examples from Africa may be considered here.

In a study of farmers' willingness to pay to contribute to tsetse control in Burkina Faso, Kamuanga et al. (2001) used a contingent valuation approach to survey 261 households. In this study, farmers are surveyed about their willingness to contribute by way of participating in a tsetse control programme, which requires farmers to spend either money or labour, or both, in setting up and maintaining traps to control tsetse flies. The authors used an open-ended format with regard to WTP questions. Twenty-three per cent of farmers were willing to pay money, 37 per cent were willing to contribute labour, and 40 per cent were willing to contribute both. However, they also found that there was a divergence between the predicted and actual contribution: only 56 per cent of those who said they would contribute labour actually contributed labour in the previous period. Also, the predicted contribution was nearly 7 days per month per household, while actual contribution was only 2.1 days per month. Thus, the respondents appeared to be exaggerating not only their willingness to contribute but also the magnitude of such contribution. Though this is just one example, it highlights the potential problem of using private WTP as a mechanism to provide public goods whereby it is difficult to exclude non-payers.

Let us contrast this with another study which finds convergence between stated and actual WTP. Urama and Hodge (2006) report a contingent valuation study conducted in South Eastern Nigeria. In this study, the willingness to pay question was framed as a contribution to a river basin restoration trust fund. The survey covered 108 face-to-face interviews with farmers using an iterative bidding process which started with an open-ended question. The starting point from the open-ended question was then increased by 10 per cent in each subsequent stage in the iterative process. The WTP values obtained were compared with another survey in the same region in which preventive expenditures by farmers to address soil and water pollution were collected. The authors found that WTP values from the contingent valuation study were fairly comparable to preventive expenditures obtained from the preventive expenditure survey. For instance, mean WTP was 925 Naira per hectare per annum, while mean preventive expenditure was 1551 Naira per hectare per annum. Thus, they found that while there is convergence in terms of predicted and actual WTP, the margin of difference is statistically significant. These results are interesting because stated WTP is smaller than actual preventive expenditures. It is plausible that lower stated WTP is a reflection of lack of trust by respondents in local institutions which would be charged with the responsibility to provide pollution reduction services.

This brings us back to what we can refer to as the 'Sagoff dilemma'; just as in the case of Girl Scout cookies, when we are eliciting WTP in CVM surveys, we cannot be sure as to what motivates the respondents to express WTP.[12] There could be many reasons, including some related to preferences for the environmental good or quality in question. The onus is on the survey designers to recognise this and to be as clear and transparent as possible in describing the WTP scenario, to try to find information on actual payment as a reference point and to be open about the limitations of the contingent valuation instrument.

Choice experiments or choice modelling

An alternative approach which shares some of the same philosophical roots as contingent valuation is known as choice experiment or choice modelling. This method has its origins in transport studies and the marketing literature. To some extent, it also appears to draw upon Lancaster's characteristics theory though this is seldom directly acknowledged as such. In a typical such study researchers construct various options (the choice set). Each option will represent a unique combination of different attributes or parameters. For example, choices with regard to environmental impacts of energy use could include packages that a citizen can choose from. Each package may provide a certain amount of energy per month. It may cost the user a certain amount per month and there may be variations from one package to another, for example in terms of how clean or green the energy is, which organisation produces and supplies the energy, whether there is any lock-in period for moving from one company to another, whether it is possible for the consumer to generate renewable energy and feed back any excess energy to the grid, and whether there is any technical or financial assistance provided to the consumer for changing their energy use pattern. Using the information collected from such surveys, the analyst tries to deduce the marginal values of different attributes and estimates the relevant welfare measure (such as compensating surplus or equivalent variation).

Choice modelling studies appear to be common with regard to choices regarding breeding of cattle in terms of the attributes of cattle such as weight gain, potential market demand, type of feed required, and resistance to disease (see, for example, Jabbar and Diedhiou, 2003; Zander and Drucker, 2008).

The present author used a choice modelling study to understand WTP for drinking water supply in Chennai in the South Indian state of Tami Nadu at a time when acute water scarcity was prevalent (reported in Anand, 2010). In that study, I wanted to explore citizen preferences for the quantity of water (hence this was one of the attributes), the role of private sector provision, willingness to share a water tap with other households, and willingness to commit to reducing water use and increasing recycling and reuse. Various options (or bundles) were created. My surveys seem to suggest that households in Chennai would prefer to receive a larger quantity of water, and to receive this via an outside tap at their own house, and as long as water quality is assured they seem indifferent to whether the public or private sector provide this service. Further, I tried to see if households considered these attributes or characteristics of various options in a hierarchical manner (by estimating a nested multinomial logit model) and found that there was no evidence of this.

The main advantage of choice studies is that they may be slightly more useful than a contingent valuation design for eliciting WTP in the case of sensitive issues where even the suggestion of a private willingness to pay question may be considered as a major shift in policy and thus result in protest votes. Also, the experimental design permits the analyst to create hypothetical options alongside real options and test preferences for aspects that do not yet exist, but that may become prevalent after the project is implemented. However, the main disadvantages are that the computational burden of models may dictate how many variables and how many choices can be used. There is also a problem of information overload on the respondents, for example while it may be quite easy to present a large number of options concerning goods or commodities that are in day-to-day use by respondents, presenting policy choices or scenarios which involve processing of abstract information may result in spurious results if too many options are presented. For instance, in the end respondents may lose interest or may become bored waiting for the researcher to finish the long monologue of description of options.

CHALLENGES AND LIMITATIONS

The purpose of environmental assessment in project appraisal is to provide information to decision takers on the nature, magnitude and distribution of the environmental impact of project investment and whether, in spite of the impacts, the project is worth doing. The purpose of environmental valuation is to provide a link between the information on magnitudes of physical quantities and monetary valuation based on how consumers value such changes. Environmental valuation does not result in measuring environmental quality in purely monetary terms – environmental valuation is an attempt merely to quantify and translate existing preferences of consumers. Where the project environmental impacts affect the production of certain environmental goods or services that are traded in markets ('marketed goods'), the change in production method can be used. Where the environmental impact in turn affects some other 'marketed good', various methods of revealed preference can be used. Where environmental impact is not directly affecting marketed goods or services, nor is it captured indirectly in the prices of other things, then citizens may need to be asked directly about their values using contingent valuation approaches. There has been considerable progress with regard to both theoretical and practical applications in developing countries. The examples discussed here suggest that it is possible to adapt and extend many of the methods considered to be within the 'mainstream' of environmental valuation. However, there are numerous philosophical as well as methodological criticisms of all the methods discussed here. Some have been discussed in the earlier sections and will not be repeated. Here, we consider some important criticisms and alternatives by way of a research agenda.

While we have already considered criticisms of individual methods above, the main criticism of environmental valuation comes from those who feel that the very act of trying to place a monetary valuation on the environment and describing benefits received from the environment as 'goods' is symptomatic of a very narrow, anthropocentric and utilitarian world-view that cannot address methodological or procedural challenges. Deliberative discussions and citizen juries are often suggested as alternatives (see Spash and Vatn, 2006; Spash, 2007). There is a need for further research into whether community-based and participatory valuation exercises can be conducted using contingent valuation type scenarios. An alternative suggested by some critics is to use the idea of capabilities and freedoms as suggested by Sen (2009) and Nussbaum (2011). On the face of it, it may appear that freedoms are anathema to the idea of conserving and protecting natural resources. However, the concept of universalism of life claims (of those present now but also those will live in the future; of humans and non-human species) within the idea of freedoms suggests that the capability approach and sustainable human development should be central to the discussions on environmental valuation (Anand and Sen, 2000; Anand, 2007).

Some studies have used alternatives such as the ecological footprint or carbon footprint. The Global Footprint Network (2010) presents data at the national level for several countries on their ecological footprint. Here, the aggregate environmental impact of all activities occurring in a nation in a given year is converted into an ecological footprint in terms of 'global hectares per capita' required to sustain all the production and consumption. It is possible to adopt a similar approach at the project level to estimate the ecological footprint of a project. However, to a critic, the ecological footprint is merely a different scale or metric compared with monetary values in the case of environmental valuation and thus, however appealing it may appear, the ecological footprint approach also suffers from some of the same philosophical and methodological limitations as cost–benefit analysis and environmental valuation. Footprints may not be able to adequately capture the stock versus flow problem in terms of various ecosystem services. Also, the calculations may not fully reflect the role of technical progress and innovative designs in reducing a footprint significantly. Further, it is one thing to conclude that globally our footprint is larger than the earth's carrying capacity; to translate this to the national, sub-national and project levels poses the problem of open economies, trade and inter-regional compensation. It does not require a sophisticated calculation to reach a conclusion that most cities have vast footprints. While the broader message of reducing the footprint is valid, detailed calculations do not necessarily help in identifying or prioritising policy options.

Another alternative is the so-called multi-criteria analysis or multi-dimensional assessment as opposed to the single criterion of monetary measure used in most of the valuation methods discussed above. In a typical multi-criteria analysis, instead of providing valuation information, a project may be appraised on various criteria for its environmental impacts. This can be done in various ways. For example, the project may be scored on a scale of 1 to 10 for each of the environmental criteria or each of the dimensions identified. Alternatively, qualitative assessments may be used, for example, with indicators such as red, orange and green or high, medium and low. Alternatively, objective indicators may be chosen and for each indicator appropriate units and scales may be used. Once again, all indicators can be normalised and transformed to produce comparable units or ratios, and from these a composite index can be calculated. Acceptable limits can be specified, for example, that to be accepted a project must score above a certain level on each of the dimensions or on aggregate. Performance on some factors can be given higher or lower weight by specifying weights. This approach has the advantage that dimensions or criteria can be chosen such that aspects that are difficult to value and those that are easy to value can both be taken into account, as opposed to only the latter points which are captured in environmental valuation. However, to a critic, these methods are as fallible as environmental valuation because the choice of criteria, dimensions, scales, units and weights is all arbitrary, and there is no correct or incorrect approach. Thus, it is quite possible to 'dress up' a project that was previously unacceptable to become acceptable simply by 'shifting the goal posts' in terms of which criteria are used and how much weight is given.

An important issue concerns the cost of and time required for conducting environmental valuation studies and whether this can add to delays in the process of project appraisal and decision making. One response is that if citizens consider the environment to be an important issue, then their preferences for environmental quality must be considered in project decisions before imposing irreversible changes. Another response can be called the 'benefit transfer' approach, that is, to develop a database of methods, case studies and results with a view to developing a potential range of values so that perhaps one day we may reach a situation whereby values generated from one study could be used as inputs in the appraisal of other projects without having to conduct a valuation study. In some cases, for example, WTP relationships estimated in one study can be used elsewhere, keeping the estimated parameters but substituting the relevant values of variables. However, given that environmental quality issues can be highly contextual and that often what people express as values in one context may be quite inappropriate in another, it is unlikely that the benefit transfer approach can replace the need for conducting environmental valuation studies. Perhaps in the early stages of the project cycle and in screening and scoping, the benefit transfer approach may be used to identify potential issues or aspects to consider.

A related issue concerns how to set standards such as quality assurance requirements by user organisations, such as development banks or finance ministries, with regard to environmental valuation studies. The Arrow–Solow blue ribbon panel is an example of standard setting for one of the valuation methods, namely, contingent valuation. In the absence of specific standards, it is difficult for users to judge whether they are getting value for money for the resources spent on environmental valuation.

A final point to make is that environmental valuation is only as good as the extent to which such information informs policy and institutional change. A clever design and a fine analysis in a valuation study without the necessary legal and institutional environment is an exercise in constructing ivory towers. Knowing the price tag of something people already have or something which is not being traded can be quite futile. Hence, environmental valuation studies must be careful not to fall into the trap of headline-grabbing but entirely useless calculations, and instead focus their attention on policy-relevant information or studies that advance our understanding of human behaviour and preference formation.

NOTES

1. See for example, Johansson (1987); Hanley and Spash (1993); Dixon et al. (1994); Weiss (1994); Bateman et al. (2002); Dasgupta (2004); van Beukering et al. (2007).
2. For an intellectual history of environmental economics and its use in cost–benefit analysis, see Pearce (2002).
3. For a discussion on the difficulty in classifying ecosystem services see Fisher et al. (2009).
4. Perhaps, in that case, option value overlaps with other dimensions of value such as existence value.
5. See Samuelsson (2010) for a discussion of existence value.
6. For a discussion on the basic model of consumer choice see Varian (1996). For a discussion on use of the consumer choice model in environmental valuation, see Johansson (1987). A number of criticisms of the rational utility maximising individual are in Sen (1984 and 1987b).
7. Sagoff (1988: 68) provides the example of the difficulty in explaining why he may have obliged and bought the Girl Scout cookies made by his neighbour's nine-year-old daughter: 'I might have wanted or preferred (1) to support the Scouts; (2) to avoid friction with my neighbour; (3) to appear generous; (4) to spare my own daughter from embarrassment among her friends; (5) to do the right thing; (6) to feel a warm glow that I did the right thing; (7) to avoid guilt; or (8) any of a hundred reasons.'
8. This issue is of relevance to other valuation methods also; see Knetsch (2007).
9. In transport models, it is quite common to think of trips originating from zones. Early transport models were based on 'gravity' models suggesting that the number of trips between two zones is directly proportional to the product of 'masses' of the two zones – in this case populations – and inversely to the square of distance.
10. The travel cost method appears to have been proposed by Harold Hotelling in a letter to the National Parks Service in the USA in 1947. See Pearce (2002: 66).
11. For example, in increasing bids, this is the point when decision changes from 'yes' to 'no'; in decreasing bids, this is the point where decision changes from 'no' to 'yes'.
12. See note 7.

9. Assessing the benefits of new or improved roads

Chris Nash

INTRODUCTION

Economic appraisal of new roads or improved roads (see for example, Coburn et al., 1960) first came into common use in the 1960s, as a relatively simplistic comparison of capital costs with road maintenance, vehicle operating costs, journey time and accident savings. This already required estimation of road maintenance and vehicle operating costs, and valuation of journey time and accident savings, and as the core of economic appraisal in the sector in the development context, these issues will be considered in the next three sections. From an early stage, there was a recognition of the importance of external costs of road schemes, both of the scheme itself and in terms of reduced external costs of traffic on alternative roads, but methods to value these costs have only more recently been regarded as sufficiently robust for this to become a part of everyday appraisal. This is the subject of the next section. We then turn to the subject of induced traffic and wider economic benefits. There has long been a belief that such benefits must exist, but again it is only recently that research has succeeded in pinpointing their nature and providing the basis for their measurement. Finally we discuss the distributive impact of road schemes, before reaching our conclusions.

VEHICLE OPERATING AND ROAD MAINTENANCE COSTS

In a developed country with a well-built and well-maintained road system, changes in vehicle operating and road maintenance costs are not usually a major part of the benefits of road projects. In a developing country, where many roads are unsealed, there are major backlogs of maintenance and severe budget constraints limit spending, this is unlikely to be the case. Since pavement damage is related mainly to axleloads, and to pavement strength, the use of heavy, perhaps overloaded vehicles on poorly built and poorly maintained roads can cause serious damage, whilst simultaneously adding significantly to fuel and vehicle maintenance costs. Thus much of the attention of organisations such as the World Bank regarding road appraisal has concerned the estimation of vehicle operating costs and life cycle maintenance costs for road networks with and without improvement projects, which may include rehabilitation of existing roads as well as their enhancement or the construction of new ones. This attention has focused heavily on the development of computer tools, such as the Highway Development and Management Tool (HDM-4) which is the latest development in a series of tools started by the World Bank. The use of this tool to examine road projects and identify marginal benefits under a budget constraint is described by Archondo-Callao (2008).

A further reason why vehicle operating costs may be important in developing countries is that road improvements may allow larger vehicles to be operated, leading to significant savings in freight transport costs.

VALUE OF TIME SAVINGS

Early studies often simply took the wage rate as the value of time savings, and this approach is still in use in some countries, including China. The argument was that for working time it represented the value of the time to the employer, whilst for non-working time it was the opportunity cost to the employee, since they could otherwise have used the time to earn more income. More recent research has found problems with both these propositions. World Bank (2005a) gives some operational rules of thumb for appraisals in developing countries.

In the case of working time, in a competitive market, employers will hire labour up to the point at which the marginal cost of labour equals the value of its marginal product. However, the marginal cost of labour may include various overheads, as well as labour-related taxes and insurance payments. It is the gross cost of labour including these elements that should be used. But if output markets are generally imperfectly competitive, this will still understate the value of the marginal product of labour. On the other hand, in situations of unemployment or underemployment, this will overstate the value of the time savings, and the shadow wage rate obviously should then be used.

A further problem is that the distinction between working and non-working time is often unclear even in developed countries; in developing countries it may be a good deal less clear. In self-employed or informal labour markets (and indeed in many other occupations as well), it may be that the person has a certain amount of work to do and works whatever hours are necessary to do it. In that case time saved travelling even in the course of work may be devoted to non-work activities. There has also been an argument that time spent travelling may be put to productive use, although that is less relevant for road travel than for other modes, and that the disutility of travel may differ from that of work, so that there is an impact on the utility of the traveller which may need to be taken into account (Hensher, 1977). Finally, there has been a long-running argument about whether small time savings (often less than five minutes and even less than a minute for small schemes) may be productively used. Often it is argued that such small time savings will not even be perceived, let alone efficiently used. On the other hand small time savings may accrue from many different sources, transport and other, and in the long run these must accumulate into time that can be usefully employed.

Despite all these concerns, the common practice remains to value working time savings at the average wage rate, often with some mark-up to represent the other costs of employing labour. What limited amount of empirical evidence there is in terms of studies of what people are actually willing to pay to save time tends to support this practice, at least for medium-distance business travel (Marks et al., 1986).

In the case of non-working time, it has to be recognised that the opportunity cost of the time is only one element of the value of time savings (the other crucial one being the disutility of travel), and that the opportunity cost of travel time is often not working – people may work fixed hours with no opportunity of overtime, or only have a certain amount of work to do, or they may prefer not to devote any time savings to work because the marginal utility of leisure activities exceeds the difference between the marginal utility of the wage and the marginal (dis)utility of work. In such cases, anyone solely concerned with finding the impact of the road scheme on GDP will ignore such time savings, but to the extent that economic appraisal is trying to find the overall impact on the welfare of all affected by the road scheme, such time savings may still have a value. Discovering this, however, requires empirical evidence on the value road users place on the time savings. This will vary with anything that affects either the opportunity cost of time or the disutility of travel – time of day, day of the week and whether the road is congested or not are obvious factors to take into account. Willingness to pay to save time must also of course be expected to be a function of income.

The first empirical studies of the value placed on time savings (for example, Beesley, 1965) looked for examples where people actually had a choice of whether to pay more to save time – toll roads versus free roads, rail versus bus, and so on – and used quite simplistic ways of analysing the data, ignoring the other elements such as the comfort of the route or mode in question that might affect the choice. Techniques for analysing such data have advanced enormously over the years, such that values of time are now typically derived from the relative weight placed on time and cost in discrete choice models estimated using logit or probit analysis (Hensher, 2001). Also, there has been a switch to the extensive use of data from stated preference experiments, in which respondents are asked to choose between hypothetical alternatives rather than being observed choosing between actual ones. The advantages of this are that alternatives can be constructed which reveal the maximum information about preferences, and that each respondent may be faced with many such choices. The majority view appears to be that, if realistic and carefully designed, such experiments are reliable, but their use remains controversial. Such studies typically yield values in the range of 25–50 per cent of the wage rate and roughly proportionate to income (Mackie et al., 2003), yielding an obvious way of transferring values from one context or country to another (simply scaling them up or down in proportion to income has been recommended for the transfer between countries of all values based on willingness to pay, whether costs or benefits; see HEATCO, 2005). However, the amount of evidence from such studies in developing countries remains limited, and transferring values from developed to developing countries is obviously uncertain, both because of the extreme differences in income often involved and because of more fundamental differences in culture and the way of life.

The value of time savings for freight traffic remains an under-researched area. Obviously drivers are treated as people travelling in working time, and an allowance for improved utilisation of vehicles may be incorporated into the estimates of operating costs. One way of estimating time values for freight is to look at the interest on the capital tied up in the freight. But there are suggestions that this may greatly underestimate the benefits of faster transits which permit changes to the supply chain affording much bigger savings (reduced stockholdings for example). It is also generally the impression that reliability is even more important than transit time itself in this context. Chronic congestion in large cities in developing countries may be a major source of unreliability, whilst rural areas may even lack all-weather roads.

ACCIDENTS

Some elements of the costs of accidents are straightforward to value in principle, even if not necessarily so in practice. Damage to property and police, ambulance and hospital treatment costs will obviously simply be valued at market or shadow prices, as will loss of working time. The difficulty with accidents is how to value the grief, pain and suffering involved. Early studies simply valued these as loss of income – even for those killed! The consensus now is that these should be valued at the willingness to pay of the population to reduce the risk of them occurring. This may be researched, as with the value of time, by finding actual situations in which people choose between paying more or incurring higher risks. Obvious examples are choice of travel mode or carrier (for instance, there are large differences between the accident records of different airlines which do not appear to be solely a matter of chance), and – outside the transport field – choice of occupation (some high-risk occupations such as working on oil rigs carry a premium relative to other occupations requiring similar skills). But to a greater extent than with travel time there is a worry as to whether those choosing are well informed on the characteristics of the modes or operators they are using, especially with regard to the risks they are taking. Thus there is a preference in recent studies for the use of the stated preference approach, in which people are directly informed of the risks, although even then there are concerns – backed by the results of some surveys – as to whether they can rationally weigh up small differences in risk (Lindberg, 2005). World Bank (2005b) gives some guidance on the incorporation of accident costs in a developing country context.

EXTERNAL COSTS

Transport has long been recognised as causing external costs, particularly in terms of its environmental impact. On the other hand, new roads can relieve some environmental costs by diverting traffic away from existing roads which may be closer to densely populated areas. Box 9.1 shows the elements of environmental costs that are considered – although not necessarily valued in money terms – in the British transport appraisal process.

As with journey time and accidents, a mixture of evidence from actual market behaviour and from hypothetical surveys is used to value these items (Maibach et al., 2008). The obvious way in which many people can trade off their living environment against cost is through the amount of rent they pay or the price they pay for their home: other things being equal, rents and property prices will be higher, the more attractive the environment. There have been many studies of the impact of noise nuisance on property values, as well as some studies of local air pollution. In the case of noise, this may be an appropriate approach: noise nuisance is readily perceived and its major cost is disamenity, although there is evidence that

---

**BOX 9.1   UK APPRAISAL SUMMARY TABLE:
ENVIRONMENT**

Noise   Heritage of historic resources
Local air quality   Biodiversity
Greenhouse gases   Water environment
Landscape   Physical fitness
Townscape   Journey ambience

Source: Department for Transport (2004).

---

high levels of noise nuisance may affect health. But the appropriateness of this approach to local air pollution is more in doubt. Whilst air pollution may cause disamenity, its major cost is its impact on health, and it is doubtful if those choosing where to live have any understanding of this. Thus the more favoured approach is the dose–response approach, whereby an attempt is made to measure directly the impact of the pollutant on health and to value that. For instance, research for the European Commission has developed the Impact Pathway method, which models in turn the level of emissions, their resulting concentration in the environment, their deposition in people's lungs (as well as on buildings and crops), and the physical impact this has. Only then does monetary valuation take place (Bickel et al., 2005).

Greenhouse gas emissions have become a major political issue in recent years (Stern, 2007). There are two alternative ways of valuing them. The marginal damage costs of additional greenhouse gases may be estimated by running world models at alternative levels of emissions, or the marginal cost of achieving politically determined constraints in terms of emission levels may be estimated. If governments have entered into binding constraints on greenhouse gases, then the latter is the more appropriate, as well as the more practical, since any change in greenhouse gases from transport will be offset by changes elsewhere in the economy. Whilst it is reasonably straightforward to estimate the change in emissions from vehicle use, if forecasts of traffic and of the future characteristics of the vehicles used have been developed, the greenhouse gases emitted from the actual construction of the scheme are typically ignored as being too difficult to measure.

The remaining costs in the list in Box 9.1 are very much more difficult to value. Both market behaviour and hypothetical surveys have been used to try to value landscape, townscape and heritage, but the problem is that each view and each historical building is unique, and it is difficult to find ways of characterising them in order to obtain values that can be generalised, whilst there is a severe risk of bias in the case of surveys of willingness to pay to avoid damage to sites known to be threatened. Loss of biodiversity raises enormous uncertainties about its long-term costs, whilst impacts on the water environment may also embody large degrees of uncertainty. None of these are currently valued in money terms in the British appraisal process, although there is research on the first two. The final two items – physical fitness and journey ambience – are rather different in nature from the other environmental costs considered and are not discussed further here.

INDUCED TRAFFIC AND WIDER ECONOMIC BENEFITS

An essential element in any normal project appraisal is the forecasting of future traffic. Normal traffic growth may be estimated from past trends, or by using elasticities with respect to price and GDP. Diversion from other roads or other modes may be estimated using diversion curves (which show the percentage using each alternative as a function of the relative time and money cost) or more complex mode split models. But it is induced traffic which presents the greatest forecasting problems (TRL, 2005).

New roads typically generate additional traffic which would not have existed in their absence. These trips may take the form of business travel, commuting, leisure trips or freight traffic. The standard approach to valuing the benefits of such trips is to use the rule of a half. Since the user was not willing to travel at the original generalised cost (that is, including all money costs and the value of the time taken) but is now, the benefit must be some fraction of the reduction in the generalised cost of the trip. Assuming a linear demand curve, that fraction will be one half.

With a very low value of time in developing countries, benefits of generated trips may appear low, although distributive weighting systems may partly offset this (see below). However, where in the absence of a road transport is so slow that regular trips to facilities such as schools and hospitals are not feasible, then the social benefits of roads may be much greater than their economic valuation implies. This may still be common in rural areas of developing countries. Of course, these benefits require not just infrastructure but access to transport services too; in countries where car ownership is out of reach of most of the rural population, this means bicycles, buses or jitney taxis (Howe and Richards, 1984).

Generated trips may also reflect the presence of wider economic benefits. Additional business travel, freight and commuting trips suggest a rise in economic activity in the area, whilst leisure trips may bring spending to the area. Surely this will bring benefits to this area over and above the consumer surplus reflected in the rule of a half.

The first point to note is that in the presence of full employment, any increased economic activity in this area will be at the expense of somewhere else. Even if there is unemployment, this is often likely to be the case. Thus any increase in employment in the area of the scheme must be set against decreases elsewhere. Only if this is a particular area of economic problems, with a lower shadow price of labour than the national level, will moving jobs here from elsewhere be a benefit. Again, this may often be the case for rural areas of developing countries. Where rural roads provide feeder services that make the transport of crops or other products to market viable from areas where this was not possible before, there may be significant wider economic benefit, equal to the difference between the value of production and the shadow priced value of inputs including labour. For instance it has been shown that improvement of access to markets in rural Nepal significantly increases land values (Jacoby, 2000). It has long been recognised that in such circumstances the only accurate way of producing transport forecasts is to forecast the change in production in the area in question, and that the desired development effect may depend on simultaneous investments in agriculture and other infrastructure (Beenhakker and Chamari, 1979). Adler (1987) has a number of case studies of rural feeder roads and World Bank (2005c) has some practical advice for operational work.

However, the rural development effect of new roads is not always beneficial. Roads carry traffic in both directions. The additional traffic may in fact reflect the movement of jobs, which previously could survive in the area because of the protection given by high transport costs, to another location to exploit economies of scale or lower costs for other reasons.

Most authors conclude that it is necessary to examine each particular case to see if the area in question has economic potential that is being held back by the level of transport costs in order to evaluate whether the road scheme may genuinely generate new economic activity that is not simply diverted from elsewhere (see, for example, World Bank, 2005d). There have been many other attempts to argue that there are wider economic benefits from road schemes. In many cases these are also transfers, or pecuniary externalities, rather than truly additional benefits. For instance a road scheme may increase property prices in the area, but this is usually simply a transfer of benefits from road users to property owners, very important when we come to consider distributive effects as discussed below, but not an additional benefit.

Similarly, road schemes which reduce freight vehicle operating costs may lead to a wider range and lower prices of goods in the shops, but this is simply the passing on of the benefit through competition in the market place to the ultimate customer.

But recent research has confirmed the possibility of three types of genuine external benefit over and above transport cost savings (Venables, 2007). These arise from:

- agglomeration economies;
- imperfect competition in output markets;
- labour market impacts.

Agglomeration economies arise from the observation that labour productivity tends to be higher in locations which are accessible to a large number of other firms. It is hypothesised that this is partly because of the opportunities for informal exchange of information that this creates, partly through the ability to match labour skills more closely to the jobs available and partly through economies of scale in the supply of inputs such as professional services, which will be more readily available locally when there is a high concentration of jobs.

These effects may be taken into account in the appraisal by measuring the elasticity of labour productivity to effective density (where effective density is the sum of employment by zone weighted by the inverse of mean generalised cost for business and commuting trips). A new road scheme will reduce this mean generalised cost. Note that this elasticity is highest in services and lowest in manufacturing (Graham, 2007).

We have already noted above that imperfect competition in output markets means that the wage rate will understate the value of the marginal product of labour, meaning that increased output resulting from reduced costs has extra value equal to the difference between price and marginal cost. British draft appraisal guidance (Department for Transport, 2009) suggests that this typically adds 10 per cent to direct benefits, but in developing countries this effect may have already been allowed for in computing the shadow price of labour.

The third impact arises when reduced commuting costs lead to an effective increase in the real wage and this calls forth an increased supply of labour. In a country with labour taxes this implies that the willingness to pay of the individual for the extra commuting journeys will understate the benefit because of the tax wedge; some of the extra income will go to the government rather than the individual.

DISTRIBUTIVE EFFECTS

In the early days of economic appraisal, it was generally seen as an application of the compensation test, in other words concerned solely with economic efficiency rather than distribution. But it is now generally accepted that project selection will affect the distribution of costs and benefits and that there are inadequate other instruments available to ensure that the overall final distribution of costs and benefits is equitable. Thus many organisations, including the British government (HM Treasury, 2003), formally include distributive weighting systems in their appraisal manual, although they are difficult to apply in practice and – as noted below – their formal use, as opposed to more qualitative assessments of distributional impacts, appears to be rare in the transport sector. World Bank (2005e) discusses these issues in the context of the transport sector.

Such an approach requires the analyst to measure the costs and benefits of the project by income group. In the case of transport projects, that is not easy. In the first round, transport projects provide benefits to road users – commuters, business and leisure travellers and freight transport companies. For commuters and leisure travellers it is possible to obtain the income distribution of users by surveys. But, as commented above, these benefits may often be passed on in the form of higher property prices, as the demand for property in the area increases, or in lower real wages as labour supply expands. Similarly, costs such as environmental costs may also be passed on through the property market.

For business and freight traffic, the likelihood that benefits will be passed on through the market is even greater. If the benefits remain where they first fall, then they will presumably increase the profits of the company concerned and thus go to the company's shareholders. But if that company trades in a competitive market, then the cost reduction will be passed on to its customers. Ultimately it will be goods and services that become cheaper, and their consumers who benefit.

It is therefore necessary to think carefully about who is the ultimate beneficiary in the case of transport projects. It must be said that careful appraisals of the distributive effects of road schemes remain relatively rare; all too often appraisals still confine quantitative analysis to the efficiency impacts. This is unfortunate in that the distributive effects of road schemes may be very important. Even in developed countries, it remains the case that road use is strongly correlated with income, and this may be even more so in developing countries.

CONCLUSION

The appraisal of road projects has improved enormously over the past few decades since its birth in the 1960s. Valuation methods have improved enormously, both in the case of time and accident savings, which have been valued in money terms since the early days of road investment appraisal, and for environmental externalities, which used to be thought too difficult to value. However, there remains a shortage of empirical evidence on these factors in the case of developing countries, and the transfer of evidence from the very different circumstances of developed countries is hazardous. The wider economic benefits of road schemes, and the extent to which these are genuine additional benefits as opposed to transfers, or pecuniary externalities, has become better understood. In addition to the long-recognised cases of generation of new economic activity particularly from rural roads in developing countries, agglomeration economics and market imperfections have been identified as sources of wider economic benefits. The need for distributive analysis has also been generally acknowledged, although less often actually realised.

Yet none of this has made the appraisal process easier, and road project appraisal remains a controversial area, in which judgement plays an important role. It cannot readily be reduced to a technical exercise following a set of instructions, but needs a good understanding of the area in which the scheme is taking place and the ability to make sensible judgements on the part of the analyst.

10. Project appraisal in health: cost effectiveness approaches

John Weiss

INTRODUCTION: THE DIFFICULTY OF BENEFIT VALUATION

Health is the classic case of a sector with 'difficult to value' benefits. Various attempts have been made to incorporate monetary values for benefits from health projects, but all suffer from some drawbacks. Private sector health projects are designed to meet commercial objectives, and their benefits to the private investor are clearly a revenue stream from patient fees. Nonetheless if they are to be assessed from a social perspective this will be inadequate as it is widely recognised that healthier individuals benefit not just themselves but the rest of society – for example through reductions in infectious disease, higher productivity and innovation.

In terms of the public sector at the simplest level some health projects may aim to save costs for the health system overall, particularly in the context of restrictions on overall health budgets. Various reorganisations for example may aim to shift health delivery from hospitals to local clinics or community health workers, with a view to saving costs. In this case, provided the impact of the project implementing such a reorganisation is purely cost saving, this provides an appropriate measure of benefits. In practice, however, reorganisations rarely have zero health consequences and once these are allowed for, the benefit valuation question is introduced.

In the development context early efforts at valuing health impacts from reduced illness focused on the change in productivity allowed by a longer period of working time with a healthier population (for example due to projects that reduced the incidence of tropical illnesses such as malaria or river blindness).[1] This approach was always recognised as being partial since it took no account of the benefits of improved health per se, either in terms of individual well-being or of the possibility of a healthier society creating external benefits not reflected in the extra productivity of individuals.

The health valuation problem is highlighted in the dilemma over how to treat a saving in human life. The productivity approach uses assumed lifetime earnings over the remaining years of working life for each individual whose death is averted by a project intervention. This procedure raises both ethical issues – why should the life of a high earner be more valuable than that of a low earner – and practical ones, relating again to the omission of the personal well-being of those affected and the incorporation of externalities. In a developed country context a number of relatively sophisticated approaches to the human life valuation problem have been developed. One focuses on observed decisions – whether of individuals or public sector decision makers – that reveal a trade-off between risk of fatality and income. Where an identifiable risk is lowered at a particular loss of income there is implicitly a valuation decision in relation to risk (for example, in taking a lower-paid but less risky job), termed 'the value of a statistical life'.[2] The main alternative approach is to survey individuals to establish their willingness to pay for lower risk. Contingent valuation surveys, for example, have been used to establish willingness to pay for lower risk of death, but although this is close in spirit to the individualistic welfare economic theory behind cost–benefit analysis, their application is complicated by the fact that responses will vary with factors like the age and wealth of respondents, the time profile of risk reduction, and the quality of life with survival. Once an estimate of willingness to pay – either through direct surveys or by observation of individual behaviour in response to risk of fatality – has been identified, it can be combined with data on change in risk levels over the total population affected. Thus, for example, if an average willingness to pay to reduce risk of death (from say 5 in 10000 to 3 in 10000) is found to be $50, then the value of a statistical life will be the average figure ($50) multiplied by the number of individuals affected (10000) divided by the lives saved (2). Thus in this instance the value of a statistical life is ($50*10000)/2, or $250000.

However, virtually all studies estimating the value of a statistical life have been for developed countries and when applied in a developing country the normal procedure is to scale the estimated value by the difference in income per capita between the country to which the estimate relates and the developing country where a health project is located.[3] This has been recognised as a highly controversial and unsatisfactory form of benefit transfer. Even accepting that such estimates are an appropriate measure of the value of a statistical life in a developed country context, the scaling down of these to lower poor country levels implies a strong ethical judgement that is highly controversial. If on average the value of a statistical life of US citizens based either on their own behaviour or their stated preference is found to be $1 million, the justification for taking 10 per cent of this value for the statistical life of citizens of a country whose income per capita happens to be 10 per cent of the US level is very weak, since the relevant preferences will be of the citizens directly exposed to risk, not those of a comparator group in a richer country.

The empirical difficulty in capturing factors like health externalities, combined with these ethical problems, means that placing monetary values on the impacts of health projects is the exception rather than the rule.[4] At least in a developing country context the standard alternative to benefit valuation in the health sector is a form of cost effectiveness analysis, and considerable effort has been made over the last two decades to develop measures of health impact that can be used in operational appraisals of health projects. The important implication of the recognition that a satisfactory monetary valuation of health benefits is not possible is that health projects should not be seen as competing directly for public funds with projects with tangible benefits which can be monetised. Thus in the public sector context, resource allocation decisions relate to obtaining maximum health impacts from a given budget. This chapter discusses some of the practical alternatives for this form of analysis in a development context.

COST EFFECTIVENESS IN HEALTH

Cost effectiveness analysis compares a stream of future impacts with the associated stream of future costs. In health the complication lies in identifying impact. Simple measures such as patients treated or bed nights are easy to identify but tell little about health outcomes. For this a more sophisticated form of measure is required which expresses the impact of an intervention in terms of a series of health outcomes (like years of life saved or days of illness avoided). A comparison between such a measure and the cost of alternative health projects or interventions has been termed a cost–utility analysis, where utility is assumed to be related only to health outcomes (Zweifel and Telser, 2009). This chapter discusses the application of this approach using three such measures, years of life gained (YLG), healthy years of life gained (HYLG) and disability adjusted years of life (DALY), and considers how such analyses can inform decision taking.[5]

A cost effectiveness indicator (*CEI*) for a health project can be defined as:

$$CEI = PV(C_w - C_{wo})/PV(HI_w - HI_{wo}) \qquad (10.1)$$

where *C* refers to costs, *HI* to health impact and the subscripts *w* and *wo* to with and without the project respectively. *PV* refers to discounted present values of both cost and impact.

Equation (10.1) requires a discount rate, and the normal procedure in health projects is to apply a time preference rate, typically in the range of 2 to 3 per cent (Gold et al., 1996). The application of an opportunity cost rate implies that project income could be reinvested productively at the chosen rate and that, in waiting, society forgoes this income stream. However, health projects do not typically create monetary income (or where they do it is only a part of total benefits), hence this rationale for discounting is not valid. Nonetheless society is likely to prefer improved health sooner rather than later, and if one assumes that time preference for health impacts matches that for monetary consumption then a standard social time preference rate (based on the declining marginal utility of income and risk avoidance) can be applied.[6]

A CEI cannot in itself determine whether a health project is a good investment. Its role is in the ranking of alternatives and selecting the one with the lowest cost per unit of outcome provided the following conditions hold:

i.   Different health impacts can be converted to an appropriate common unit.
ii.   Alternatives are divisible – so that several more cost-effective smaller alternatives can replace one large less cost-effective project in reaching the same number of patients more cheaply.
iii.   The budget for health projects is fixed so that more patients cannot be treated by expanding the budget.
iv.   Cost effectiveness ratios are calculated on a marginal, not average, basis whenever the cost per unit of impact is not constant.[7]

Where the divisibility condition does not hold there is the possibility of implausible implicit valuations of health effects. Put simply, if we can save ten lives at a cost of $1 million or five lives at a cost of $0.4 million, the respective cost effectiveness ratios are $0.1million/life for the larger alternative and $0.08/life for the smaller. If we opt for the more cost-effective smaller alternative we are saying we would rather save $0.6 million than save five lives, which is an implicit valuation of less than $0.12 million per life saved. Where the smaller programme can be expanded to cover more people this is not an issue, but where it cannot, the implicit valuation problem remains. Similarly, where budgets are fixed the choice of not expanding them is again setting off saving of lives against saving of cost. Decision takers and the wider community may be highly uncomfortable if the full implications of some cost-saving decisions were known and cost effectiveness analysis cannot address this.

It might be argued that these implicit valuations provide a revealed preference measure of the monetary benefits of health effects which would allow full cost–benefit calculation of many types of health project. The flaw in this argument, however, is that it requires informed and consistent decision taking, and since decision takers are often unaware of many implicit valuations this will have only limited relevance in practical appraisals.

Equation (10.1) can be estimated most simply using a narrow definition of health impact based on the specific goal of a project, for example relating to the number of patients served (such as children immunised or pregnant mothers seen), the medical staff provided (such as nurses or doctors trained) or the inputs provided (such as the number of bed nights or operations). This is a process approach to cost effectiveness since the process of providing a given type of health service is assumed to have a clear and constant relation with health outcomes. Thus different projects can be compared, for example by costs per hospital bed or overall costs per patient seen, without regard to differential health consequences. Although simple to apply, this approach is simplistic in this basic assumption and cannot be applied realistically in comparisons between different types of health project. For this reason a series of more complex indicators of health impact have been developed for application in equation (10.1).

YEARS OF LIFE GAINED

Of these indicators the simplest is based on deaths averted or years of life gained (YLG). Use of this indicator allows a comparison between different ways of saving life (for example preventive or curative treatment). Thus the comparison across projects is by discounted costs per discounted year of life saved.[8] This requires an estimate of expected duration of life with and without a project for all those patients who will be treated, which in turn involves data by each disease or condition the project will address. The key data are combined in equation (10.2). YLGs can be given by any unit of population (such as 1000 of the population):

$$YLG = IN * CF * SR * PV \, (ad..ar) \qquad (10.2)$$

where IN is the incidence of the condition (new cases per 1000 of population); CF is the percentage case fatality rate; SR is the probability of survival without the condition between the years ao (the average age of onset) and ad (average age of death for those suffering from the condition); PV is present value; ad is as above; and ar is the average age of death without the condition, so $PV(ad..ar)$ is the discounted present value of years survived between ad and ar.

To apply this approach in comparisons between projects requires assumptions about how effective they will be in reducing incidence (*IN*) of different conditions and in extending the average age of premature death (*ad*) where treatment is not fully effective. National life expectancy tables will be required to identify expected age at death for someone without the condition at age *ad*, although use of such tables typically will assume no further improvements in the absence of the project. Cost effectiveness comparisons will thus be of the form:

$$CEI = PV\,(C_w - C_{wo})/PV\,(YLG) \qquad (10.3)$$

where, as before, C_w and C_{wo} are costs with and without the project, *PV* refers to present values and *YLG* refers to years saved.

YLG has an advantage over process indicators (like bed nights, for example) in that it is based on health outcomes; however, it is inadequate where projects create significant morbidity in addition to mortality effects. Hence to compare projects to combat chronic diseases with large morbidity but relatively minor mortality impacts, several alternative indicators have been developed.

HEALTHY YEARS OF LIFE GAINED

As the simplest of this range of alternative indicators, healthy years of life gained (HYLG) is the sum of the years of life saved by a project plus the years no longer affected by illness, with the latter years weighted to make them comparable to years of life saved. This is also referred to as quality adjusted years of life (QALY). The formula for HYLG requires estimates for years affected by disease or disability before premature death (YD) plus years of chronic disability for those who do not die prematurely (YCD) plus years lost to temporary illness from the same condition (YT). Calculation of these health outcomes requires information on:

- the degree to which those suffering from a condition suffer disability from its onset to premature death, where the latter is relevant;
- the proportion of those suffering who survive but are permanently affected;
- the severity of their chronic condition.

With such data the following formulae apply:

$$YD = IN^*CF^*SR^*w1^*PV\,(ao..\,ad) \qquad (10.4)$$

where *YD* is years of life affected by a condition before premature death; *IN* and *CF* are as in equation (10.2); *ao* and *ad* are the average age at the onset of the condition and the average age of premature death from it, respectively; *SR* is the probability of survival without the condition between the ages of *ao* and *ad*; *w*1 is the disability weight attached to a year of morbidity for years *ao* to *ad*; and *PV* is the present value of the discounted stream of years survived between *ao* and *ad*.

$$YCD = IN*PD*w2* \, PV \, (ao.. \, ar) \tag{10.5}$$

where *YCD* is years of chronic disability; *IN* is as in equation (10.2); *PD* is the percentage of those affected by a condition, who do not die prematurely but remain permanently ill; *w*2 is the disability weight attached to a year of morbidity from age *ao* to normal expected death *ar*; and *PV* is the present value of the discounted stream of years survived from *ao* to *ar*.[9]

$$YT = PV \, (IN*(1 - CF - PD)*t*w3)) \tag{10.6}$$

where *YT* is years of temporary disability or ill-health; *IN*, *CF* and *PD* are as defined in equations (10.2), (10.4) and (10.5); $(1 - CF - PD)$ is the proportion of those affected at age *ao* who suffer temporary ill-health; *t* is the proportion of a year affected by ill-health; *w*3 is the disability weight attached to a year of temporary ill-health; and $PV \, (IN*(1 - CF - PD)*t*w3)$ is the present value of $(IN*(1 - CF - PD)*t*w3)$.

Total HYLG is thus:

$$HYLG = YLG + YD + YCD + YT \tag{10.7}$$

and the cost effectiveness comparison between projects is now based on:

$$CEI = PV \, (C_w - C_{wo})/PV(HYLG) \tag{10.8}$$

where *PV(HYLG)* is the present value of healthy years of life gained as a result of a project.

Use of the HYLG requires additional information on health outcomes but critically the use of disability weights (*w*1, *w*2, *w*3), which convert years of ill-health saved to an equivalent in healthy years saved.

The best-known HYLG indicator is the QALY routinely used in the UK, for example in cost effectiveness studies for the National Institute of Clinical Excellence (NICE) in its assessment of treatments to be offered by the National Health Service. QALYs represent levels of quality of life enjoyed by individuals in different health states. The

Table 10.1   EQ-5D health state valuations

Health state	Description	Valuation
11111	No problems.	1.000
11221	No problems walking; no problems with self-care; some problems performing usual activities; some pain or discomfort; not anxious or depressed.	0.760
22222	Some problems walking; some problems washing or dressing; some problems performing usual activities; moderate pain or discomfort; moderately anxious or depressed.	0.516
12321	No problems walking; some problems washing or dressing; unable to perform usual activities; some pain or discomfort; not anxious or depressed.	0.329
21123	Some problems walking; no problems with self-care; no problems performing usual activities; moderate pain or discomfort; extremely anxious or depressed.	0.222
23322	Some problems walking; unable to wash or dress; unable to perform usual activities; moderate pain or discomfort; moderately anxious or depressed.	0.079
33332	Confined to bed; unable to wash or dress; unable to perform usual activities; extreme pain or discomfort; moderately anxious or depressed.	−0.429

Source: Phillips (2009, Table 1).

weights used run from 1.0 for perfect health to negative values for severe disability.[10] The weighting scheme used by NICE follows the EQ-5D which assesses the ability of individuals to function in five dimensions relating to mobility, pain, self-care, anxiety/depression and usual activities. Each dimension has three levels relating to the severity of problems. Weights for these conditions are derived from responses from a random sample of the population who state their preferences in a choice-based method of valuation (the time-trade-off method) (Phillips, 2009). The time-trade-off in effect asks individuals how many weeks or months of normal health equate to a year of a particular health condition. Thus if nine months of normal health is deemed equivalent to a year suffering from diabetes, the latter condition has a weight of 0.75. Table 10.1 illustrates a sample of these weights for a range of health states based on a description of patient conditions.

Because they refer to a gain in health, the objective of a health project will be to maximise the HYLGs or QALYs for a given health budget; thus HYLGs (or QALYs) gained as a result of an intervention are summed and compared with project cost. Because of the subjectivity of such a weighting system, HYLGs (such as QALYs) are a more contentious indicator than the simpler YLG.[11]

DISABILITY ADJUSTED LIFE YEARS

The Disability Adjusted Life Year (DALY) indicator is similar to the HYLG except that it adds another level of complexity by using not only subjective disability weights, but in addition weights for years of life saved at different ages.[12] DALYs represent levels of loss caused by ill-health and the sum of DALYs is a benefit in terms of losses avoided. If society's view of the merit of saving an extra year of life is influenced by the productivity of those affected (which is a controversial view), then saving the lives of those of working age will create a higher social gain than saving the lives of the elderly and the very young. The original DALY age weighting gave a weight of more than 1.0 to those aged 9 to 54 and weights of below 1.0 to those aged below 9 and above 54.

Table 10.2 gives the disability weights used in the original DALY analysis. How particular conditions are classified in relation to these is subjective and typically is based on expert opinion rather than patient responses to surveys (as for QALYs for example). Apart from the different origins of the disability weights and the age weighting adjustment, DALYs

Table 10.2   DALY disability weights

Class	Description of condition	Weight
1	Limited ability to perform at least one activity in one of the following areas: recreation, education, procreation, occupation.	0.096
2	Limited ability to perform most activities in one of the following areas: recreation, education, procreation, occupation.	0.220
3	Limited ability to perform most activities in two or more of the following areas: recreation, education, procreation, occupation.	0.400
4	Limited ability to perform most activities in all of the following areas: recreation, education, procreation, occupation.	0.600
5	Needs assistance with instrumental activities of daily living such as meal preparation, shopping or housework.	0.810
6	Needs assistance with activities of daily living such as eating, personal hygiene or toilet use.	0.920

Note: Limited ability is defined as 50 per cent reduction in normal ability.

Source: Murray (1994).

differ from QALYs in that the impact of a health project is in terms of DALYs saved (that is, ill-health avoided) rather than the extra quality adjusted years gained. Whilst the reference condition (weight of unity) of the QALY is perfect health, for the DALY the reference condition with a weight of unity is death. Where there are no age weights applied in the DALY indicator and the disability weights are equivalent (so with a weight of 0.10 for a year of life with a serious health condition in the QALY system the weight for the same condition in the DALY system is 0.90) the equivalence is:

$$(1 - Q) = D$$

where Q is the sum of the QALYs from a project and D is the sum of the DALYs from the same project.

Thus whilst the objective of health planning using the QALY measure is to maximise QALYs for a given budget, for the same budget it is to minimise DALYs.

As noted above, in the calculation of DALYs disability weights are combined with age weights which are derived from the formula:

$$ax = Cx*e^{-bx} \qquad (10.9)$$

or

$$ax = Cx/e^{bx}$$

where ax is the age weight for year x; C is a constant specified so the total burden of disease in healthy years is the same with and without age weights (which requires that some age weights are below 1.0 and some above). The parameter b is required to derive a function of this form. The original study set b at 0.04 and C at 0.1624.

With e at 2.7314, application of equation (10.9) and these values for b and C gives a set of age weights. For example for year 10:

$$ax = (0.1624*10)/(2.7314^{0.04*10}) = 1.086$$

Similarly for year 60:

$$ax = (0.1624*60)/(2.7314^{0.04*60}) = 0.874$$

Thus DALY calculations involve the product of two sets of weights for years of life saved – a disability weight that reflects the severity of the condition averted times an age weight reflecting the productivity of a healthy year at that age. Thus, for example, for the most serious condition in Table 10.1, a healthy year of life gained at age 10 is valued at 0.92*1.086, which gives an overall weight of 1.0. However, the same serious condition averted at age 60 has an overall weight of 0.92*0.844, which equals 0.78, implying that averting the condition in someone aged 60 has a 22 per cent lower social worth than averting the same condition in someone aged 10. Use of the DALY requires application of this combination of weights to each year saved over the patient's lifetime and summing for all patients treated.

It should be noted that the DALY approach is controversial. It not only involves expert judgement on the severity of conditions, but also differentiates the seriousness of a condition by the age of the patient. This means that, for example, a year of life saved for someone who would otherwise be healthy prevents the loss of fewer DALYs than saving the life of someone with a disability whose weighted year of life saved is less than unity because of their disability. Similarly, saving one year of life of someone aged 30 prevents the loss of more DALYs than saving the life of a child. Critics have suggested these are inherently inequitable criteria to apply in resource allocation decisions where costs per DALY saved become a means of distinguishing between health alternatives (Anand and Hanson, 1998).

The definition of total DALYs requires that equations for *YLG*, *YD*, *YCD* and *YT* are amended by incorporating age weights. As with healthy years of life estimates, whenever there are both mortality and morbidity impacts the total DALY will be the sum of years of life gained, years affected by disability before premature death, years of chronic disability for those who do not die prematurely and years of temporary disability. The expressions for *YLG*, *YD*, *YCD* and *YT* are as before except that now each year saved has a weight that allows for age differences. Using the subscript *d* to denote DALY calculations, the earlier equations become as follows:

$$YLG_d = IN*CF*SR*PV\,(wa(ad..ar)) \qquad (10.10)$$

$$YD_d = IN*CF*SR*w1*PV\,(wa(ao..\,ad)) \qquad (10.11)$$

$$YCD_d = IN*PD*w2*PV\,(wa(ao..\,ar)) \qquad (10.12)$$

$$YT_d = PV\,(IN*(1 - CF - PD)*t*w3*wa) \qquad (10.13)$$

where all terms are as above and *wa* is the age weight which differs for each year of life.

Table 10.3   Cost per DALY averted for selected health interventions in low and middle income countries

Intervention	US$/DALY
Coronary bypass graft	37000
Drug and psychosocial treatment of depression	1699
Polypill to prevent heart disease	409
Improved emergency obstetric care	127
Tuberculosis treatment	102
Basic childhood vaccines	7

Source: Jamison et al. (2006).

Therefore, for example, in equation (10.10) the expression $PV(wa(ad.. ar))$ is the present value of the age weighted and disability weighted expected years survived between ages ad and ar.

The total DALY indicator is:

$$DALY = YLG_d + YD_d + YCD_d + YT_d \qquad (10.14)$$

and the cost effectiveness of a project is measured as:

$$CEI = PV(C_w - C_{wo})/PV(DALY) \qquad (10.15)$$

where $PV(DALY)$ is the present value of years of life gained in DALYs.

Measures of project impact, whether YLG, HYLG or DALY, are typically estimated per unit of population (for example per 1000) and once the total population to be reached by a project has been estimated, total impact in years gained can be estimated.

Costs per DALY have been estimated for various health interventions in developing countries (see for example Table 10.3). They continue to be used in the planning of the health sector.[13] For example, Hutton et al. (2009) report on estimates of costs per DALY averted from malaria as a result of preventive treatment of infants in Tanzania and Mozambique, with maximum figures of US$12 per DALY in Tanzania and $92 in Mozambique. Similarly, Ortega et al. (2009) examine the cost effectiveness of a rotavirus immunisation programme for infants in Egypt, reporting a cost per DALY of US$363.

Table 10.3 reveals a wide range of costs – from the minimal for children's vaccine to the very high for heart treatment. A similarly wide range of cost per healthy year of life gained from different forms of treatment is reported in WHO (2010, Table 4.2) where it is pointed out that the

Table 10.4   Estimated costs per healthy year gained (selected countries)

Country (currency)	Condition	Costs/HYLG current	Costs/HYLG optimal
Zambia (US$)	Malaria drug treatment	10.7	8.6
Thailand (Baht)	Cardiovascular disease prevention	300 000	2 185
Nigeria (Naira)	Schizophrenia	210 544	67 113
	Depression	104 586	62 095
	Epilepsy	13 339	10 507

Source: WHO (2010, Table 4.2).

potential range is from US$10 to $100 000 and that current costs could be reduced by adopting an optimal mix of treatment (see Table 10.4).

Interpretation of results such as these requires care. They simply reflect the cost of treatment and on their own say nothing about priorities, although they make clear that certain treatments for infants, mothers and children can have large health impacts at very low cost. Some interventions are found to be very low cost per DALY averted; for example, Griffiths et al. (2004) report that neonatal immunisation against tetanus in Pakistan has a cost of only US$3.6 per DALY. A simple rule of thumb has been put forward as a rough screening device (WHO, 2002). This states that a very cost-effective intervention is one where cost per DALY is no more than average income per capita in the country concerned. Interventions that cost up to three times per capita income are still considered cost effective but those that exceed this are deemed not cost effective. Such rules can be no more than guidelines since taken literally they imply that new facilities to carry out coronary bypass operations would not be introduced in poor countries. Any society has an obligation to treat all its citizens, but the cost per DALY data give an indication of priorities, and the data in Table 10.3 suggest that nearly 5000 children would benefit for every heart surgery patient treated.[14]

CONCLUSION

Cost effectiveness calculations can be used to rank activities and to select alternative interventions. In doing this a cut-off rate in terms of cost per unit of impact can be established. All interventions that cost more than this need not be rejected automatically. To do so would imply an implicit valuation that may or may not be acceptable; for example if a normal intervention costs $10 million per year of life saved, rejecting one that costs $11 million but which treats a particular condition or patient group implies that a year of life for those affected is worth less than $11 million. If extra funds could be found to expand the budget the project may still be deemed worthwhile. Cost effectiveness calculations provide an important check on the efficiency with which projects convert resources into health outcomes. On their own, however, they cannot determine whether a project is worthwhile in the sense of social benefits exceeding social costs. This would require monetisation of health benefits and, as noted at the outset, this remains an area of considerable controversy. Hence priorities within the health sector will need to be identified on broad social and medical grounds and once these are identified cost effectiveness appraisals can be applied to ensure efficiency in the way in which these objectives are to be achieved.

NOTES

1. See for example Kim and Benton (1995). It is notable that this study is concerned with the low initial internal rate of return of the project to remove river blindness when higher labour productivity alone is treated as benefits. To generate a return above 6 per cent benefits from bringing new land into cultivation are added. The concern arises because once monetary values are placed on benefits, health projects appear to be competing with directly productive projects for scarce funding and thus require a return above the perceived opportunity cost of capital.
2. For example, Cropper et al. (1992) is an influential illustration of a revealed preference approach to the valuation of life by focusing on the decisions of the US Environment Planning Agency in restricting the use of pesticides to reduce the risk of cancers; the decision to forgo use of pesticides had a cost in lower output which was compared with reduced cancer risk to obtain an implicit value for lower risk.
3. Pearce et al. (2006, Chapter 14) have a good survey of these issues. Their Table 14.1 brings together the results of some of the major studies estimating a statistical value of life which mostly use either contingent valuation surveys or wage rate data. All of the studies covered are for developed countries.
4. Zweifel and Telser (2009) survey approaches to benefit valuation in health. They argue (p. 48) that the vast majority of health cost–benefit studies (they suggest 90 per cent) do not meet the full standards of cost–benefit analysis in that they do not adequately measure health benefits.
5. The discussion draws heavily on ADB (2000) with which the author was closely involved.
6. The DALY calculations referred to below use a discount rate of 3 per cent for example.
7. Hammer (1993) in the Appendix gives numerical examples of how uncritical use of cost effectiveness comparisons can give misleading results.
8. LeFevre et al. (2010) examining the cost effectiveness of skin treatment for pre-term infants in Bangladesh is an example of cost effectiveness analysis using years of life gained (or its equivalent years of life lost averted) as the health impact.
9. Survival probabilities are implicit in the estimate of *ar*.
10. The implication of a negative weight is that saving a year of very severe disability is worse than death, which has a weight of 0.

11. Hammer (1993, Table 1) reports a wide range of estimates of cost per QALY from alternative treatments for malaria from different developing countries. These appear to arise from a combination of differences of methodology in what type of costs are included as well as differences in the incidence and severity of the condition.
12. Sassi (2006) compares the derivation of DALYs and QALYs. The technical basis for DALYs is explained in Murray and Lopez (1994) and Murray (1994) with the main statement of the method and its implications for the global burden of disease in Murray and Lopez (1996).
13. The WHO has adopted this approach to cost effectiveness in its CHOICE programme; see Tan-Torres et al. (2003).
14. The comparison is not quite in the ratio 37 000 to 7, since the age weighting in the DALY will skew the benefits in years saved in favour of the young.

11. Measuring benefits from education

David Potts

INTRODUCTION

The argument for using cost–benefit analysis (CBA) in the social sectors is less widely accepted than for other sectors. In the education sector in particular there are certain levels of education where issues of basic needs and human rights are concerned. The second UN Millennium Development Goal is to 'ensure that, by 2015, children everywhere will be able to complete a full course of primary schooling'. Surely the issue then is not *whether* to provide primary education but *how* to. Most countries also have a target to widen access to secondary education with the intention eventually to provide universal access. What then is the need for CBA if education is regarded as a merit good?

While such arguments have some validity, there are still questions to be asked about the efficiency of expenditure on education, and the tools available to the investment analyst can be used to answer them. The first question to consider is whether it is ultimately intended that a particular level of education should be open to universal access. Clearly this is not the case for higher education or for vocational based technical education. For both these activities a major reason for expansion of provision is to provide the skills necessary for economic development and the extent of access will depend to some extent on the skill requirements of the economy. However, even for primary and secondary education there are some questions to be asked. In a context of limited education budgets how do we decide on the extent to which additional funds are allocated between secondary and tertiary levels? The answer may have implications for the speed with which universal access to secondary education is achieved. Even at the primary education level we must address the issue of educational outcomes. The purpose of education is not the physical placement of children in schools but the achievement of desired learning outcomes. If that is the case, at the very least, there must be some comparison of cost with measures of educational achievement and the justification for spending more than the minimum may need to be made on the basis of the cost effectiveness of activities in relation to the achievement of learning outcomes.

Given the above propositions it can be argued that there is a justification for the use of CBA at least for some higher levels of education and there is also a need for a means to establish the cost effectiveness of education spending at all levels and to determine priorities in the allocation of funds. This chapter therefore starts by discussing the theoretical basis for CBA in education derived from the human capital concept and reviews its application in developing countries both as a policy tool and for the appraisal of projects and programmes. It then discusses the potential use of cost effectiveness analysis in cases where CBA may not be appropriate or may be difficult to use.

HUMAN CAPITAL THEORY AND THE BENEFITS OF EDUCATION

The ideas underlying the human capital concept can be traced back to Adam Smith but the term was first used by Pigou (1928), and modern applications can be traced to Becker (1964) and Mincer (1974). According to Becker, investment in human capital could be analogous to investment in physical capital and so in principle it should be possible to estimate a return to education and training in the same way as the return to a machine. By investing in education or training, a worker is able to achieve a higher level of productivity, and this will be reflected in a higher wage or salary. The crucial underlying assumptions are that the labour market works in such a way that higher productivity is reflected in higher wages and that the effect of education on human productivity can be separated from other factors. Mincer used US census data to relate years of education and work experience to earnings, and his method of constructing an earnings function is often described as the 'Mincerian method'.

Early criticisms of human capital theory pointed to the probability that earnings differentials would be affected by differences in factors such as innate ability, motivation, social class and gender (Merrett, 1966: 290). It was also argued that education might be used as a 'screening' device by employers in job selection and that it was not in itself the major source of additional productivity (Arrow, 1973). Attempts to measure the value of education on the basis of the earnings of those with and without a particular level of education also overlook the possibility that both groups might be affected by differing levels of unemployment. Association of increased earnings with different levels of education therefore has to include an 'alpha coefficient' to allow for the proportion of observed earnings differentials that could be attributed to factors other than educational differences. Typically rate of return studies have adjusted the earnings differential downward by a factor of about one-third to take account of these factors. An alternative approach is to use sensitivity analysis to test the effect of varying assumptions about the 'alpha factor' (Woodall, 2004: 51–2).

The assumption that the price paid for different categories of labour reflects the productivity of the workers is potentially problematic, particularly in a developing country context, where labour markets may be highly imperfect. In principle some allowance for labour market imperfections can be made through the use of shadow wage rates but these are rarely applied in practice to skilled labour. Arguably the opportunity cost of skilled labour in developing countries is fairly close to the market wage (see Chapter 3 in this volume for some of the issues relating to such an assumption). In the case of unskilled labour it is possible to use shadow wage rate estimates, if they are available, or to make direct estimates of productivity (e.g. of smallholder farmers with and without education) (Woodall, 2004: 55). Overall, although labour markets are not perfect indicators of productivity, they can usually provide some indication as long as there is due recognition of the margin of error in the data used and some care taken about the interpretation of the results.

Studies influenced by Mincer's work have been undertaken in many countries. Much of the developing country literature is associated with the work of Psacharopoulos (e.g. Psacharopoulos, 1973, 1981, 1985, 1994, 1995; Psacharopoulos and Patrinos, 2004). These studies have been influential in guiding the policies of international agencies, particularly the World Bank, toward the education sector, but they have also been criticised for shortcomings in the data used and for failing to take sufficient account of changes in the labour market (Bennell, 1996a, 1996b, 1998; Appleton and Teal, 1998). Particular concerns were expressed about the legitimacy of any general conclusions drawn from a collection of studies that were not always comparable in terms of data and approach. More recently, in an African context, Diagne and Diene (2011) have raised concerns about the comparability and specifications of the models used and the range of countries to which they have been applied.

An important question to consider in the case of educational costs and benefits is that of who pays and who gains. In most societies the government subsidises education up to a certain level and so the costs of education, including the opportunity cost of forgone earnings during the education process, are shared between the person being educated and the government (and ultimately taxpayers). If we just consider educational benefits as the incremental salary of the educated person, it would appear that the benefits of education only accrue to the individual. However, this

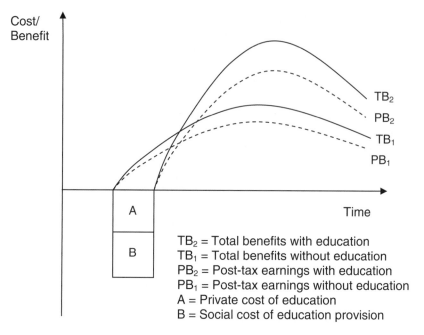

Figure 11.1   Education costs and benefits

is not entirely true because a proportion of the additional income will be taxed or spent on goods that are taxed, so there is some positive return to the government from the additional income earned. Furthermore it can be argued that there are external benefits associated with education because of the greater contribution made by educated people both to civil society and to the welfare of their children. Finally it is also argued that there are consumption benefits from education to the educated person in terms of enjoyment of the education process itself and the effect of enhanced understanding on subsequent enjoyment of other activities (Woodall, 2004: 39–40). While there are clearly methodological difficulties in measuring some of these benefits, authors that have tried to do so have concluded that they are substantial (Haveman and Wolfe, 1984; McMahon, 1999). McMahon (p. 7) suggested that the externality effects of education accounted for 38–40 per cent of the total effects on economic growth.

Figure 11.1 illustrates the measurement of educational costs and benefits. Lines TB_1 and TB_2 respectively represent the total benefits to society without and with a particular level of education. This includes tax revenue to the government and any external benefits to society derived from education. Lines PB_1 and PB_2 represent private benefits to the individual concerned. Areas A and B respectively represent the private and social costs (or government subsidy) of education during the period when the education takes place. If the non-monetary benefits of education to the individual that are not measured in the change in income are given a monetary equivalent value and also included, the lines PB_2 and TB_2 will be raised.

In principle an annual net benefit stream can be derived both for the individual and for society on an annual basis, taking account of changes in income over time as well as the probability of surviving to a particular age. Thus net private benefits (NPB) for any year t are given by:

$$NPB_t = PB_{2t} - PB_{1t} - A_t \qquad (11.1)$$

and net social benefits (NSB) are given by:

$$NSB_t = TB_{2t} - TB_{1t} - A_t - B_t \qquad (11.2)$$

These net benefits can then be discounted at an appropriate social rate of discount to derive an NPV, and an internal rate of return can also be calculated. Thus the private NPV_P is given by:

$$NPV_P = \sum_{t=a}^{n} \frac{NPB_t}{(1 + r)^t} \qquad (11.3)$$

where t refers to time in years; a refers to the year when the level of education under consideration starts; n refers to the life expectancy of the person from the time of commencement of education; and r refers to the rate of discount.

In principle such a calculation could take account of the possibility that life expectancy also varies with education level by setting a zero level of benefit for years beyond the expected lifespan. The private rate of return to education (PRORE) is the discount rate at which NPV_P is equal to zero. Similarly NPV_S, the social NPV, is given by:

$$NPV_S = \sum_{t=0}^{n} \frac{NSB_t}{(1 + r)^t} \qquad (11.4)$$

and the social rate of return to education (SRORE) is the discount rate at which NPV_S is equal to zero. The fiscal impact FI of the education level in year t is given by:

$$FI_t = NSB_t - NPB_t - NPX_t \qquad (11.5)$$

where NPX_t refers to net externalities that accrue to private individuals.

The size of the net public subsidy (*PS*) is given by:

$$PS = NPV_P + NPV_{PX} - NPV_S \qquad (11.6)$$

where NPV_{PX} refers to the NPV of any external benefits that accrue to private individuals. The net public subsidy is positive (i.e. the fiscal impact is negative) if the total social NPV is less than the sum of the private NPVs.

In practice the rate of return approach has been used mainly for policy analysis and the SRORE for a particular level of education has been calculated and used to justify prioritisation of particular levels. Woodall (2004: 73) describes this approach, where lifetime earnings profiles are computed with and without a particular level of education, as the 'complete method'. Over time, for some levels of education, the net public subsidy might be negative if tax revenue or revenue from the repayment of student loans is large enough but, in an economy where public sector funding is constrained in the short term, the timing of the fiscal impact may be as important as the present value over the longer period.

Some of the studies conducted have been criticised for adopting fairly crude assumptions about age–earnings profiles. In particular estimates based on Mincerian earnings functions have tended to assume a flat age–earnings profile (Woodall, 2004: 78–9). Psacharopoulos (1981) argued that use of such an assumption made little difference to the resulting rate of return, but clearly the validity of this judgement depends on the actual data, which are unknown, so the crudity of the assumptions will have some implications for the reliability of the result.

The alternative to assuming a flat earnings function is to investigate age–earnings profiles for workers of different ages and different levels of education over a long period. Since it is only possible to collect data on past earnings, there is an underlying assumption that the patterns of the past will continue in the future. Such an assumption can be modified to a certain extent if there is sufficient information to identify trends in earnings differentials. Part of the value of the comparative studies collected and updated by Psacharopoulos is that they do give some indication of changes over time, subject to the limitations imposed by the comparability of the data. To get a very reliable indication of what is happening it is necessary to have data going back for a long period and this is often problematic in developing countries, hence the tendency to use short-cut methods.

A particular issue that may be relevant to the definition of social returns is the implication of rent-seeking behaviour for the assumption that a higher salary implies higher *social* productivity. Pritchett (2001) has pointed to a macro–micro paradox in that macroeconomic estimates of the contribution of education to economic growth often do not support the microeconomic indicators of the returns to different levels of education. If a higher salary is earned for activities that increase the transaction costs for other economic activities it cannot be regarded as socially productive. Pritchett also points to the possibility that, in some cases, additional education may not impart the necessary skills that would lead to the higher productivity expected from higher earnings, a point that is consistent with Arrow's 'screening' observation, whereby educational achievement is used for screening job applicants although the content of the education may not be relevant to the job. Teal (2011) investigates the processes by which higher education links to accumulation of other forms of capital and argues that investment in technology is required to realise the desired growth impact from a more highly skilled labour force. This is especially important when expansion of higher education increases the proportion of the highly educated workforce going to the private sector.

EMPIRICAL RESULTS OF POLICY STUDIES

Despite the reservations some observers have about the reliability and comparability of many of the studies included in the global results reported by Psacharopoulos, such studies have been used widely to inform policy choices, in particular prioritisation of public expenditure in the education sector and analysis of options for financing the sector. There is a fairly general consensus that returns to all levels of education in developing countries are quite high and this has been used to argue the case for greater priority for the education sector in general and primary education in particular (Woodall, 2004: 103–5).

As might be expected, initial research suggested that social rates of return were highest for primary education and lowest for higher education (Psacharopoulos, 1985: 586), indicating diminishing returns to incremental education. Social rates of return were also higher for developing countries than for developed countries, again consistent with diminishing returns as education becomes more widely available. Private returns were highest for primary education but similar for secondary and higher education, raising some potential equity questions about the level of subsidisation of higher education. Mingat and Tan (1996) found that social returns to different levels of education depended on the level of economic development of the country concerned, with primary education giving the highest returns in the poorest countries, whereas in middle-income countries the highest returns went to secondary education and in high-income countries the highest returns went to higher education. This is consistent with the existence of fairly universal primary education in middle-income countries and fairly universal secondary education in high-income countries.

The most recent global survey (Psacharopoulos and Patrinos, 2004) suggests that returns to all levels of education have fallen slightly, again consistent with diminishing returns, with the greatest fall occurring in primary education. One reason for the decline in the return to primary education has been the shift towards universal primary education and the implied loss of its scarcity value (Jimenez and Patrinos, 2009: 90). The evidence on high social returns to primary education was used to argue the case for greater emphasis of public sector financing in developing countries on primary education and lower levels of subsidy to higher education.

The debate on subsidisation of higher education is not straightforward. Subsidisation facilitates access to those who would otherwise be unable to afford to undergo higher education and without it access to the poor would be almost impossible. However, in the absence of effective systems to recover the costs either from taxation of the higher incomes earned by graduates or from repayment of student loans, subsidisation of higher education may result in the use of government revenue to subsidise either those who are already relatively rich or those who will eventually become so, hence the concerns about equity.

Initially it was often assumed that the return to education for women would be lower than for men because of the lower levels of both earnings and labour force participation. However, the most recent study by Psacharopoulos and Patrinos suggests that the return to education for women is slightly higher than for men, partly because lower labour force participation without education reduces the cost of forgone earnings. If the greater externalities associated with female education are also taken into account, particularly in the areas of health and nutrition (Schultz, 1995, 1999), it would appear that investment in women's education gives greater overall returns than education of men. However, the focus on directly productive labour and consequent undervaluation of traditionally female household tasks could work in the reverse direction by underestimating the opportunity cost of women's time.

Rates of return have also been used in the debate about public sector investment in vocational training as an alternative to general secondary education. A study by Psacharopoulos and Loxley (1985) based on Tanzanian data argued that vocational education was expensive and did not give greater benefits than general secondary education. This study provided some of the evidence underlying a shift away from funding vocational education by the World Bank (World Bank, 1995). The evidence for this shift was criticised by Bennell and Sogerstrom (1998) on similar grounds to the criticisms Bennell made of the unreliability of the global rate of return studies. A more recent study (Kahyarara and Teal, 2008), also relating to Tanzania, concluded that vocational education could give better returns at lower levels of education but lower returns than for higher levels of general education. This was explained by the shape of the earnings function, and the authors argued that the issue was not so much a dichotomous choice as the choice of appropriate investments at different levels of education. It might therefore be argued that we should be careful about drawing general conclusions about the global desirability of particular types or levels of education without specifying the context in which such generalisations are valid.

Despite the limitations involved in benefit estimation and the consequent issues of comparability it appears that CBA can have a useful role in providing both some quantitative evidence for the existence of significant social returns and a rationale for prioritising expenditure. Jimenez and Patrinos (2009: 100) argue that CBA is 'crucial in informing the tough choices that policy makers need to make'. Woodall (2004: 117) suggests that CBA serves 'a useful practical purpose' in reminding policy makers of opportunity cost and the importance of comparing alternatives. We must nevertheless be fully aware of the limitations of the assumptions we use and careful about contextualising any wider conclusions drawn on the impact of education levels on economic performance. Improved skills derived from better education may be a necessary but not necessarily a sufficient condition for economic growth.

USE OF COST–BENEFIT ANALYSIS IN THE APPRAISAL OF EDUCATION PROJECTS

Although CBA techniques have been used quite extensively in the debates about education policy they have not been used so extensively for appraisal of education projects. Even in the World Bank relatively few educational projects were subjected to CBA until the 1990s (Vawda et al., 2003). It appeared that difficulties associated with measurement of the externalities associated with education projects were used as a rationale for not requiring CBA in this sector. However, Vawda et al. (2003: 648) quoted a 1994 memorandum from Graham Donaldson of the Operations Evaluation Department, stating:

> As far as I can tell no education projects have been subject to formal ex ante cost benefit analysis in the past two decades. . . .Having reviewed agriculture sector and education sector projects for the better part of 10 years I am struck by the fact that agriculture is subject to cost benefit analysis and education is not. I can see no reason for this anomaly – the assumptions to be made in

estimating an ERR for education are no more challenging (or heroic) than those for agriculture. There is an established literature going back to the 1950s dealing with the application of cost–benefit to education projects.

Vawda et al. reported a significant shift in the extent of the use of quantitative analysis for education projects, including CBA, in the 1990s and evidence of a correlation between the quality of the initial appraisal and the quality of project outcomes. This suggests that the process of undertaking a CBA or a systematic cost effectiveness analysis (CEA) helps to improve both the design and the implementation of education projects, providing a strong argument for their use.

One of the reasons why CBA is not used very much in the education sector is that much of the planning for the sector is done on a programme basis rather than through individual projects. This may be one reason why so many of the studies in the sector have related to prioritisation of levels of education rather than individual projects. Nevertheless there have been a number of CBA studies of education projects, some of which have been published.

One of the most well known CBA studies is that of the Mauritius Higher Education Project (Belli et al., 1999; also referred to in Belli et al., 2001). In this study the earnings of graduates at different education levels were compared with their potential earnings without that level of education. Due to data limitations flat earnings profiles were assumed, and there appears to have been no attempt to control for other factors that might account for differences in earnings. Nevertheless the analysis was subjected to risk analysis and the positive results seemed to be robust. Woodall (2004: 99–100) refers to another World Bank project for improvement of higher education in Vietnam which adopted a similar approach to estimating the benefits from improved education on the basis of higher lifetime earnings.

Belli et al. (2001) also refer to cases of school amalgamation in Barbados and school improvement options in Brazil where the main objective was to reduce the costs associated with existing educational facilities, in particular the cost of drop-outs and repetition. The Brazilian case is described in detail in Harbison and Hanushek (1992). In neither of the cases was there an attempt to value any change in educational outcomes and therefore these cases might be regarded more as examples of CEA than of CBA. Jimenez and Patrinos (2009) refer to the case of a school building project in Ethiopia involving analysis of the use of different building materials. Again this might be regarded more as a form of CEA since the educational outcomes were not valued. It should be noted that both costs and benefits should be measured in shadow prices for educational CBA to ensure consistency across sectors in the appraisal process. However, in general it appears that the use of CBA for education projects is relatively rare and is mainly applied to investment in higher and technical/vocational education or for comparing alternative project designs where it may be thought of more as a form of CEA.

COST EFFECTIVENESS ANALYSIS AND MEASUREMENT OF EDUCATIONAL OUTCOMES

In principle cost effectiveness analysis requires a measure of costs in money terms and a measure of outcomes in some other units, preferably quanti-fiable. Where outcomes are the same, CEA is simply an exercise in least cost estimation; however, it is rarely the case that outcomes are exactly the same and there are also questions as to whose costs are counted. For example the Barbados school amalgamation project does not appear to have taken any account of the travel costs to school for parents and children. Amalgamation of schools means fewer schools and therefore a greater average distance for pupils to travel. In the case of the Ethiopian school construction programme there appears to have been an unstated assumption of equivalent educational outcomes although it could be argued that schools requiring more maintenance are more likely to be subject to disruption and therefore may not give the same outcome. In conducting any economic cost effectiveness analysis of education projects it is therefore important to consider both the costs to all the stakeholders and any possible differences in educational outcomes.

In the education sector, measuring the costs to the organisation imple-menting the project or programme does not involve any particular prob-lems beyond the standard issues involved in cost estimation. However, measuring the costs to parents and students is more problematic since it requires survey data. For example measuring the costs involved in a school amalgamation project would need accurate data on the distance from home to school and costs of whatever modes of transport are used, including the opportunity cost of time. It therefore needs to be clear from whose perspective the CEA is conducted. A financial perspective would consider only the costs of the implementing organisation and its view of the desired outcomes. An economic perspective would include the costs of parents and students and should also take some account of their views on desired outcomes. In principle the costs measured in the CEA should also be valued at shadow prices.

The most important issues, however, are those of measuring educational outcomes and attributing these outcomes to particular interventions. Levin and McEwan (2001: 108) suggest that measurement of outcomes must relate as closely as possible to the stated objectives of the project or programme. In the case of the education sector, learning outcomes are likely to be conceptualised in terms of knowledge or skills gained and measured through some form of test. For example Harbison and Hanushek (1992) used tests in basic skills in Portuguese and mathematics for their analysis of the effectiveness of various measures to improve school conditions in north-east Brazil. The major limitation of such approaches is that some skills are easier to measure than others and it is therefore the skills that are easier to measure that tend to be emphasised. As a result, the impact of educational programmes on basic literacy and numeracy may receive much greater attention than other skills that are more difficult to measure. This would not take account of some of the major externalities associated with education such as its impact on health and nutrition as a result of education in these areas.

The second issue is that of attribution. To what extent can any change in educational outcomes be attributed to a specific project or programme rather than to other factors related to the environment in which the programme is conducted? Jimenez and Patrinos (2009: 98) point out that the attribution issue can be addressed by the use of impact evaluations of earlier projects; however, such practice is not undertaken in the majority of cases. Presumably part of the problem is the lack of adequate impact evaluations to refer to.

Glewwe and Kremer (2006) reviewed evidence on the relationship between resources and educational outcomes and reported mixed results. However, perhaps their most important conclusion was that educational spending needs to address the inefficiencies in the existing system if it is to be effective. This would suggest that the starting point has to be a rigorous analysis of that system and that an inadequate understanding of the context will lead to inappropriate identification of solutions. In other words a correct formulation of the problems facing the sector is required in order to come up with a cost-effective solution.

CONCLUSION

In theory CBA can be used in the analysis of education projects and programmes, and methods have been established for the estimation of benefits on the basis of human capital theory. Attempts have also been made to identify and quantify some of the most important externalities associated with education. In practice CBA has been used relatively rarely for education projects although it has been used quite extensively to inform the debates on education policy both in terms of sector priorities and the extent to which the state subsidises different levels of education. It is most relevant for the levels where universal access is not an objective and the extent of provision is influenced by economic considerations related to workforce requirements. It can also be used to inform issues related to programme and project design but in these cases it is most likely to be a form of least cost analysis.

In the areas of primary and general secondary education it is unlikely that CBA will be used because the most important question is *how* to implement full access, not whether to do so. This then becomes a cost effectiveness question. To make CEA useful it is important to have a good understanding of the existing situation, in particular the weaknesses in the system of delivery. In the context of constrained budgets it is important to ensure that any additional funds are used to tackle clearly identified problems. For such a process to be operationally useful it is also important to have a clear idea of what the desired outcomes are and how the proposed expenditure will contribute to them.

Not surprisingly there is some evidence to suggest that the very process of thinking through the design and appraisal of investment in the sector in a systematic way that relates inputs to expected outcomes tends to deliver better performance. The justification for the use of CBA or CEA therefore lies not just in the results of the calculations but at least as much in the process of getting them.

12. Cost–benefit analysis traditions: the approach of EU regional policy*

Massimo Florio and Silvia Vignetti

INTRODUCTION

As discussed extensively in Chapter 1, cost–benefit analysis (CBA) developed in a particular way in the context of project planning in poor countries. One of the innovative developments in the literature and practice of recent years has been the attempt to apply these CBA techniques to analysis of infrastructure projects in the European Union (EU), funded as part of EU regional policy. Since the principal aim of these funds is to help the development of the less developed regions of the EU, some of the key concerns raised in the developing country context – the use of shadow prices, the calculation of a shadow wage, the monetisation of non-market impacts, the choice of a social discount rate and the use of welfare weights – have also been addressed in work for the European Commission.

In the 2007–13 programming period the EU Structural Funds and the Cohesion Fund will contribute through grants to the infrastructure plans of 27 countries, including some former transition economies. Additional funds are assisting Turkey, Croatia and other candidate and potential candidate countries. The EU seven-year budget supporting this effort will draw from a provision of around EUR 350 billion for cohesion policy (see Table 12.1).

Some researchers have been critical of the effectiveness of this EU funding mechanism. In particular, the Sapir Report (Sapir et al., 2004) has proposed a wide reform to concentrate available EU resources on the new member states (the so-called re-nationalisation of EU regional policy), and to entirely delegate the project planning to them, with the argument that local actors know what to do with capital subsidies better than Brussels. However, this proposal has been rejected by the EU members for two reasons. First, some infrastructure, for example the trans-European networks in energy and transport, needs supra-national coordination. Second, the EC is in a unique position to collate infrastructure knowledge across countries and regions, and is less captured by local interests.

Table 12.1   EU Cohesion Policy 2007–13 (EUR 347.41 billion, current prices)

Programmes and instruments	Eligibility	Priorities	Allocations (%)
Convergence objective			81.54
Regional and national programmes ERDF ESF	Regions with a GDP/ head <75% of average EU25 Statistical effect: regions with a GDP/ head <75% of EU15 and >75% of EU25	● innovation; ● environment/risk prevention; ● accessibility; ● infrastructure; ● human resources; ● administrative capacity;	70.5 5.0
Cohesion Fund including phasing-out	Member states GNI/ head <90% EU25 average	● transport (TENs); ● sustainable transport; ● environment; ● renewable energy	23.2
Regional competitiveness and employment objective			15.95
Regional programmes (ERDF) and national programmes (ESF)	Member states suggest a list of regions (NUTS I or II) 'Phasing-in' regions covered by objective 1 between 2000 and 2006 and not covered by the convergence objective	● innovation; ● environment/risk prevention; ● accessibility; ● European Employment Strategy	78.9 21.14
European territorial cooperation objective			2.52
Cross-border and transnational programmes and networks (ERDF)	Border regions and large transnational cooperation regions	● innovation; ● environment/risk prevention; ● accessibility; ● culture, education	● 73.86 cross-border cooperation ● 20.95 transnational cooperation ● 5.19 interregional cooperation

Source: Author processing DG REGIO data.

This coordination–benchmarking mechanism has an intrinsic value that would be entirely lost by full re-nationalisation of planning and evaluation (Florio, 2007a). The core of the potential added value of a multi-government co-financing mechanism for infrastructure investment lies in its information/incentive structure, when there is *ex ante* appraisal and *ex post* project evaluation by evaluators who report information to the different actors. CBA lies at the heart of this framework, and is now firmly embodied in the EU regulations.

In the rest of this chapter we: (a) briefly present some institutional features of EU infrastructure funding, particularly grants by the Structural Funds and the Cohesion Fund; (b) show the way a specific CBA approach has been suggested in the EC Guide to Cost–Benefit Analysis (European Commission, 2008);[1] and (c) discuss the relationship between this Guide and earlier literature on project appraisal in developed and developing economies. The chapter is concluded by indications for further research needs on CBA in the context of developed economies.

THE STRUCTURAL FUNDS AND THE COHESION FUND[2]

The EU Structural Funds (SF) are financial instruments that offer Community assistance, mainly in the form of capital grants, to different kinds of regional programmes and projects. In the framework of the 2007–13 Cohesion Policy there are three main objectives. The first and by far the most important in terms of funds available under the Cohesion Policy (almost 82 per cent) is the objective of supporting the convergence of sustainable economic growth in lagging regions. Most of these regions are located in the recently accessed members, but there are also some relatively underdeveloped regions in some rich countries in the EU-15.[3] A second objective is to increase the competitiveness of and employment in the remaining regions. Many of them, while located in the core areas of Europe, face high unemployment and have had relatively modest economic growth in recent years. Third, there is an objective of territorial cooperation that is relevant for some EU regions. EU assistance to achieve these objectives revolves around a small number of financial instruments, each with a set of operating rules, eligibility conditions, and co-financing rates. The most important of these funds is the European Regional Development Fund (ERDF). The ERDF has a very wide range of possible intervention areas (including for example research and development and support for small and medium enterprises, as well as infrastructure activities) especially in the Convergence regions (defined as those where GDP per capita is below the threshold of 75 per cent of the EU average), while in the Competitiveness regions it focuses on three priorities: innovation and the knowledge economy; environment and risk prevention; and accessibility (transport and telecommunication services of general economic interest). Finally, under the Territorial Cooperation objective, the priorities are cross-border, transnational and interregional cooperation, as well as networking of regions.

While the ERDF is in a broad sense targeted at infrastructure and productive investment, the European Social Fund (ESF) is mainly concerned with human capital, including support to vocational training and education programmes, both public and private.

Lastly, the Cohesion Fund (CF) was established in 1993 under the Maastricht Treaty to promote economic and social cohesion and solidarity between EU member states. It co-funds projects in the field of the environment and trans-European transport infrastructure networks. Member states eligible for CF assistance are those whose per capita gross national income (GNI) measured in purchasing power parity is less than 90 per cent of the EU average. Ceilings for EU co-financing are different according to the region and the fund (the overall 'macroeconomic' cap at national level for EU grants is 4 per cent of GDP per year). Moreover, ERDF finance, in the form of a grant, can be combined with loans by the European Investment Bank (EIB), and with other sources of loan or equity finance. Table 12.2 shows the leverage effect of the SF. It is important to understand, however, that the grant mechanism is often critical, and thus the usual screening activity by banks is more limited than in purely private projects.

In this chapter we focus on revenue-generating public projects.[4] For these projects the EC contributes to filling the gap between the present value of investment costs and the present value of the net revenues collected by the project by the approval of an EU grant. We turn now to explaining the current funding mechanism and its problems.

GRANT MECHANISMS AND PROJECT APPRAISAL

Project selection and *ex ante* appraisal within this very broad framework is normally the sole responsibility of the national authorities. However, for major projects (with a total investment cost of more than EUR 50 million (or 25 million for environmental projects and 10 million in the case of IPA projects), the EC requires member states to submit a cost–benefit analysis (CBA) before a final decision is taken. The analysis must include, amongst other requirements:

*Table 12.2   Leverage effect of Structural Funds on public and private
expenditure under Objective 1, 1994–99 and 2000–06 (EUR)*

	1994–99		2000–06	
	National public funds per euro of SF	Private funds per euro of SF	National public funds per euro of SF	Private funds per euro of SF
BE	0.77	1.18	1.02	1.43
DE	0.37	1.53	0.58	0.02
EL	0.52	0.28	0.5	0.48
ES	0.51	–	0.52	0.04
FR	0.54	0.23	0.88	0.33
IE	0.43	0.34	0.76	0.25
IT	1.40	–	0.89	0.45

Notes:
* Based on actual expenditure 1994–2000 for ES and IT.
For 1994–99, national public funds include private funds.
EU11: excluding FI, SE.

Source: Third Report on Economic and Social Cohesion: A New Partnership for
Cohesion Convergence Competitiveness Cooperation, Statistical Annex to Part 4, 'Impact
and added value of structural policies', European Commission (2004: 180).

- a cost–benefit analysis;
- a risk assessment;
- an analysis of the expected socio-economic impact on the sector and region concerned;
- an analysis of the environmental impact;
- justification for the use of public funds;
- a project financing plan.

In addition to relying on the governments of the member states to produce this information and to conduct an *ex ante* project analysis, the SF regulations state that the EC is responsible for *ex post* evaluation: it can appoint independent experts that will re-assess its benefits and costs after the completion of the project.

Hence, there is a clear provision for both *ex ante* appraisal and *ex post* evaluation in the SF regulations, but there is, however, no clear link between the investment co-financing decision and such assessments (except in rather extreme situations when fraud is discovered). Florio and Vignetti (2005) suggest that without a 'contractual' link between appraisal and co-financing, a misallocation of these funds may arise.

Occasional observation shows that there may be, however, some informal punishment for regional governments who are thought to have disclosed insufficient information *ex ante* (so the co-financing decision by the EC is delayed) or when an *ex post* evaluation discovers an unsatisfactory outcome. One of these mechanisms is the loss of reputation by the managing authority, so consequently their new project funding requests are subject to more intensive scrutiny by the Commission. There are, however, some shortcomings that are built into the SF allocation mechanism.

Figure 12.1 shows how the EC evaluation and grant decision framework currently works for major investment projects (2007–13). First, the applicant should show to the EC that, after a suitable CBA, the economic net present value (ENPV) is expected to be positive; if it is expected to be negative, the project usually is supposed to be rejected. Second, for revenue-generating projects, financial profitability is assessed in order to establish whether the project needs a grant and to what extent this applies. Third, under the so-called 'funding gap method', the EU grant co-finances the portion of the investment cost which is not covered by the future net revenues. The funding gap rate R is simply:

$$R = (DIC - DNR)/DIC \qquad (12.1)$$

where DIC is the net present value (NPV) of investment costs, and DNR is the NPV of net revenue (the difference between discounted revenues and discounted operating costs plus the discounted residual value). Then, the decision amount (DA), 'the amount to which the co-financing rate for the priority axis applies' (Article 41.2), is:

$$DA = EC*R \qquad (12.2)$$

where EC is the eligible cost. The maximum EU grant is given by:

$$EU\ grant = DA*Max\ CRpa \qquad (12.3)$$

where $Max\ CRpa$ is the maximum co-funding rate fixed for priority activities by the Commission.

In principle, projects expecting a positive financial net present value (FNPV) have no funding gap and thus do not generally receive a grant from the SF.[5] The rationale of the 'funding gap' approach is to determine the project's self-financing ratio, so as to grant the investor no less and no more than what is actually needed to implement a socially beneficial, but financially loss-making, project. The problem with this approach is

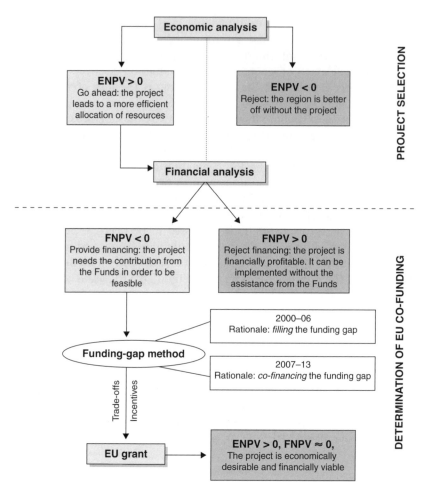

Source: Mairate and Angelini (2007).

Figure 12.1   The allocation of funds to the projects: CBA and the funding-gap method

obvious: the applicant has a clear incentive to exaggerate expected costs and to underestimate revenues, in order to maximise the EU grant.

Thus, if the total investment cost is EUR 100 million, and the ceiling is 80 per cent, the grant is simply a linear function of *DNR/DIC*. In other words, just the part of the investment cost that will not be covered by future net revenues is eligible for co-financing, given one initial threshold. The EU grant does not *fill* the whole funding gap (as it did in the period

2000–06) but will only *co-finance* it, with national public finances having to cover the difference. The EC expects that this feature of the mechanism will create stronger incentives for the member state to find additional sources of finance, such as public–private partnerships. Cella and Florio (2007) discuss the incentive issues involved and propose alternative mechanisms. It is important, however, to notice a positive feature of the project appraisal framework as it has been currently designed. If a project proposer exaggerates the economic benefits of a project, for example the demand for transport services, this will also raise its financial return (at least for revenue-generating projects) and this will decrease the EC grant, and in some cases it will rule it out because the project will appear financially viable and thus will not qualify for a grant. Thus, the combination of financial and economic appraisal in one evaluation frame is an advantage. In the rest of this chapter we focus on CBA issues in the specific context of these funding arrangements.

SOME CBA 'RULES OF THE GAME' UNDER THE EU STRUCTURAL FUNDS

The EC Guide (European Commission, 2008) (henceforth the Guide) was designed as a simple, operational document. It is currently used by perhaps one thousand project teams, which are involved in the preparation of applications to the EC for assistance under the SF. What follows explains why some decisions were made by the team in charge of drafting the new edition of the Guide.[6] We focus on the following issues: (a) use of shadow prices and conversion factors; (b) a shadow wage; (c) monetisation of non-market impacts; (d) the social discount rate; (e) the marginal cost of public funds; and (f) welfare weights.

Unlike several guidelines in some member states, for example the British 'Green Book' (HM Treasury, 2003), the Guide insists on the fundamental intuition that observed prices may differ from the social opportunity cost of some goods. While this point is well established in CBA theory,[7] in practice it has been taken seriously only in project appraisal in poor or developing countries, particularly following the seminal work of Little and Mirrlees (1974). In fact, shadow pricing has often been seen as an issue mainly related to market distortions in countries affected by trade barriers. As such, it has been dismissed as unimportant within developed economies when it was perceived that such barriers were falling, following international free trade agreements. There are two objections to this tendency to dismiss shadow pricing, an attitude which, as far as we know, was never supported by rigorous empirical analysis. First, there is a serious misunderstanding about

Table 12.3   Electricity price dispersion for industry and households in the EU, 2005, EUR

Electricity		2005
Industry (annual	Average	6.74
consumption: 2000 MWh)	Median price	6.46
	Coeff. of variation (%)	18.1
	Max/min. ratio	2.20
Households (annual	Average	10.65
consumption: 3500 kWh)	Median price	9.00
	Coeff. of variation (%)	23.5
	Max/min. ratio	2.50

Source: European Commission (2008).

shadow prices. Some practitioners tend to assume that when markets are in equilibrium, this ensures the social optimality of observed prices. In other words, shadow prices are seen as virtual market prices in those markets that are out of equilibrium. While this may be correct in some cases, it is not the general rule. Shadow prices are defined as the marginal social welfare change (in a numeraire) caused by the additional net availability of a good. In a general equilibrium framework this implies the need for a social welfare function, a policy linking changes in production plans in the public sector (broadly defined) to changes in the behaviour of the private sector, including any indirect effects on welfare. While this is an ambitious definition in terms of information needs, it is the only general one that allows defining in an unambiguous way what a shadow price is, hence what CBA is. Thus, the fact that a country is open to trade, as happens within the EU, does not ensure that observed prices can be taken as the best proxy for shadow prices. The second objection, of a more practical nature, is that even within the EU, where trade barriers have been officially removed, there still are significant barriers that prevent the less ambitious assumption that market prices work well as shadow prices. The Guide shows this with a simple example for electricity prices (see Table 12.3).

Despite all the efforts by the EU to create an internal market for electricity, with privatisation and liberalisation on a national basis, cross-border trade of electricity is still limited. This happens due to both a lack of physical interconnection of infrastructure and national legislation that prevents the full tradability of electricity. Thus, given also different energy inputs (such as coal, nuclear, hydro, thermal) and different regulatory arrangements, a household can pay 250 per cent more for a kWh in one

EU member state than a comparable household elsewhere. Now, suppose that the country where the electricity price is higher asks for an EU grant to support an investment in electricity generation. Benefits, if measured by market instead of shadow prices, are likely to be very much higher in this country than elsewhere in the EU. This is exactly the situation that led Ian Little in the 1950s to consider that planning in India, a federal country with different electricity tariffs at state level, needed the use of shadow prices. Thus, surprisingly, the reasoning that was relevant to India fifty years ago is still relevant in contemporary Europe, and cannot be dismissed because formally the EU trade is free. Moreover, in a social perspective, the opportunity cost of electricity is also related to important environmental issues. Thus, a kWh produced with less impact on CO_2 or other pollutants is more desirable than otherwise, and this fact is not always captured by the emission permits mechanism. This environmental cost should also enter into the shadow price of electricity. Moreover, a social planner may have specific energy-saving objectives or objectives relating to access for disadvantaged users that in principle may also need to be incorporated in the valuation of electricity.

The example of electricity is far from exceptional. A second important example is food and all prices related to the agriculture chain. Here the Common Agricultural Policy creates a wedge between border prices and internal prices, but also a very complex pattern of internal prices across EU member states. Moreover, there may be additional objectives and constraints related to food safety that need to be considered and possibly included in CBA. Thus, an EU grant to a water project in a specific region needs to use prices that differ from observed prices, because those prices are distorted in the traditional meaning of being affected by both (external) trade barriers and (internal) subsidies and regulations. This fact is well known to CBA practitioners in developing countries, and, surprisingly, has been neglected in developed economies.

A third example is telecommunications, where recently the EC itself needed to intervene to contain rents in mobile communications related to 'roaming', which is a form of virtual trade barrier not officially acknowledged as such. Thus, surprisingly, everybody seems to agree that CBA is needed in traditional transport services, where tariffs apparently do not capture well costs and benefits for society, but many practitioners tend to forget that, for example, prices of energy, communications, or food in the EU can also be distorted and may be a poor guide to social value. Thus the Guide restates some well-known shortcuts for computing shadow prices such as the use of border prices when appropriate for tradable goods and willingness to pay or long-run marginal costs for non-tradables (see Chapter 1 in this volume).

In practice, it is not yet known how far the project appraisal teams will comply with this aspect of the Guide, and how far conversion factors (ratios of shadow to observed market prices) will be introduced in project analysis in the EU, but it is important that this view is restated, thus linking CBA in developing and developed economies.

An important shadow price that is often neglected in CBA as applied to developed countries is related to the social opportunity cost of labour. This was briefly discussed in Florio (2006), and the Guide suggests using region-specific conversion factors. The rationale for re-introducing the shadow wage rate in the EU is a matter of consistency with the overall objective of regional policy. In fact, the overarching goal of this policy is to achieve both growth and the convergence of European regions, and labour is a core ingredient in a growth perspective. Table 12.4 shows that officially recorded unemployment is substantial, and unevenly distributed across EU regions.

Moreover, it is well known that in some countries, particularly in transition economies in Central and Eastern Europe, there is sizeable hidden unemployment in agriculture, meaning that the social cost of displacing a worker from rural activities may be limited. This is far from being captured by observed wages, because, for example, infrastructure projects assisted by EU grants need to comply with legislation on social insurance and other forms of minimum wages gross of taxes and contributions. Even if the EU is officially open to internal movements of the workforce, different types of barriers make it difficult and undesirable to have huge migration flows from one country to another.

In recent research Del Bo et al. (2011) went back to shadow wage theory and identified four types of labour market conditions at the regional level. They assume that the labour market is in equilibrium in mainly urban, high-income contexts, where unemployment is low, rural activities are minimal, and migration flows are of modest importance. In these regions in principle a conversion factor of observed wages near to 1 seems sensible, hence the shadow wage and the actual wage coincide. There are, however, other urban contexts where unemployment is high, and a quasi-Keynesian labour market, affected by nominal rigidities, may be a more appropriate description when migration is modest. Third, in other regions there may be dualism in an urban context, with part of the workforce drawn from informal urban activities. This is more similar to a Little–Mirrlees context, with the difference that the informal sector is not agriculture. Finally, there are regions (for example in Romania or Bulgaria) where rural activities are still very important, but are plagued by very low productivity.

Table 12.4 shows the four types of regions, their key characteristics and a tentative estimate of the average labour conversion factor for each type

Table 12.4   Labour market, average shadow wages and conversion factors:
preliminary estimates

Labour market	No. obs	Mean	St. dev.	Min.	Max.
FSE regions	63				
GDP per capita (€ PPP)		33094	9331	23200	83200
Unemployment (%)		4.05	1.21	2.10	8.10
Long-term unemployment (%)		1.11	0.58	0.36	3.46
Rurality		0.03	0.02	0.00	0.09
Annual net migration (%)		0.40	0.35	−0.39	1.28
Shadow wage (€)		45239	10739	13871	66528
Conversion factor		0.99	0.00	0.99	1.00
ULD regions	129				
GDP per capita (€ PPP)		24271	5128	13900	47800
Unemployment (%)		6.36	1.62	3.40	10.50
Long-term unemployment (%)		2.32	1.10	0.51	4.91
Rurality		0.04	0.04	0.00	0.23
Annual net migration (%)		0.58	0.58	−0.55	2.67
Shadow wage		27143	10266	3255	50486
Conversion factor		0.80	0.08	0.61	0.97
QKU regions	52				
GDP per capita (€ PPP)		18654	7366	9800	55000
Unemployment (%)		11.87	2.94	7.80	20.30
Long-term unemployment (%)		6.35	2.39	2.48	11.81
Rurality		0.07	0.05	0.00	0.18
Annual net migration (%)		−0.06	0.40	−0.79	1.06
Shadow wage (€)		12111	8858	3494	53107
Conversion factor		0.54	0.16	0.23	0.89
RLD regions	22				
GDP per capita (€ PPP)		10400	3503	6400	18900
Unemployment (%)		8.27	1.99	4.30	12.1
Long-term unemployment (%)		4.45	1.32	1.82	7.06
Rurality		0.30	0.07	0.19	0.42
Annual net migration (%)		−0.39	0.40	−1.05	0.41
Shadow wage (€)		5217	3351	1591	13929
Conversion factor		0.62	0.13	0.36	0.84

Notes:
FSE: fairly socially efficient; ULD: urban labour dualism; QKU: quasi-Keynesian
unemployment; RLD: rural labour dualism.
Rurality is the proportion of the labour force employed in agriculture.

Source: Del Bo et al. (2011).

of region. In urban labour markets characterised by dualism (ULD) a mean labour conversion factor is estimated at 0.8, whilst for rural economies with dualistic labour markets (RLD) it is close to 0.6, which is similar to that often used in poor labour surplus developing economies.

Some goods are entirely removed from market transactions, for a number of reasons, the most important class of these being environmental goods (or bads). This is probably the only area where CBA has progressed significantly in recent decades and Pearce et al. (2006) review the recent literature. The Guide insists on shadow pricing externalities, because, without this, any CBA would not be meaningful or consistent with the fundamental objectives of EU regional policy. The Guide also dismisses the objection that has been advanced against this recommendation, that as the environmental legislation of the EU already imposes the achievement of certain environmental or safety standards as compulsory for projects, there is no need to incorporate environmental effects in CBA. Thus, one may think that because a certain quality of drinking water is prescribed, there is no need to dwell on giving a shadow price to the safety or quality of water, and that just cost-effectiveness analysis is needed. This objection can be rejected by looking into the options that are open to project investors. In fact, while a certain minimum quality or maximum emission standards are required by EU legislation, this is not the end of the story. For example, a sewage system can be designed in different ways and for the same investment cost can achieve different environmental targets. If exceeding the minimum standard in terms of physical emissions is desirable, for a project that exceeds the minimum we need to assign a social value to this achievement. This social value can be high or low, linear or decreasing with quantity, but simply ignoring what happens beyond the legal quantity threshold is inadequate. Given the difficulty of estimation in this area, the Guide suggests taking advantage of the substantial literature on estimation of values of non-market goods, with the 'benefit transfer approach' (see Atkinson, 2006). This approach, if well managed, is practical and sensible. It uses as benchmark values estimations done elsewhere and adapted to local conditions with appropriate transfer functions.

The social discount rate is a core parameter in CBA, and probably the one that has attracted the greatest interest in recent theoretical and applied literature (see also Chapter 10 in this volume). Among the different possible approaches, the new edition of the Guide takes the view that the social time preference rate (STPR) approach is the most relevant one. The key concepts here are the growth rate of per capita income or consumption, the elasticity of marginal social welfare with respect to this variable and a pure time preference rate.[8] The standard formula is:

Table 12.5 Indicative social discount rates for selected EU countries based on the STPR approach

Non-CF countries	g	e	p	SDR
Austria	1.9	1.63	1.0	4.1
Denmark	1.9	1.28	1.1	3.5
France	2.0	1.26	0.9	3.4
Italy	1.3	1.79	1.0	3.3
Germany	1.3	1.61	1.0	3.1
The Netherlands	1.3	1.44	0.9	2.8
Sweden	2.5	1.20	1.1	4.1
CF countries	**g**	**e**	**p**	**SDR**
Czech Rep.	3.5	1.31	1.1	5.7
Hungary	4.0	1.68	1.4	8.1
Poland	3.8	1.12	1.0	5.3
Slovakia	4.5	1.48	1.0	7.7

Source: European Commission (2008).

$$SDR = eg + p \qquad\qquad (12.4)$$

where *SDR* is the social discount rate, *g* is a growth rate of an appropriate macroeconomic variable (usually GDP because no long-term estimates are available for private consumption), *e* is the elasticity of marginal social welfare with respect to the variable, and *p* is a rate of pure time preference.

Florio (2006) suggested using a 3.5 per cent rate as a benchmark value for the *SDR* in the more developed regions of the EU, and 5.5 per cent for the remaining regions. Table 12.5, taken from the Guide, reports estimates for different member states that justify these suggestions. An estimate for *e* can be based on the ratio $\log(1 - t)/\log(1 - T/Y)$, where *t* is the marginal income tax rate, *T* is total income tax liability, and *Y* is total taxable income.[9] This gives estimates of *e* in the range of 1.10–1.80, without clear differences between EU-15 and EU-12 countries. One way of estimating *p*, although it remains controversial, is by looking into mortality rates, based on the idea that individuals discount the future against the present because their expected survival rate declines with age. The range in Table 12.5 is between 0.9 and 1.4, with the average a little higher in the EU-12. What actually drives the estimates of the SDR is principally differences in the growth rate.

The objective of regional policy is convergence of the 27 member states' income in the long run. Given the wide differences in current conditions, g in the EU-12 can be forecast at around 4 per cent per annum, which is twice the likely long-term growth rate in the EU-15 countries. In fact, for the countries considered in the table, the range for g is 1.3 to 4.5 per cent. Thus simple computation suggests that with p around 1 per cent for all the member states, and e around 1–1.5, a reasonable range of values of the SDR is 3–4 per cent for the EU-15, and 5–6 per cent for the EU-12. The Guide suggested an intermediate benchmark value for each group, leaving it up to each member state to estimate country-specific values, if they wish to. As it happens, the 3.5 per cent SDR is the same as suggested by the UK Green Book (albeit with different data, and declining over time, see below). We just mention here that the Guide team, after some consultation with the EC services, decided not to offer an estimate of the Marginal Cost of Public Funds (MCPF) and suggested $MCPF = 1$ as a default rule when a national estimate is not available (this will be the most likely case). Estimation here depends critically upon a number of fiscal parameters, not easily available in several countries (see Dahlby, 2008 and Hashimzade and Myles, 2009 for a discussion). Moreover, the problem here is complicated because EU funds are granted under an assumption of 'additionality', meaning that in principle they do not displace domestic public funding. Hence it is the EU, not national taxpayers, that suffers the burden of distortionary taxation. In fact, a weighted average of net contributions to the EU budget implies combining different tax sources across countries. This is not the end of the story, because additionality varies across countries, with some partial evidence of displacement of domestic spending, but no systematic evidence. Thus the team concluded that the calculation of the MCPF in this context raised too many problems. The Guide departs from the Harberger and Jenkins (2002) view that distribution issues do not count in CBA. Given that a substantial part of the EU funds is targeted to infrastructure for delivery of public services, such as water, waste collection or electricity distribution, it was important to stress a concern for social affordability of the services and more generally to focus on poverty issues potentially addressed or worsened by the projects. The suggestion was here flexible, pointing out that in principle it is possible to use distribution weights based on regional income or consumption of the type:

$$W = (C^{average}/C^{group})^e \tag{12.5}$$

where $C^{average}$ is national average consumption, C^{group} is consumption in a given region, and e is the constant elasticity of marginal social utility of consumption. In practice, welfare weights are seldom used, but the

Guide insists that the distribution characteristics of a project at least be looked into, even if changes in consumption are not formally adjusted by weights.

While the above remarks have covered some CBA issues treated in the Guide only selectively, they can give the reader some of the core concepts that were adopted. We turn now to compare the EU Guide with a recent UK government publication on CBA.

A COMPARISON WITH THE UK 'GREEN BOOK'

In this section we comment on differences between the EU Guide and the UK Green Book (HM Treasury, 2003). The latter is perhaps the best-known example of a serious tradition of public investment appraisal at a national level in developed countries, and is the latest edition of guidelines that have been compulsory for all departments in the UK for decades.

In spite of minor semantic differences, the key similarities between the two guides include: the legitimacy of public intervention to address market failures; the concept of a social opportunity cost of inputs and outputs; the need to consider different options from the beginning of the appraisal process; the focus on valuing as far as possible cost and benefits; the concept of discounting by the social time preference rate (STPR); a consideration of distributional impact; and a wide discussion of risk and uncertainty.

Despite these important conceptual similarities, there are also important differences.

The Green Book (like several other national guidelines in the EU and elsewhere that we cannot review here) does not recommend explicitly using shadow prices: 'Cost and benefits should be normally based on market prices as they reflect the best alternative uses that the good can be put to (the opportunity cost). However market prices may need to be adjusted for tax differences between options' (point 5.11, p. 19). This position is slightly qualified in a subsequent statement:

> Real or estimated market prices provide the first point of reference for the value of the benefits. There are a few exceptions [. . .] if the market is dominated by monopoly suppliers, or is significantly distorted by taxes and subsidies, prices will not reflect the opportunity cost and adjustments may be required [. . .] An example of this is the effect of EU subsidies on the market for agricultural land. (point 5.26, p. 21)

We have explained before why this position, albeit simple and practical, may be too restrictive. In fact, once it is admitted that 'monopoly' prices deserve special consideration, it is just a logical step to pay a similar atten-tion to oligopoly prices. As it happens, most of the key services of general interest (for example water, telecommunications, energy, transport, health and education) are oligopolies. Moreover, market failures of the types mentioned elsewhere by the Green Book (Annex I, pp. 51 ff.) are wide-spread in all economies (certainly not just in developing economies). Thus, the fact that the Green Book is reluctant to deal with shadow pricing (it is just mentioned in the Glossary, p. 105), while the UK government uses this idea in its guidelines for assistance in developing countries (ODA, 1988), seems to be an unjustified asymmetry of approach. The EU Guide, being targeted to several member states and to wide disparities in regional devel-opment, could not avoid using a more general perspective on the concept of opportunity cost as an alternative to market prices.

An example of why the position of the Green Book on shadow prices leads to a cumbersome approach is the treatment of the opportunity cost of labour. This is not explicitly dealt with in the main text of the Green Book, but is treated in Annex I, under the heading of Additionality (of government interventions). In this more general discussion the Green Book deals with such issues as 'leakage', 'deadweight', 'displacement' and 'substitution' effects. For example it states that:

> The appropriate area for analysis of displacement effects will depend on the type of project. In the case of employment displacement, the area considered should usually be the local labour market [. . .]. The effect of net employment and net output is likely to be much smaller than the direct employment and output effects of the project. Evidence should support the assessment of the scale and importance of any net employment and net output benefits, taking account of multiplier effects. (p. 54)

In contrast, the EC Guide insists on the use of a shadow wage, possibly region-specific, and to avoid the recourse to income multipliers. In fact, it is well known that shadow prices in principle are sufficient statistics for these effects in a general equilibrium framework, and in practice their use would be efficient. While in principle there is a clear conceptual relation-ship between shadow wages and income multipliers, it is noteworthy that what the Green Book says would imply a 'local' analysis of the 'with–without project' change of the economy, which is usually difficult to apply. Moreover, it would delegate to a project appraisal team the calculation of average marginal effects that are best done in some central planning office.

For example, consider this statement by the Green Book: 'The net benefit of an intervention equals the gross benefit less the benefits that would have occurred in the absence of interventions (the 'deadweight') less the negative impacts elsewhere (including 'displacement' of activity), plus multiplier effects' (p. 54). While there is nothing wrong in this statement, and similar concepts are used in the EC Guide, clearly it is of paramount practical importance to see the implications of using shadow wages (and shadow prices in general) against using the 'net benefit' approach. If the project analyst is instructed by the government or a planning office to use a shadow wage (or a conversion factor for the observed wage) there is no need in general to embark on the difficult route of estimating deadweight and displacement effects. If no shadow wage is available when appraising a hospital project, for example, in fact it is right to ask the evaluators whether in future the local labour market would have evolved in such a way as to show a different unemployment rate from the one expected if the hospital is built, and to ask them where new employees will be drawn from. In practice the data will not be available to address this, and any error incurred either in ignoring the difference between gross and net effects, or in guessing them with very imprecise data, will often be much greater than using a shadow wage, which is a planning parameter based on more aggregate information.

One crucial difference between the EC Guide and the Green Book is the strong emphasis in the former on having a consistent financial and economic analysis, in order to take advantage of the two perspectives. While the Green Book certainly does not confuse financial and economic concepts, in fact its treatment of the differences is very limited (see for example Box 3.1, p. 73 and in Annex 3, where a cost-effectiveness cash flow analysis and a limited CBA are presented on office space options). Thus, it is not made explicit if the same social discount rate should be applied when focusing on cash flows in financial analysis. In fact the worked example in Annex 3 uses a 3.5 per cent discount rate in both the cost effectiveness and the cost–benefit analysis, where the former seems to be just a projection of cash flows. The EC Guide, while ending up with similar real rates for the two concepts, carefully distinguishes between the justification for the financial discount rate (based on a portfolio of long-term financial assets) and the social discount rate (based on the social time preference approach). Moreover, it devotes much of its space to five worked project examples (railway, highway, water, waste treatment and manufacturing projects) with financial, economic and risk analysis to show how important the differences are when we move from one perspective of appraisal to the other. The Guide suggests that it is important to distinguish clearly between the financial and economic effects of a project, given the need to consider the different financial conditions and regional contexts in the member states.

CONCLUSIONS

In conclusion, the contribution of the EC Guide as compared with some national traditions in CBA in Europe probably lies in suggesting that there is no need to have an entirely different framework for project appraisal in less developed economies and in more mature ones. Having to deal at the same time with countries as different as Sweden and Bulgaria, it was necessary to try to establish a common appraisal language for these diverse countries, leaving it up to analysts and planners in the countries concerned to estimate country-specific parameters and develop country-specific solutions to problems in particular sectors. While one does not need to be over-optimistic about the overall quality of appraisal that this process under the EU SF will generate, it was interesting to build a bridge between different traditions in social cost–benefit analysis.

There are a number of open research issues on project appraisal, and CBA in the EU Cohesion policy in particular, which would deserve further investigation. We present here some of the most urgent.

The first issue regards the need for adopting shared national (in some cases perhaps even regional) parameters for CBA (shadow prices and shadow wages, the value of time, the value of the most common environmental costs and benefits) to be used consistently by appraisal teams. The advantage is not only in terms of efficiency for practitioners who can be provided with a ready-to-use set of relevant values for economic analysis, but mainly in terms of consistency and comparability of different projects implemented in the same context or sector. Currently it could easily be the case that two projects in the same region and sector, say transport, are evaluated on the basis of different parameters. For example different values of time might be used to estimate social benefits. In terms of the overall planning exercise, the use of a consistent set of parameters would enhance the soundness of analysis and the reliability of a coordinated assessment. Attempts to produce some kind of generally applicable suggested values of parameters have already been made (see for example the HEATCO[10] project), but not in a systematic way. Originally, in a first draft of the cohesion regulations, it was provided that the European Commission and member states would produce agreed national parameters for performing CBA. This provision was dropped in the last version of the Regulation.[11] We still hope that some national initiatives are promoted in order to produce consistent sets of parameters.

Second, given the importance of the climate change issue for regional development and for the appraisal of major infrastructure projects (especially for the transport and energy sectors), some specific rules should be explored for the assessment of climate-related effects. The discount rate is crucial for estimating the social cost of carbon, a typical indicator for the desirable level of climate policy, and a case has been made for the use of a long-term, declining SDR. The rationale is the increasing uncertainty about the future when long-term effects are considered.[12] This is something the Green Book clearly put forward, by suggesting that, for costs and benefits accruing more than 30 years into the future, discount rates to be used range from 3.5 per cent (in a 0–30 years horizon) to 3.0 per cent (for a 31–75 years horizon), to 1 per cent (in the case of a 301+ years horizon).[13] In the same vein, recent literature discusses the role of aversion to risk and to income inequality as determinants of the discount rate when analysing climate change.[14]

Third, the complex subject of the marginal cost of public funds in a multi-country framework remains an open issue. Different fiscal systems and the application of the additionality principle (which in fact requires that EU public funds rather than national public funds be the marginal source of funding) not only make the calculation of an appropriate value difficult from a practical point of view, but also raise challenging theoretical issues.

Lastly, the right incentives are needed to implement a good CBA, which requires time, effort and adequate human capital. Linking CBA and incentive theory[15] is an important task for the future. These issues are relevant for either developed and developing economies, and a unique general framework is needed.

NOTES

*   This chapter draws from material in Florio and Vignetti (2010).
1.   This is the fourth edition of guidelines prepared by a team led by one of the authors, Florio.
2.   This section and the following draw from Cella and Florio (2007).
3.   Particularly in Italy (the Mezzogiorno), in Germany (the Eastern Länder of the former DDR), in Spain, Greece, Portugal, and in the overseas French and Portuguese islands.
4.   According to Article 55 of Reg. 1083/2006, these are defined as 'any operation involving an investment in infrastructure the use of which is subject to charges borne directly by users or any operation involving the sale or rent of land or buildings or any other provision of service against payment'.
5.   Special rules apply to productive investments under state aid regimes.
6.   The team acted with the support of a Steering Committee including officers from several Directorates-General (DGs) of the EC, the European Investment Bank, and particularly the Evaluation Unit, DG Regional Policy. However, the team was free to propose its preferred approach and in general there was no disagreement on substantial issues. What follows, is of course, a personal interpretation of some specific issues.
7.   See for example Drèze and Stern (1987).
8.   See for example Evans (2007) for a discussion and recent estimates for the EU.
9.   See Evans (2007) for details on the derivation of the formula.

10. Developing Harmonised European Approaches for Transport Costing and Project Assessment, http://heatco.ier.uni-stuttgart.de/.
11. Art. 40 of Reg. 1083/2006 simply says that 'the Commission shall provide indicative guidance on the methodology to be used in carrying out the cost–benefit analysis'. This was done by the Guide and a previous working document (European Commission, 2006).
12. One strand of the recent literature proposes as an alternative method to adjust instead future environmental benefits for rising willingness to pay (the theoretical foundation for a lower environmental discount rate) for enviromental benefits and to discount those benefits at the consumption discount rate (see Kögel, 2009).
13. See the Green Book, Annex 6, p. 99. The Stern Review (Stern, 2007) suggests a 0.1 per cent discount rate.
14. See for example Atkinson et al. (2009). The authors find that individual preferences over these dimensions are weakly correlated in the context of climate change, with large heterogeneity over preferences. In the light of these findings, it is suggested that modellers present policy makers with a range of optimal policies corresponding to different degrees of risk aversion, spatial inequality aversion and temporal inequality aversion, since a single value for each would conceal important ethical disagreements.
15. See Cella and Florio (2007) for a discussion and an example.

Bibliography

Abiad, A., P. Kannan and J. Lee (2009), 'Evaluating historical CGER assessments: how well have they predicted subsequent exchange rate movements?', *IMF Working Paper*, 09/32, Washington, DC: International Monetary Fund.

Adler, H. (1987), *Economic Appraisal of Transport Projects*, Baltimore, MD: Johns Hopkins University Press.

Akinleye, S., O. Olubanjo and O. Adenrele (2005), 'Hedonic price analysis of sheep and goat market in Lagos State, Nigeria', *African Journal of Livestock Extension*, **4**, 15–19.

Anand, P. (2007), 'Capability, sustainability, and collective action: an examination of a river dispute', *The Journal of Human Development*, **8** (1), 109–32.

Anand, P. (2010), *Scarcity, Entitlements and the Economics of Water in Developing Countries*, Cheltenham, UK and Northampton, MA, USA: Edward Elgar Publishing.

Anand, S. and K. Hanson (1998), 'DALYs: efficiency versus equity', *World Development*, **26** (2), 307–10.

Anand, S. and A. Sen (2000), 'Human development and economic sustainability', *World Development*, **28** (12), 2029–49.

Andersson, P., S. Crone, J. Stage and J. Stage (2005), 'Potential monopoly rents from international wildlife tourism: an example from Uganda's gorilla tourism', *Eastern Africa Social Science Research Review*, **21** (1), 1–18.

Appleton, S. and F. Teal (1998), 'Human capital and economic development', *Economic Research Papers*, 39, African Development Bank.

Archondo-Callao, R. (2008), 'Applying the HDM-4 model to strategic planning of road works', *World Bank Transport Paper*, TP20, Washington, DC: World Bank.

Arrow, K. (1963), *Social Choice and Individual Values*, 2nd edn, London: Wiley.

Arrow, K. (1966), 'Discounting in public investment criteria', in A. Knesee and S. Smith (eds), *Water Research*, Baltimore, MD: Johns Hopkins University Press.

Arrow, K. (1973), 'Higher education as a filter', *Journal of Public Economics*, **2** (3), 193–216.

Arrow, K. and A. Fisher (1974), 'Environmental preservation, uncertainty and irreversibility', *Quarterly Journal of Economics*, **88** (2), 312–19.

Arrow, K. and R. Lind (1970), 'Uncertainty and the evaluation of public investment decisions', *American Economic Review*, **60** (3), 364–78.

Arrow, K., R. Solow, P. Portney, E. Leamer, R. Radner and H. Schuman (1993), 'Report of the NOAA panel on contingent valuation', *Federal Register*, **58** (10), 4601–14.

Asian Development Bank (ADB) (1997), *Guidelines for the Economic Analysis of Projects*, Manila: ADB.

Asian Development Bank (ADB) (1999), *Fighting Poverty in Asia and the Pacific: The Poverty Reduction Strategy*, Manila: ADB.

Asian Development Bank (ADB) (2000), *Handbook for the Economic Analysis of Health Projects*, Manila: ADB.

Asian Development Bank (ADB) (2001), *Handbook for Integrating Poverty Impact in Economic Analysis of Projects*, Manila: ADB.

Asian Development Bank (ADB) (2002), *Handbook for Integrating Risk Analysis in the Economic Analysis of Projects*, Manila: ADB.

Asian Development Bank (ADB) (2006), *Poverty Handbook: Analysis and Processes to Support ADB Operations*, Manila: ADB.

Asian Development Bank (ADB) (2009), *The Economics of Climate Change in South East Asia: a Regional Review*, Manila: ADB.

Atkinson, A. and N. Stern (1974), 'Pigou, taxation and public goods', *Review of Economic Studies*, **41** (125), 119–28.

Atkinson, G. (2006), 'Environmental valuation and benefits transfer', in M. Florio (ed.), *Cost–Benefit Analysis and Incentives in Evaluation*, Cheltenham, UK and Northampton, MA, USA: Edward Elgar Publishing.

Atkinson, G., S. Dietz, J. Helgeson, C. Hepburn and H. Saelen (2009), 'Siblings, not triplets: social preferences for risk, inequality and time in discounting climate change', *Economics e-journal*, Special Issue 'Discounting the Long-run Future and Sustainable Development', **3** (2009–26), available at: http://www.economics-ejournal.org/economics/journalarticles/2009-26.

Auerbach, A. and M. Feldstein (eds) (1987), *Handbook of Public Economics*, Vol. II, Amsterdam: North-Holland.

Barrett, C., S. Sherlund and A. Adesina (2008), 'Shadow wages, allocative inefficiency, and labour supply in smallholder agriculture', *Agricultural Economics*, **38** (1), 21–34.

Bateman, I., K. Willis and K. Arrow (eds) (2002), *Valuing Environmental Preferences: Theory and Practice of the Contingent Valuation Method in the US, EU, and Developing Countries*, New York: Oxford University Press.

Bateman, I., A. Munro, B. Rhodes, C. Starmer and R. Sugden (1997), 'Does part–whole bias exist? An experimental investigation', *The Economic Journal*, **107** (441), 322–32.

Baumol, W. (1952), *Welfare Economics and the Theory of the State*, Cambridge, MA: Harvard University Press.

Baumol, W. (1968), 'On the social rate of discount', *American Economic Review*, **58** (4), 788–802.

Becker, G. (1964), *Human Capital: A Theoretical and Empirical Analysis, with Special Reference to Education*, Chicago, IL: University of Chicago Press.

Beenhakker, H. and A. Chamari (1979), *Identification and Appraisal of Rural Road Projects*, Washington, DC: World Bank.

Beesley, M. (1965), 'The value of time spent in travelling: some new evidence', *Economica*, **32** (126), 174–85.

Belli, P., Q. Khan and G. Psacharopoulos (1999), 'Assessing a higher education project: a Mauritius feasibility study', *Applied Economics*, **31** (1), 27–35.

Belli, P., J. Anderson, H. Barnum, J. Dixon and Jee-Peng Tan (2001), *Economic Analysis of Investment Operations: Analytical Tools and Practical Applications*, Washington, DC: World Bank Institute.

Bello, M. and V. Bello (2008), 'Willingness to pay for better environmental services: evidence from the Nigerian real estate market', *Journal of African Real Estate Research*, **1** (1), 19–27.

Bennell, P. (1996a), 'Rates of return to education: does the conventional pattern prevail in sub-Saharan Africa?', *World Development*, **24** (1), 183–99.

Bennell, P. (1996b), 'Using and abusing rates of return: a critique of the World Bank's 1995 education sector review', *International Journal of Education Development*, **16** (3), 235–48.

Bennell, P. (1998), 'Rates of return to education in Asia: a review of the evidence', *Education Economics*, **6** (2), 107–20.

Bennell, P. and J. Sogerstrom (1998), 'Vocational education and training in developing countries: has the World Bank got it right?', *International Journal of Education Development*, **18** (4), 271–87.

Bhagwati, J. (1988), 'Export promoting protection: endogenous monopoly and price disparity', *Pakistan Development Review*, **27** (1), 1–5.

Biçak, H., G. Jenkins, C. Kuo and M. Mphahlele (2004), 'An operational guide to the estimation of the economic opportunity cost of labour in South Africa', *South African Journal of Economics*, **72** (5), 1057–68.

Bickel, P., S. Schmid and R. Friedrich (2005), 'Environmental costs', in

C. Nash and B. Matthews (eds), *Measuring the Marginal Social Cost of Transport*, Research in Transportation Economics, Volume 14, Elsevier.

Birdsall, N. and A. Steer (1993), 'Act now on global warming – but don't cook the books', *Finance and Development*, **30** (1), 6–8.

Bishop, R. and T. Heberlein (1979), 'Measuring values of extra-market goods: are indirect methods biased?', *American Journal of Agricultural Economics*, **61** (5), 926–30.

Bohm-Bawerk, E. (1887), *A Positive Theory of Capital*, trans. W. Smart (1991), London: Macmillan.

Brazer, V., R. Mead and F. Xiao (2006), 'Valuing health impacts of air pollution in Hong Kong', *Ecological Economics*, **17**, 85–102.

Brent, R. (2006), *Applied Cost–Benefit Analysis*, Cheltenham, UK and Northampton, MA, USA: Edward Elgar Publishing.

Brent, R. (ed.) (2009), *Handbook of Research on Cost–Benefit Analysis*, Cheltenham, UK and Northampton, MA, USA: Edward Elgar Publishing.

Brookshire, D., M. Thayer, W. Schulze and R. D'Arge (1982), 'Valuing public goods: a comparison of survey and hedonic approaches', *American Economic Review*, **72** (1), 165–77.

Brown, G. (1992), 'Replacement costs of birds and mammals', report commissioned by State of Alaska, available at: http://www.evostc.state.ak.us/facts/economic.cfm.

Brown, K. and D. Pearce (1994), 'The economic value of non-market benefits of tropical forests: carbon storage', in J. Weiss (ed.), *The Economics of Project Appraisal and the Environment*, Aldershot, UK and Brookfield, VT, USA: Edward Elgar Publishing.

Buchanan, J. (ed.) (1961), *Public Finances: Needs, Sources and Utilization*, Princeton, NJ: Princeton University Press.

Burke, L., S. Greenhalgh, D. Prager and E. Cooper (2008), *Coastal Capital: Economic Valuation of Coral Reefs in Tobago and St Lucia*, Washington, DC: World Resources Institute.

Burness, H., R. Cummings, E. Gorman and R. Lindsfort (1982), 'US reclamation policy and Indian water rights', *Natural Resources Journal*, **20** (1980), 807–26.

Buyinza, M., M. Bukenya and M. Nabalegwa (2007), 'Economic valuation of Bujagali Falls Recreational Park, Uganda', *Journal of Park and Recreation Administration*, **25** (2), 12–28.

Campbell, H. and R. Brown (2003), *Benefit–Cost Analysis*, Cambridge, UK: Cambridge University Press.

Capelle-Blancard, G. and M. Laguna (2010), 'How does the stock market respond to chemical disasters?', *Journal of Environmental Economics and Management*, **59** (2), 192–205.

Carson, R. (1997), 'Contingent valuation: theoretical advances and empirical tests since the NOAA panel', *American Journal of Agricultural Economics*, **79** (5), 1501–7.

Carson, R., R. Mitchell, M. Hanemann, R. Kopp and S. Presser (2003), 'Contingent valuation and lost passive use: damages from the Exxon Valdez oil spill', *Environmental and Resource Economics*, **25** (3), 257–86.

Carson, R., R. Mitchell, W. Hanemann, R. Kopp, S. Presser and P. Ruud (1992), *A Contingent Valuation Study of Lost Passive Use Values Resulting from the Exxon Valdez Oil Spill*, Report to the Attorney General of the State of Alaska.

Cella, M. and M. Florio (2007), 'Hierarchical contracting in grant decisions: ex-ante and ex-post evaluation in the context of the EU Structural Funds', *Working Paper 22*, University of Milan, Research Papers in Economics, Business, and Statistics.

Cervini, H. (2003), 'Shadow prices for Colombia', in E. Londero (ed.), *Shadow Prices for Project Appraisal*, Cheltenham, UK and Northampton, MA, USA: Edward Elgar Publishing, pp. 177–241.

Chambers, R. and G. Conway (1992), 'Sustainable rural livelihoods: practical concepts for the 21st century', *IDS Discussion Paper 296*, Brighton: IDS.

Chen, W., H. Hong, Y. Liu, L. Zhang, X. Hou and M. Raymond (2004), 'Recreation demand and economic value: an application of travel cost method for Xiamen Island', *China Economic Review*, **15** (4), 398–406.

Choynowski, P. (2002), 'Measuring willingness to pay for electricity', *EDR Technical Note* 3, Manila: ADB.

Clark, P., L. Bartolini, T. Bayoumi and S. Symansky (1994), 'Exchange rates and economic fundamentals', *IMF Occasional Paper* 115, Washington, DC: International Monetary Fund.

Clarke, R. and A. Low (1993), 'Risk analysis in project planning: a simple spreadsheet application using Monte Carlo techniques', *Project Appraisal*, **8** (3), 141–6.

Cline, W. (1993), 'Give greenhouse abatement a fair chance', *Finance and Development*, **30** (1), 3–5.

Cmnd 3437 (1967), *Nationalised Industries: A Review of Economic and Financial Objectives*, London: HMSO.

Cmnd 7131 (1978), *The Nationalised Industries*, London: HMSO.

Coburn, T., M. Beesley and D. Reynolds (1960), 'The London–Birmingham motorway', *Road Research Laboratory Technical Paper*, 46, London: HMSO.

Cornelisse, P. and C. Tilanus (1966), 'The semi-input–output method with an application to Turkish data', *De Economist*, **114** (9/10), 521–33.

Costanza, R., R. d'Arge, R. de Groot, S. Farber, M. Grasso, B. Hannon, K. Limburg, S. Naeem, R. O'Neill, J. Paruelo, R. Raskin, P. Sutton and M. van den Belt (1997), 'The value of the world's ecosystem services and natural capital', *Nature*, **387**, 253–60.

Cropper, M., W. Evans, S. Beradi, M. Ducla-Soares and P. Portney (1992), 'The determinants of pesticide regulation: a statistical analysis of EPA decision-making', *Journal of Political Economy*, **100** (1), 175–97.

Cummings, R., H. Burness and R. Norton (1981), *The Proposed Waste Isolation Pilot Project (WIPP) and Impacts in the State of New Mexico: a Socio-economic Analysis, EMO-2-67-1139*, Albuquerque, NM: University of New Mexico.

Cummings, R., D. Brookshire, W. Schulze and M. Walbert (1986), *Valuing Environmental Goods: A State of the Arts Assessment of the Contingent Valuation Method*, Washington, DC: Institute for Policy Research.

Curry, S. and R. Lucking (1991), 'Report on shadow prices for Sri Lanka: a report prepared for National Planning Department, Ministry of Policy Planning and Implementation', Development and Project Planning Centre: University of Bradford (mimeo).

Curry, S. and J. Weiss (2000), *Project Analysis in Developing Countries*, London: Macmillan.

Dahlby, B. (2008), *The Marginal Cost of Public Funds: Theory and Applications*, Boston, MA: The MIT Press.

Dasgupta, P. (1972), 'A comparative analysis of the UNIDO Guidelines and the OECD Manual', *Bulletin of the Oxford University Institute of Economics and Statistics*, **34** (1), 33–51.

Dasgupta, P. (2004), *Human Well-being and the Natural Environment*, Oxford: Oxford University Press.

Day, B. (2002), 'Valuing visits to game parks in South Africa', in D. Pearce, C. Pearce and C. Palmer (eds), *Valuing the Environment in Developing Countries: Case Studies*, Cheltenham, UK and Northampton, MA, USA: Edward Elgar Publishing.

Deininger, K., L. Squire and S. Basu (1998), 'Does economic analysis improve the quality of foreign assistance?', *World Bank Economic Review*, **12** (3), 385–418.

Del Bo, C., C. Fiorio and M. Florio (2009), 'Shadow wages for the EU regions', paper presented at the VIII Milan European Economy Workshop, 11–12 June, University of Milan.

Del Bo, C., C. Fiorio and M. Florio (2011), 'Shadow wages for the EU regions', *Fiscal Studies*, **32** (1), 109–43.

Department for Transport (2004), 'The appraisal process: TAG 2.5', *Transport Analysis Guidance (TAG)*, available at: http://www.dft.gov.uk/webtag/documents/archive/1104/unit2.5.pdf.

Department for Transport (2009), 'The wider impacts sub-objective: TAG 3.5.14' (draft), *Transport Analysis Guidance (TAG)*, available at: http://www.dft.gov.uk/webtag/documents/expert/pdf/unit3.5.14c.pdf.

Desvousges, W., F. Johnson, R. Dunford, K. Boyle, S. Hudson and K. Wilson (2010), *Measuring Nonuse Damages Using Contingent Valuation: An Experimental Evaluation of Accuracy*, 2nd edn, Research Triangle Park, NC: RTI International, available at: http://www.rti.org/rtipress.

Devarajan, S., L. Squire and S. Suthiwart-Narueput (1996), 'Project appraisal at the World Bank', in C. Kirkpatrick and J. Weiss (eds), *Cost–benefit Analysis and Project Appraisal in Developing Countries*, Cheltenham, UK and Northampton, MA, USA: Edward Elgar Publishing, pp. 35–53.

Devarajan, S., L. Squire and S. Suthiwart-Narueput (1997), 'Beyond rate of return: reorienting project appraisal', *World Bank Research Observer*, **12** (1), 35–46.

Diagne, A. and B. Diene (2011), 'Estimating returns to higher education: a survey of models, methods and empirical evidence', *Journal of African Economies*, **20**, AERC Supplement 3.

Diamond, P. and J. Hausman (1994), 'Contingent valuation: is some number better than no number?', *Journal of Economic Perspectives*, **8** (4), 45–64.

Diamond, P. and J. Mirrlees (1971), 'Optimal taxation and public production', *American Economic Review*, **61** (8), 8–27 (Part 1), 261–78 (Part 2).

Dinwiddy, C. and F. Teal (1996), *Principles of Cost–Benefit Analysis for Developing Countries*, Cambridge, UK: Cambridge University Press.

Dixit, A. (1968), 'Optimal development in the labour surplus economy', *Review of Economic Studies*, **35** (1), 23–34.

Dixit, A. and R. Pindyck (1994), *Investment Under Uncertainty*, Princeton, NJ: Princeton University Press.

Dixon, J., R. Carpenter, L. Fallon and P. Sherman (1994), *Economic Analysis of Environmental Impacts*, London: Earthscan.

Dondur, N. (1996), 'National economic parameters for Hungary', *Project Appraisal*, **11** (1), 41–50.

Douthwaite, R. (1992), *The Growth Illusion: How Economic Growth has Enriched the Few, Impoverished the Many and Endangered the Planet*, Dublin: Lilliput.

Drèze, J. and N. Stern (1987), 'The theory of cost–benefit analysis', in A. Auerbach and M. Feldstein (eds), *Handbook of Public Economics*, Vol. II, Amsterdam: North-Holland.

Driver, R. and P. Westaway (2004), 'Concepts of equilibrium exchange rates', *Bank of England Publications Working Paper*, 248, London: Bank of England.

Dury, S. and V. Meuriot (2010), 'Do urban African dwellers pay a premium for food quality, and if so, how much?', *Review of Agricultural and Environmental Studies*, **91** (4), 417–33.

Eckstein, O. (1961), 'A survey in the theory of public expenditure', in J. Buchanan (ed.), *Public Finances: Needs, Sources and Utilization*, Princeton, NJ: Princeton University Press.

Edwards, A. (1989), 'Labour supply price, market wage, and the social opportunity cost of labour', *Economic Development and Cultural Change*, **38** (1), 31–43.

Edwards, S. (1988), *Exchange Rate Misalignment in Developing Countries*, Baltimore, MD: Johns Hopkins University Press.

Edwards, S. (1989), *Real Exchange Rates, Devaluation, and Adjustment*, Cambridge, MA: MIT Press.

Ellis, F. (2000), *Rural Livelihoods and Diversity in Developing Countries*, Oxford: Oxford University Press.

European Commission (2004), *Third Report on Economic and Social Cohesion: A New Partnership for Cohesion: Convergence, Competitiveness, Co-operation*, Brussels: EU, available at: http://ec.europa.eu/regional_policy/sources/docoffic/official/reports/cohesion3/cohesion3_en.htm.

European Commission (2006), 'Guidance on the methodology for carrying out cost–benefit analysis', *Working Document No. 4*, Brussels: EU, available at: http://ec.europa.eu/regional_policy/sources/docoffic/2007/working/wd4_cost_en.pdf.

European Commission (2007), *Growing Regions, Growing Europe: Fourth Report on Economic and Social Cohesion*, Brussels: EU, available at: http://ec.europa.eu/regional_policy/sources/docoffic/official/reports/cohesion4/pdf/4cr_en.pdf.

European Commission (2008), *Guide to Cost–Benefit Analysis of Investment Projects*, Brussels: EU, available at: http://ec.europa.eu/regional_policy/sources/docgener/guides/cost/guide2008_en.pdf.

Evans, A. (2000), *Poverty Reduction in the 1990s: An Evaluation of Strategy and Performance*, Washington, DC: World Bank.

Evans, D. (2004), 'A social discount rate for France', *Applied Economics Letters*, **11** (13), 803–808.

Evans, D. (2005), 'The elasticity of marginal utility of consumption: estimates for twenty OECD countries', *Fiscal Studies*, **26** (2), 197–224.

Evans, D. (2007), 'Social discount rates for the European Union: new estimates', in M. Florio (ed.), *Cost–Benefit Analysis and Incentives in Evaluation*, Cheltenham, UK and Northampton, MA, USA: Edward Elgar Publishing.

Evans, D. and H. Sezer (2003), 'A time preference measure of the social rate of discount for the UK', *Applied Economics*, **34** (15), 1925–34.

Evans, D. and H. Sezer (2004), 'Social discount rate for six countries', *Applied Economics Letters*, **11** (9), 557–60.

Evans, D. and H. Sezer (2005), 'Social discount rates for member countries of the EU', *Journal of Economic Studies*, **32** (1), 47–59.

Fane, G. (1991), 'The social opportunity cost of foreign exchange: a partial defence of Harberger et al.', *Economic Record*, **67** (4), 307–16.

Faustman, Martin (1849), 'On the determination of the value which forest land and immature stands possess for forestry', in M. Gane (ed.) (1968), 'Martin Faustman and the evolution of discounted cash flow: two articles from the original German of 1849 (translated by W. Linnard)', *Commonwealth Paper No. 42*, Oxford: Commonwealth Forestry Institute.

Fehr, E. and K. Hoff (2011), 'Introduction: tastes, castes and culture: the influence of society on preferences', *The Economic Journal*, **121** (556), F396–412.

Feldstein, M. (1964), 'The social time preference rate in cost–benefit analysis', *Economic Journal*, **74** (294), 360–79.

Feldstein, M. (1972), 'The inadequacy of weighted discount rates', in R. Layard (ed.), *Cost–Benefit Analysis*, Harmondsworth: Penguin.

Fellner, W. (ed.) (1967), *Ten Economic Essays in the Tradition of Irving Fisher*, New York: Wiley.

Financial Times (2007), 'Interview with Sir Nicholas Stern', 19 June, London.

Fisher, B., R. Turner and P. Morling (2009), 'Defining and classifying ecosystem services for decision making', *Ecological Economics*, **68**, 643–53.

Fisher, I. (1907), *The Rate of Interest*, New York: Macmillan.

Fisher, I. (1930), *The Theory of Interest*, New York: Macmillan.

Fitzgerald, E. (1976), 'The urban service sector, the supply of wage goods and the shadow wage rate', *Oxford Economic Papers, New Series*, **28** (2), 228–39.

Fitzgerald, E. (1978), *Public Sector Investment Planning for Developing Countries*, London: Macmillan.

Florio, M. (2006), 'Cost–benefit analysis and the European Union Cohesion Fund: on the social cost of capital and labour', *Regional Studies*, **40** (2), 211–24.

Florio, M. (2007a), 'Multi-government cost–benefit analysis: shadow prices and incentives', in M. Florio (ed.), *Cost–Benefit Analysis and Incentives in Evaluation*, Cheltenham, UK and Northampton, MA, USA: Edward Elgar Publishing.

Florio, M. (ed.) (2007b), *Cost-Benefit Analysis and Incentives in Evaluation*, Cheltenham, UK and Northampton, MA, USA: Edward Elgar Publishing.

Florio, M. and S. Vignetti (2004), 'Cost benefit analysis, development planning and the EU cohesion fund: learning from experience', *Working Paper* 2004–31, Dipartimento di Economia Politica e Aziendale, Università degli Studi di Milano.

Florio, M. and S. Vignetti (2005), 'Cost–benefit analysis of infrastructure projects in an enlarged European Union: an incentive oriented approach', *Economic Change and Restructuring*, **38** (3), 179–210.

Florio, M. and S. Vignetti (2010), 'Intellectual bridges across project evaluation traditions: the contribution of EU regional policy', *Cuadernos Economicos de ICE*, **80**, 29–48.

Freeman, A. (1979), 'Hedonic prices, property values and measuring environmental benefits: a survey of the issues', *Scandinavian Journal of Economics*, **81** (2), 154–73.

Freeman, A. (2003), *The Measurement of Environmental and Resource Values: Theory and Methods*, 2nd edn, Washington, DC: Resources for the Future.

Fujimura, M. and J. Weiss (2000), 'Integration of poverty impact in project economic analysis: issues in theory and practice', *EDRC Methodology Series No. 2*, Manila: ADB.

Gajewski, G. and M. Luppino (2003), 'Poverty reduction and road projects: a prospective estimation method', Working Paper, available at: http://www.louisberger.com/Insights/~/media/Files/LBG/PDF/Insights/gajewski_poverty_and_roads.pdf.

Gajewski, G. and M. Luppino (2004), 'Methods in distribution and poverty impact analysis of projects: practices and clarifications', paper presented at 79th Annual Conference of Western Economic Association International, Vancouver.

Gajewski, G., M. Luppino, M. Ihara and L. Luppino (2004), 'Estimating the poverty reduction potential of roads projects in regions experiencing institutional instability due to conflict and post-conflict conditions', paper presented at the Conference of the European Association for Evolutionary Political Economy, Crete.

Gittinger, J. (1972), *The Economic Analysis of Agricultural Projects*, Baltimore, MD: Johns Hopkins University Press.

Glewwe, P. and M. Kremer (2006), 'School teachers and educational outcomes in developing countries', in E. Hanushek and F. Welch (eds), *Handbook of the Economics of Education*, Vol. 2, Amsterdam: Elsevier.

Global Footprint Network (2010), *Ecological Footprint Atlas of the World 2010*, Oakland, CA: Global Footprint Network.

Gold, M., J. Siegel, L. Russel and M. Weinstein (1996), *Cost Effectiveness in Health and Medicine*, New York: Oxford University Press.

Gollier, C. (2002), 'Time horizon and the discount rate', IDEI, University of Toulouse (mimeo).

Gómez, C. (1979), 'Estimation of the national accounting parameters at efficiency prices for Dominican Republic', *Papers on Project Analysis*, No. 8, Washington, DC: Inter-American Development Bank.

Graaff, J. de V. (1957), *Theoretical Welfare Economics*, Cambridge, UK: Cambridge University Press.

Graham, D. (2007), 'Agglomeration, productivity and transport investment', *Journal of Transport Economics and Policy*, **41** (3), 317–43.

Grennes, T. (1984), *International Economics*, Englewood Cliffs, NJ: Prentice Hall.

Griffiths, U., L. Wolfson, A. Quddus, M. Younus and R. Hafiz (2004), 'Incremental cost effectiveness of supplementary immunization activities to prevent neonatal tetanus in Pakistan', *Bulletin of the World Health Organization*, **82** (9), 643–51.

Guo, J., C. Hepburn, R. Tol and I. Anthoff (2006), 'Discounting and the social cost of carbon – a closer look at uncertainty', *Environmental Science and Policy*, **9** (3), 205–16.

Hammer, J. (1993), 'The economics of malaria control', *World Bank Research Observer*, **8** (1), 1–22.

Hanemann, W., J. Loomis and B. Kanninen (1991), 'Statistical efficiency of double-bounded dichotomous choice contingent valuation', *American Journal of Agricultural Economics*, **73** (4), 1255–63.

Hanley, N. and C. Spash (1993), *Cost–Benefit Analysis and the Environment*, Aldershot, UK and Brookfield, VT, USA: Edward Elgar Publishing.

Hansard (1989), 'Investment', **150** (79), column 187, 5 April, London: HMSO.

Hansen, J. (1974), 'A guide to the *Guidelines*: the UNIDO method of economic project evaluation', *Staff Working Paper*, No. 166, Washington, DC: World Bank.

Hanushek, E. and F. Welch (eds) (2006), *Handbook of the Economics of Education*, Vol. 2, Amsterdam: Elsevier.

Harberger, A. (1965), 'Survey of literature on cost–benefit analysis for industrial project evaluation', reprinted in A. Harberger (1968), *Project Evaluation: Collected Papers*, London: Macmillan.

Harberger, A. (1971), 'On measuring the social opportunity cost of labour', *International Labour Review*, **103** (6), 559–79.

Harberger, A. (1973), *Project Evaluation: Collected Papers*, Chicago, IL: Markham.

Harberger, A. (1977), 'On the UNIDO Guidelines for Social Project Evaluation', in H. Schwartz and R. Berney (eds), *Social and Economic Dimensions of Project Evaluation*, Washington, DC: Inter-American Development Bank.

Harberger, A. (1978), 'On the use of distributional weights in social cost–benefit analysis', *Journal of Political Economy*, **86** (2), 87–120.

Harberger, A. (1985), 'Crisis fiscal e internacional de Panamá: ¿un problema o dos?' (Panama's fiscal and international crisis: one problem or two?), Panama: Ministerio de Planificación y Política Económica.

Harberger, A. (1986), 'Economic adjustment and the real exchange rate', in S. Edwards and L. Ahamed (eds), *Economic Adjustment and Exchange Rates in Developing Countries*, Chicago, IL: University of Chicago Press.

Harberger, A. and G. Jenkins (eds) (2002), *Cost–Benefit Analysis*, Cheltenham, UK and Northampton, MA, USA: Edward Elgar Publishing.

Harbison, R. and E. Hanushek (1992), *Educational Performance of the Poor: Lessons from Rural Northeast Brazil*, Oxford: Oxford University Press.

Hards, S. (2011), 'Social practice and the evolution of personal environmental values', *Environmental Values*, **20** (1), 23–42.

Harris, J. and M. Todaro (1970), 'Migration and development: a two sector analysis', *American Economic Review*, **60** (1), 126–42.

Hashimzade, N. and G. Myles (2009), 'Cost–benefit analysis and the marginal cost of public funds', paper presented at the VIII Milan European Economy Workshop, 11–12 June, University of Milan.

Hausman, J. (ed.) (1993), *Contingent Valuation: a Critical Assessment*, Amsterdam: North-Holland.

Haveman, R. and B. Wolfe (1984), 'Schooling and economic well-being: the role of nonmarket effects', *Journal of Human Resources*, **19** (3), 377–407.

HEATCO (2005), 'Deliverable 5', available at: http://heatco.ier.uni-stuttgart.de/HEATCO_D5.pdf.

Henderson, P. (1965), 'Notes on the public sector investment criteria in the UK', *Bulletin of the Oxford University Institute of Statistics*, **27** (1), 55–89.

Hensher, D. (1977), *Value of Business Travel Time*, Oxford: Pergamon Press.

Hensher, D. (2001), 'Measurement of the valuation of travel time savings', *Journal of Transport Economics and Policy (JTEP)*, **35** (1), 71–98.

Hicks, J. (1939a), *Value and Capital: An Inquiry into some Fundamental Principles of Economic Theory*, Oxford: Clarendon Press.

Hicks, J. (1939b), 'The foundations of welfare economics', *Economic Journal*, **49** (196), 696–712.

Hicks, J. (1965), *Capital Growth*, Oxford: Oxford University Press.

Hicks, J. (1975), 'The scope and status of welfare economics', *Oxford Economic Papers*, **27** (3), 307–26.

Hinkle, L. and P. Montiel (eds) (1999), *Exchange Rate Misalignment: Concepts and Measurement for Developing Countries*, Oxford: Oxford University Press.

Hirshleifer, J. (1958), 'On the theory of the optimal investment decision', *Journal of Political Economy*, **66** (4), 329–52.

Hirshleifer, J., J. De-Haven and J. Milliman (1960), *Water Supply, Economics, Technology and Policy*, Chicago, IL: University of Chicago Press.

HM Treasury (1984), *Investment Appraisal in the Public Sector – A Technical Guide for Government Departments*, London: HMSO.

HM Treasury (2003), *The Green Book: Appraisal and Evaluation in Central Government*, London: HM Treasury, available at: http://www.hm-treasury.gov.uk/data_greenbook_index.htm.

Honohan, P. (1998), 'Key issues of cost–benefit methodology for Irish industrial policy', *General Research Series*, available at: http://homepage.eircom.net/~phonohan/costbenefit.pdf.

Hosking, S.G. (ed.) (2010), *The Valuation of Estuary Services in South Africa Specifically Regarding Changes to Estuary Services as a Result of Reductions to Fresh Water Inflows – Main Report*, Report to the Water Research Commission, Nelson Mandela Metropolitan University.

Hotelling, H. (1931), 'The economics of exhaustible resources', *Journal of Political Economy*, **39** (2), 137–75.

Howe, J. and P. Richards (1984), *Rural Roads and Poverty Alleviation*, London: Intermediate Technology Development Group.

Humavindu, M. (2008), 'Estimating national economic parameters for Namibia', *Umea Economic Studies*, No. 744, Umea, Sweden: Umea University.

Humavindu, M. and J. Stage (2003), 'Hedonic pricing in Windhoek townships', *Environment and Development Economics*, **8**, 391–404.

Hutton, G., D. Schellenberg, F. Tediosi, E. Macete, E. Kahiqwa, X. Mas, M. Trapero, M. Tanner, A. Trilla, P. Alonso and C. Menendez (2009), 'Cost effectiveness of malaria intermittent preventive treatment in infants (IPTi) in Mozambique and the United Republic of Tanzania', *Bulletin of the World Health Organization*, **87** (2), 123–9.

Independent Evaluation Group (IEG) (2010), *Cost–Benefit Analysis in World Bank Projects*, Washington, DC: World Bank, available at: http://siteresources.worldbank.org/EXTOED/Resources/cba_full_report.pdf.

Inter-American Development Bank (IDB) (2001), 'Social equity/poverty reduction and poverty targeted investment criteria, an advisory note prepared by Poverty and Inequality Unit', Washington, DC: Inter-American Development Bank.

Irvin, G. (1978), *Modern Cost–Benefit Methods*, London: Macmillan.

Jabbar, M. and M. Diedhiou (2003), 'Does breed matter to cattle farmers and buyers? Evidence from West Africa', *Ecological Economics*, **45**, 461–72.

Jacoby, H. (1993), 'Shadow wages and peasant family labour supply: an econometric application to the Peruvian Sierra', *Review of Economic Studies*, **60** (4), 903–21.

Jacoby, H. (2000), 'Access to markets and the benefits of rural roads', *Economic Journal*, **110** (465), 713–37.

James, L. and R. Lee (1971), *Economics of Water Resources Planning*, Bombay: McGraw Hill.

Jamison, D., J. Breman, A. Measham, G. Alleyne, M. Claeson, D. Evans, P. Jha, A. Mills and P. Musgrove (eds) (2006), *Disease Control Priorities in Developing Countries*, 2nd edn, New York: Oxford University Press.

Jenkins, G. (1997), 'Project analysis and the World Bank', *American Economic Review*, **87** (2), 38–42.

Jenkins, G. (1999), 'Evaluation of stakeholder impacts in cost–benefit analysis', *Impact Assessment and Project Appraisal*, **17** (2), 87–96.

Jenkins, G. and A. Harberger (1994), 'Cost–benefit analysis of investment decisions', Harvard Institute of International Development (mimeo).

Jevons, W. (1871), *The Theory of Political Economy*, London: Macmillan.

Jimenez, E. and H. Patrinos (2009), 'Can cost–benefit analysis guide education policy in developing countries?', in R. Brent (ed.), *Handbook of Research on Cost–Benefit Analysis*, Cheltenham, UK and Northampton, MA, USA: Edward Elgar Publishing.

Johansson, P. (1987), *Cost–Benefit Analysis of Environmental Change*, Cambridge: Cambridge University Press.

Johnson, J. (1987), 'Estimating accounting prices for project appraisal in the Philippines', *Economics Department Working Paper*, Manila: Asian Development Bank (mimeo).

Joshi, H. (1972), 'World prices as shadow prices: a critique', *Bulletin of the Oxford University Institute of Economics and Statistics*, **34** (1), 53–73.

Journal of Economic Perspectives (1994), 'Symposia on contingent valuation', *Journal of Economic Perspectives*, **8** (4).

Kahnemann, D. and J. Knetsch (1992), 'Valuing public goods: the purchase of moral satisfaction', *Journal of Environmental Economics and Management*, **22** (1), 57–70.

Kahyarara, G. and F. Teal (2008), 'The returns to vocational training and academic education: evidence from Tanzania', *World Development*, **36** (11), 2223–42.

Kamuanga, M., B. Swallow, H. Sigue and B. Bauer (2001), 'Evaluating contingent and actual contributions to a local public good: tsetse control in the Yale agro-pastoral zone, Burkina Faso', *Ecological Economics*, **39**, 115–30.

Keynes, J. (1925), 'The economic consequences of Mr. Churchill', in J. Keynes (1978), *Collected Writings*, Vol. 9, Cambridge: Cambridge University Press.

Kim, A. and B. Benton (1995), 'Cost–benefit analysis of the onchocerciasis control program', *World Bank Technical Paper*, 282, Washington, DC: World Bank.

Kirkpatrick, C. and J. MacArthur (1990), 'Shadow pricing unemployed labour in developed economies: an approach at estimation', *Project Appraisal*, **5** (2), 101–12.

Kirkpatrick, C. and J. Weiss (eds) (1996), *Cost–Benefit Analysis and Project Appraisal in Developing Countries*, Cheltenham, UK and Brookfield, VT, USA: Edward Elgar Publishing.

Knesee, A. and S. Smith (eds) (1966), *Water Research*, Baltimore, MD: Johns Hopkins University Press.

Knetsch, J. (2007), 'Biased valuations, damage assessments, and policy choices: the choice of measure matters', *Ecological Economics*, **63**, 684–9.

Kögel, T. (2009), 'On the relation between discounting of climate change and Edgeworth–Pareto substitutability', *Economics e-journal*, Special Issue 'Discounting the Long-run Future and Sustainable Development', **3** (2009–26), available at: http://www.economics-ejournal.org/economics/journalarticles/2009-27/view.

Kreander, N., R. Gray, D. Power and C. Sinclair (2005), 'Evaluating the performance of ethical and non-ethical funds: a matched pair analysis', *Journal of Business Finance and Accounting*, **32** (7), 1465–93.

Krishna, K., R. Erzan and L. Tan (1994), 'Rent sharing in the multi-fibre arrangement: theory and evidence from US apparel imports from Hong Kong', *Review of International Economics*, **2** (1), 62–73.

Krishna, K., W. Martin and L. Tan (1995), 'Imputing licence prices: limitations of a cost-based approach', mimeo, conference on Empirical Investigations in International Trade, Purdue University, November.

Krutilla, J. and C. Eckstein (1958), *Multipurpose River Development*, Baltimore, MD: Johns Hopkins University Press.

Kuhn, T. (1962), *Public Enterprise and Transport Problems*, Los Angeles, CA: California University Press.

Kula, E. (1984), 'Derivation of social time preference rates for the USA and Canada', *Quarterly Journal of Economics*, **99** (4), 873–83.

Kula, E. (1998), *Time Discounting and Future Generations – the Harmful Effects of an Untrue Economic Theory*, Westport, CT and London: Quorum.

Kula, E. (2008), 'Is contemporary interest rate in conflict with Islamic ethics?', *Kyklos*, **61** (1), 45–64.

Kula, E. (2011), 'Dual discounting in cost–benefit analysis for environmental impacts', *Environmental Impact Assessment Review*, **31** (3), 180–86.

Lal, D. (1973), 'Disutility of effort, migration, and the shadow wage-rate', *Oxford Economic Papers, New Series*, **25** (1), 112–26.

Lal, D. (1980), *Prices for Planning*, London: Heinemann.

Lancaster, K. (1966), 'A new approach to consumer theory', *The Journal of Political Economy*, **74** (2), 132–57.

Landauer, C. (1947), *The Theory of National Economic Planning*, San Francisco, CA: University of California Press.

Layard, R. (ed.) (1972), *Cost–Benefit Analysis*, Harmondsworth: Penguin.

Layard, R. and S. Glaister (eds) (1994), *Cost–Benefit Analysis*, 2nd edn, Cambridge: Cambridge University Press.

Le, K. (2009), 'Shadow wage and shadow income in farmers' labour supply functions', *American Journal of Agricultural Economics*, **91** (3), 685–96.

Lee, J., G. Milesi-Ferreti, J. Ostry, A. Prati and L. Ricci (2008), 'Exchange Rate Assessments: CGER Methodologies', *IMF Occasional Papers*, 261, Washington, DC: International Monetary Fund.

LeFevre, A., S. Shillcutt, S. Saha, N. Ahmed, A. Chowdhury, P. Law, R. Black, M. Santoshama and G. Darmstadt (2010), 'Skin barrier enhancing emollients among pre-term infants in Bangladesh', *Bulletin of the World Health Organization*, **88**, 104–12.

Leontief, W. (1956), 'Factor proportions and the structure of American trade: further theoretical and empirical analysis', in W. Leontief (ed.) (1986), *Input–Output Economics*, 2nd edn, New York: Oxford University Press.

Levin, H. and P. McEwan (2001), *Cost Effectiveness Analysis*, London: Sage.

Lewis, W. (1954), 'Economic development with unlimited supplies of labour', *Manchester School*, **22** (2), 139–91.

Lindberg, G. (2005), 'Accident costs', in C. Nash and B. Matthews (eds), *Measuring the Marginal Social Cost of Transport*, Research in Transportation Economics, Volume 14, Elsevier.

Linn, J. (1977), 'Economic and social analysis of projects: a case-study of Ivory Coast', *World Bank Staff Working Paper*, 253, Washington, DC: World Bank.

Little, I. (1950 [1960]), *A Critique of Welfare Economics*, 1st edn 1950, 2nd edn 1960, Oxford: Oxford University Press.

Little, I. and J. Mirrlees (1968), *Manual of Industrial Project Analysis in Developing Countries*, Vol. 2, Paris: OECD.

Little, I. and J. Mirrlees (1974), *Project Appraisal and Planning for Developing Countries*, London: Heinemann Educational.

Little, I. and J. Mirrlees (1991), 'Project appraisal and planning twenty years on', in *Proceedings of the World Bank Annual Conference on Development Economics 1990*, Washington, DC: World Bank.

Little, I. and J. Mirrlees (1994), 'The costs and benefits of analysis: project appraisal and planning twenty years on', in R. Layard and S. Glaister (eds), *Cost–Benefit Analysis*, 2nd edn, Cambridge: Cambridge University Press.

Livingstone, I. and M. Tribe (1995), 'Projects with long time horizons: their economic appraisal and the discount rate', *Project Appraisal*, **10** (2), 66–76.

Loewenstein, G. (ed.) (2007), *Exotic Preferences: Behavioural Economics and Human Motivation*, New York: Oxford University Press.

Loewenstein, G., L. Thompson and M. Bazerman (2007), 'Social utility and decision making in interpersonal contexts', in G. Loewenstein (ed.), *Exotic Preferences: Behavioural Economics and Human Motivation*, New York: Oxford University Press.

Logan, S., W. Schulze, S. Ben-David and D. Brookshire (1978), *Development and Application of a Risk Assessment Method for Radioactive Waste Management – Volume 3, Economic Analysis*, Washington, DC: US Environmental Protection Agency.

Londero, E. (1994), 'Estimating the accounting price of foreign exchange: an input–output approach', *Economic Systems Research*, **6** (4), 415–34.

Londero, E. (1995), 'Reflections on estimating distributional effects', in C. Kirkpatrick and J. Weiss (eds), *Cost–Benefit Analysis and Project Appraisal in Developing Countries*, Aldershot, UK and Brookfield, VT, USA: Edward Elgar Publishing, pp. 54–74.

Londero, E. (1996a), *Benefits and Beneficiaries: An Introduction to Estimating Distributional Effects in Cost–Benefit Analysis*, 2nd edn (1st edn 1987), Washington, DC: Inter-American Development Bank.

Londero, E. (1996b), 'Shadow pricing rules for partially traded goods', *Project Appraisal*, **11** (3), 169–82.

Londero, E. (1997), 'Trade liberalization with a fixed exchange rate', *International Trade Journal*, **11** (2), 247–76.

Londero, E. (2001), 'By-products', *Economic Systems Research*, **13** (1), 35–45.

Londero, E. (2003a), *Shadow Prices for Project Appraisal*, Cheltenham, UK and Northampton, MA, USA: Edward Elgar Publishing.

Londero, E. (2003b), 'Trade liberalization and adjustment in Argentina', *Journal of International Trade and Economic Development*, **12** (3), 225–46.

Londero, E. and R. Soto (1987), 'CALPAN: a microcomputer program for calculating accounting prices using input–output techniques. User's manual', *Papers on Project Analysis*, No. 30, Washington, DC: Inter-American Development Bank (revised edition 1991).

Londero, E., S. Teitel, H. Cervini, R. Parot and J. Lenicov (1998), *Resources, Industrialization and Exports in Latin America. The Primary Input Content of Sustained Exports of Manufactures from Argentina, Colombia and Venezuela*, London: Palgrave Macmillan.

Lucking, R. (1993), 'Technical problems in the appraisal of projects using semi-input–output methodology', *Project Appraisal*, **8** (2), 113–24.

Lumby, S. and G. Jones (1994), *Investment Appraisal and Financial Decisions*, 6th edn, London: Chapman and Hall.

Maass, A. (ed.) (1962), *Design of Water-Resource Systems*, Cambridge, MA: Harvard University Press.

MacArthur, J. (1978), 'Appraising the distributional aspects of rural development projects: a Kenya case study', *World Development*, **6** (2), 167–93.

MacArthur, J. (1994), 'Estimating efficiency prices through semi-input–output methods – a review of practice in available studies', *Journal of International Development*, **6** (1), 19–43.

McKenzie, G. (1983), *Measuring Economic Welfare: New Methods*, Cambridge: Cambridge University Press.

Mackie, P., M. Wardman, A. Fowkes, G. Whelan, J. Nellthorp and J. Bates (2003), *Value of Travel Time Savings in the UK Department for Transport*, Institute for Transport Studies, University of Leeds in association with John Bates Services, available at: http://eprints.whiterose.ac.uk/2079/.

Maclennan, D. (1977), 'Some thoughts on the nature and purpose of hedonic price functions', *Urban Studies*, **14** (1), 59–71.

McMahon, W. (1999), *Education and Development: Measuring the Social Benefits*, Oxford: Oxford University Press.

Maddison, A. (2001), *The World Economy – A Millennial Perspective*, Paris: OECD.

Maddock, N. and F. Wilson (eds) (1994), *Project Design for Agricultural Development*, Aldershot: Avebury.

Maibach, M., C. Schreyer, H. van Essen, B. Boon, R. Smokers, A. Sachroten, C. Doll, B. Pawlowska and M. Bak (2008), *Handbook for the Estimation of External Costs in the Transport Sector*, Delft: CE Delft, available at: http://ec.europa.eu/transport/sustainable/doc/2008_costs_handbook.pdf.

Mairate, A. and F. Angelini (2007), 'Cost–benefit analysis and EU cohesion policy', in M. Florio (ed.) (2007), *Cost–Benefit Analysis and Incentives in Evaluation*, Cheltenham, UK and Northampton, MA, USA: Edward Elgar Publishing.

Malpezzi, S. (2003), 'Hedonic pricing models: a selective and applied review', in A. O'Sullivan and K. Gibb (eds), *Housing Economics and Public Policy: Essays in Honour of Duncan Maclennan*, Oxford: Blackwell Science.

Marglin, S. (1962), 'Economic factors affecting system design', in A. Maass (ed.), *Design of Water-Resource Systems*, Cambridge, MA: Harvard University Press.

Marglin, S. (1963), 'The opportunity cost of public investment', *Quarterly Journal of Economics*, **77** (1), 274–89.

Marglin, S. (1967), *Public Investment Criteria*, London: Unwin.

Markandya, A. and D. Pearce (1988), 'Environmental considerations and the choice of the discount rate in developing countries', *Environment Department Working Paper*, 3, Washington, DC: World Bank.

Marks, P., T.S. Fowkes and C.A. Nash (1986), 'Valuing long distance business travel time savings for evaluation: a methodological review and application', Sussex University: Proceedings of the Seminar held at the PTRC Summer Annual Meeting, available at: http://trid.trb.org/view.aspx?id=294540.

Marshall, A. (1899), *Elements of Economics of Industry*, 3rd edn, London: Macmillan.

Matete, M. and R. Hassan (2006), 'Integrated ecological economics accounting approach to evaluation of inter-basin water transfers: an application to the Lesotho Highlands Water Project', *Ecological Economics*, **60**, 246–59.

Mejía, F. (1989), 'Estimación de precios de cuenta para la República Dominicana' (Estimating accounting prices for the Dominican Republic), *Monografías de Análisis de Proyectos*, 36, Washington, DC: Inter-American Development Bank.

Menon, M., F. Preali and F. Rosati (2005), 'The shadow wage of child labour: an application to Nepal', *Understanding Children's Work Working Paper*, ILO, UNICEF and World Bank, available at: http://www.childtrafficking.com/Docs/womanemp_familywelfare_childlabour_070402.pdf.

Merrett, S. (1966), 'The rate of return to education: a critique', *Oxford Economic Papers*, **18** (3), 289–303.

Mincer, J. (1974), *Schooling, Experience and Earnings*, New York: Columbia University Press.

Mingat, A. and Jee-Peng Tan (1996), 'The full social returns to education: estimates based on countries' economic growth performance', *Human Capital Development Working Paper*, 73, Washington, DC: World Bank.

Ministry of Economic Development and Co-operation (MEDaC) of Ethiopia (1998), *National Parameters and Economic Analysis for the Public Investment Programme in Ethiopia*, Addis Ababa: MEDaC.

Ministry of Overseas Development (1977), *A Guide to Economic Appraisal in Developing Countries*, London: HMSO.

Mishan, E. (1981), *Introduction to Normative Economics*, Oxford: Oxford University Press.

Mishan, E. (1982), 'The new controversy about the rationale of economic evaluation', *Journal of Economic Issues*, **16** (1), 29–47.

Mishan, E. (1988), *Cost–Benefit Analysis*, 4th edn, London: Unwin Hyman.

Mitchell, R. and R. Carson (1989), *Using Surveys to Value Public Goods: The Contingent Valuation Method*, Washington, DC: Resources for the Future.

Mosley, P. (2001), 'A simple technology for poverty-oriented project assessment', *Impact Assessment and Project Appraisal*, **19** (1), 53–67.

Murray, C. (1994), 'Quantifying the global burden of disease: the technical basis for disability adjusted life years', in C. Murray and A. Lopez (eds), *Global Comparative Assessments in the Health Sector*, Geneva: WHO.

Murray, C. and A. Lopez (eds) (1994), *Global Comparative Assessments in the Health Sector*, Geneva: WHO.

Murray, C. and A. Lopez (eds) (1996), *The Global Burden of Disease*, Boston, MA: Harvard School of Public Health.

Nash, C. and B. Matthews (eds) (2005), *Measuring the Marginal Social Cost of Transport*, Research in Transportation Economics, Volume 14, Elsevier.

Nieves, G. (2001), 'Estimación de precios sombra a partir del análisis input–output: aplicación a la economía Española' (Estimation of shadow prices through input–output analysis: application to the Spanish economy), *Papeles de Trabajo del Instituto de Estudios Fiscales, Series Economía*, No. 26, available at: http://www.ief.es/documentos/recursos/publicaciones/papeles_trabajo/2001_26.pdf.

Nussbaum, M. (2011), *Creating Capabilities: the Human Development Approach*, Cambridge, MA: Harvard University Press.

OECD (1980), *Radiological Significance and Management of Tritium, Carbon-14, Krypton-85, and Iodine arising from the Nuclear Fuel Cycle*, Paris: OECD Nuclear Energy Agency, Expert Group.

Orr, S. (2006), 'Values, preferences, and the citizen–consumer distinction in cost benefit analysis', *Politics, Philosophy and Economics*, **5** (3), 377–400.

Ortega, O., N. El-Sayed, J. Sanders, Z. Abd-Rabou, L. Antil, J. Bresee, A. Mansour, I. Nakhla and M. Riddle (2009), 'Cost benefit analysis of rotavirus immunization program in the Arab Republic of Egypt', *Journal of Infectious Diseases*, **200** (Supplement 1), S92–S98.

O'Sullivan, A. and K. Gibb (eds) (2003), *Housing Economics and Public Policy: Essays in Honour of Duncan Maclennan*, Oxford: Blackwell Science.

Overseas Development Agency (ODA) (1988), *Appraisal of Projects in Developing Countries. A Guide for Economists*, 3rd edn, London: HMSO.

OXERA (2002), 'A social time preference rate for use in long-term discounting', Report for the Office of the Deputy Prime Minister, Department for Transport and Department for the Environment, Food and Rural Affairs, Oxford: OXERA, available at: http://www.commu nities.gov.uk/documents/corporate/pdf/146862.pdf.

Page, J. (1982), 'Shadow prices for trade strategy and investment planning in Egypt', *World Bank Staff Working Papers*, 521, Washington, DC: World Bank.

Pearce, D. (1991), *Blueprint 2 – Greening the World Economy*, London: Earthscan.

Pearce, D. (2002), 'An intellectual history of environmental economics', *Annual Review of Energy and Economics*, **27**, 57–81.

Pearce, D. and K. Turner (1990), *Economics of Natural Resources and the Environment*, London: Harvester Wheatsheaf.

Pearce, D., G. Atkinson and S. Mourato (2006), *Cost Benefit Analysis and the Environment: Recent Developments*, Paris: OECD.

Pearce, D., A. Markyanda and E. Barbier (1990), *Sustainable Development*, Aldershot, UK and Brookfield, VT, USA: Edward Elgar Publishing.

Pearce, D., C. Pearce and C. Palmer (eds) (2002), *Valuing the Environment in Developing Countries: Case Studies*, Cheltenham, UK and Northampton, MA, USA: Edward Elgar Publishing.

Perkins, F. (1994), *Practical Cost Benefit Analysis*, Melbourne: Macmillan.

Phillips, C. (2009), 'What is a QALY?', *What is series: Health Economics*, Hayward Medical Communications, UK, available at: http://www. medicine.ox.ac.uk/bandolier/painres/download/whatis/QALY.pdf.

Pigou, A. (1928), *A Study in Public Finance*, London: Macmillan.

Pigou, A. (1929), *The Economics of Welfare*, London: Macmillan.

Plottu, E. and B. Plottu (2007), 'The concept of total economic value of environment: a reconsideration within a hierarchical rationality', *Ecological Economics*, **61** (1), 52–61.

Potts, D. (1994), 'Real interest rates and the pattern of agricultural investment', in N. Maddock and F. Wilson (eds), *Project Design for Agricultural Development*, Aldershot: Avebury, pp. 173–83.

Potts, D. (1995), 'Economic analysis for the public investment programme in Lithuania', Development and Project Planning Centre, University of Bradford (mimeo).

Potts, D. (1996a), 'Economic analysis for the public investment programme in Latvia', Development and Project Planning Centre, University of Bradford (mimeo).

Potts, D. (1996b), 'Estimating shadow prices in a transitional economy: the case of Lithuania', in C. Kirkpatrick and J. Weiss (eds), *Cost–Benefit Analysis and Project Appraisal in Developing Countries*, Cheltenham, UK and Brookfield, VT, USA: Edward Elgar Publishing, pp. 299–310.

Potts, D. (1996c), 'When prices change: consistency in the financial analysis of projects', *Project Appraisal*, **11** (1), 27–40.

Potts, D. (1999), 'Forget the weights, who gets the benefits? How to bring a poverty focus to the economic analysis of projects', *Journal of International Development*, **11** (4), 581–95.

Potts, D. (2001), 'Simple technology or unnecessary complication? A critique of the "poverty elasticity of aid" measure for project assessment', *Impact Assessment and Project Appraisal*, **19** (1), 69–72.

Potts, D. (2002), *Project Planning and Analysis for Development*, Boulder, CO: Lynne Rienner.

Potts, D. (2003), 'Applying distribution analysis: the Mufima case study revisited', in D. Potts, P. Ryan and A. Toner (eds), *Development Planning and Poverty Reduction*, London: Palgrave Macmillan, pp. 218–30.

Potts, D. (2008), 'Assessing the impact of regeneration spending: lessons from the United Kingdom and the wider world', *Education, Knowledge and Economy*, **2** (3), 213–22.

Potts, D., P. Ryan and A. Toner (eds) (2003), *Development Planning and Poverty Reduction*, London: Palgrave Macmillan.

Pouliquen, L. (1970), 'Risk analysis in project appraisal', *World Bank Staff Working Paper*, 11, Washington, DC: World Bank.

Powers, T. (ed.) (1981), *Estimating Accounting Prices for Project Appraisal*, Washington, DC: Inter-American Development Bank.

Powers, T. (1989), 'A practical application: the IDB experience', paper presented at The Impact of Development Projects on Poverty seminar organised by the OECD Development Centre and the Inter-American Development Bank, Paris.

Powers, T. and E. Howard (1979), 'A methodology for measuring and recording the distributional effects of projects in the Bank's portfolio', *Papers on Project Analysis*, 10, Washington, DC: Inter-American Development Bank.

President's Water Resources Council (1962), 'Policies, standards and procedures in the formulation, evaluation and review of plans for use and development of water related land resources', 87th Congress, 2nd session, Senate Document, Washington, DC: US Government Printing Office.

Price, C. (1984), 'The sum of discounted consumption flows', *Environment and Planning*, **16** (6), 829–37.

Price, C. (1993), *Time Discounting and Value*, Oxford: Blackwell.

Price, C. (1996a), 'Discounting and project appraisal: from the bizarre to the ridiculous', in C. Kirkpatrick and J. Weiss (eds), *Cost–Benefit Analysis and Project Appraisal in Developing Countries*, Cheltenham, UK and Brookfield, VT, USA: Edward Elgar Publishing.

Price, C. (1996b), 'Long time horizons, low discount rates and moderate investment criteria', *Project Appraisal*, **11** (3), 157–68.

Pritchett, L. (2001), 'Where has all the education gone?', *World Bank Economic Review*, **15** (3), 367–91.

Psacharopoulos, G. (1973), *Returns to Education: An International Comparison*, Amsterdam: Elsevier.

Psacharopoulos, G. (1981), 'Returns to education: an updated international comparison', *Comparative Education*, **17** (3), 321–41.

Psacharopoulos, G. (1985), 'Returns to education: a further international update and implications', *Journal of Human Resources*, **20** (4), 583–604.

Psacharopoulos, G. (1994), 'Returns to investment in education: a global update', *World Development*, **22** (9), 1325–43.

Psacharopoulos, G. (1995), 'The profitability of investment in education: concepts and methods', *HCO Working Papers*, 63, Washington, DC: World Bank.

Psacharopoulos, G. and J. Loxley (1985), *Diversified Secondary Education and Development: Evidence from Colombia and Tanzania*, Oxford: Oxford University Press.

Psacharopoulos, G. and H. Patrinos (2002), 'Returns to investment in education: a further update', *World Bank Policy Research Working Paper*, 2881, Washington, DC: World Bank.

Psacharopoulos, G. and H. Patrinos (2004), 'Returns to investment in education: a further update', *Education Economics*, **12** (2), 111–34.

Rabin, M. (2006), 'The experimental study of social preferences', *Social Research: an International Quarterly*, **73** (2), 405–28.

Rae, J. (1905), *The Social Theory of Capital*, London: Macmillan.

Ramsey, F. (1928), 'A mathematical theory of saving', *Economic Journal*, **38** (152), 543–59.

Ray, A. (1984), *Cost–Benefit Analysis: Issues and Methodologies*, Baltimore, MD: Johns Hopkins University Press.

Richards, K. and C. Stokes (2004), 'A review of carbon sequestration cost studies', *Climate Change*, **63**, 1–48.

Saerbeck, R. (1988), 'Estimating accounting price ratios with a semi-input–output table: Botswana', *Project Appraisal*, **3** (4), 190–98.

Sagoff, M. (1988), *Economy of the Earth: Philosophy, Law, and the Environment*, Cambridge: Cambridge University Press.

Saleh, I. (2004), 'Estimating shadow wage rates for economic project appraisal', *Pakistan Development Review*, **43** (3), 253–66.

Samuelson, P. (1967), 'Irving Fisher and the theory of capital', in W. Fellner (ed.), *Ten Economic Essays in the Tradition of Irving Fisher*, New York: Wiley.

Samuelsson, L. (2010), 'Reasons and values in environmental ethics', *Environmental Values*, **19**, 517–35.

Sandmo, A. (1997), 'Redistribution and the marginal cost of public funds', *Norwegian School of Economics and Business Administration Discussion Paper*, 08/97.

Sapir, A., P. Aghion, G. Bertola, M. Hellwig, J. Pisani-Ferry, D. Rosati, J. Viñals and H. Wallace (2004), *An Agenda for a Growing Europe – The 'Sapir Report'*, Oxford: Oxford University Press.

Sassi, F. (2006), 'Calculating QALYs, comparing QALY and DALY calculations', *Health Policy and Planning*, **21** (5), 402–8.

Savvides, S. (1994), 'Risk analysis in investment appraisal', *Project Appraisal*, **9** (1), 3–18.

Schultz, T.P. (1995), 'Investment in the schooling and health of women and men: quantities and returns', in T.P. Schultz (ed.), *Investment in Women's Human Capital*, Chicago, IL: University of Chicago Press.

Schultz, T.P. (1999), 'Health and schooling investments in Africa', *Journal of Economic Perspectives*, **13** (3), 67–88.

Schultz, T.W. (1964), *Transforming Traditional Agriculture*, New Haven, CT: Yale University Press.

Schwartz, H. and R. Berney (eds) (1977), *Social and Economic Dimensions of Project Evaluation*, Washington, DC: Inter-American Development Bank.

Scoones, I. (2009), 'Livelihoods perspectives and rural development', *Journal of Peasant Studies*, **36** (1), 171–96.

Scott, M., J. MacArthur and D. Newbery (1976), *Project Appraisal in Practice*, London: Heinemann.

Sen, A. (1966), 'Peasants and dualism with or without surplus labour', *Journal of Political Economy*, **74** (5), 424–50.

Sen, A. (1967), 'Isolation, assurance and the social rate of discount', *Quarterly Journal of Economics*, **81** (1), 112–24.

Sen, A. (1972), 'Control areas and accounting prices: an approach to economic evaluation', *Economic Journal*, **82** (325 suppl.), 486–501.

Sen, A. (1973), 'Behaviour and the concept of preference', *Economica*, **40** (159), 241–59.

Sen, A. (1977), 'Rational fools: a critique of the behavioral foundations of economic theory', *Philosophy and Public Affairs*, **6** (4), 317–44.

Sen, A. (1984), *Choice, Welfare and Measurement*, Cambridge, MA: Belknap Press for Harvard University Press.

Sen, A. (1987a), *On Ethics and Economics*, New York: Basil Blackwell.

Sen, A. (1987b), *Resources, Values and Development*, Cambridge, MA: Belknap Press for Harvard University Press.

Sen, A.K. (2009), *The Idea of Justice*, London: Allen Lane.

Sieper, E. (1981), 'The structure of general equilibrium shadow pricing rules for a tax-distorted economy', *Centre of Policy Studies Discussion Paper*, 4, Melbourne: Monash University.

Silva Neto, A. da (1993), 'Estimates of national parameters for the economic analysis of projects in Brazil', *Project Appraisal*, **8** (4), 231–9.

Silva Neto, A. da (1996), 'The income-distributional effects of a mining project in Brazil', in C. Kirkpatrick and J. Weiss (eds), *Cost–Benefit Analysis and Project Appraisal in Developing Countries*, Cheltenham, UK and Brookfield, VT, USA: Edward Elgar Publishing, pp. 206–32.

Skoufias, E. (1994), 'Using shadow wages to estimate labour supply of agricultural households', *American Journal of Agricultural Economics*, **76** (2), 215–27.

Smith, D. (2006), 'Pendulum swinging on cut in interest rate', *The Sunday Times*, Business Section, 5 February, London.

Solow, R. (1974), 'The economics of resources or the resources of economics', *American Economic Review*, **64** (2), 1–14.

Spash, C. (2007), 'Deliberative monetary valuation (DMV): issues in combining economic and political processes to value environmental change', *Ecological Economics*, **63**, 690–99.

Spash, C. and A. Vatn (2006), 'Transferring environmental value estimates: issues and alternatives', *Ecological Economics*, **60**, 379–88.

Squire, L. (1989), 'Project evaluation in theory and practice', in H. Chenery and T. Srinivasan (eds), *Handbook of Development Economics*, Vol. II, Amsterdam: North-Holland.

Squire, L. and H. van der Tak (1975), *Economic Analysis of Projects*, Baltimore, MD: Johns Hopkins University Press.

Standard Life (2010), *Ethical funds newsletter*, edition 13.

Stern, N. (2007), *The Economics of Climate Change: the Stern Review*, Cambridge: Cambridge University Press.

Stewart, F. and P. Streeten (1972), 'Little–Mirrlees methods and project appraisal', *Bulletin of the Oxford University Institute of Economics and Statistics*, **34** (1), 75–91.

Swales, K. (1997), 'A cost benefit approach to the evaluation of regional selective assistance', *Fiscal Studies*, **18** (1), 73–84.

Tan, T. (1997), 'Measuring the costs and benefits of foreign direct investment', *Asian Economic Journal*, **11** (3), 227–41.

Tan, T. and J. MacArthur (1995), 'An extended semi-input–output method for estimating shadow prices', *Project Appraisal*, **10** (1), 39–48.

Tan-Torres, E., R. Baltussen, T. Adam, R. Hutubessy, A. Acharya, D. Evans and C. Murray (eds) (2003), *Making Choices in Health: WHO Guide to Cost Effectiveness Analysis*, Geneva: WHO.

Teal, F. (2011), 'Higher education and economic development in Africa: a review of channels and interactions', *Journal of African Economics*, **20**, AERC Supplement 3.

Tinbergen, J. (1956), 'The optimum rate of saving', *Economic Journal*, **66** (264), 603–9.

Tinbergen, J. and H. Bos (1962), *Mathematical Models of Economic Growth*, New York: McGraw Hill.

Tol, R. (2003), 'On dual rate discounting', *Economic Modelling*, **21**, 95–8.

Transport and Road Research Laboratory (TRL) (2005), *Overseas Road Note 5: A Guide to Road Project Appraisal*, revised edn, London: DFID, available at: http://www.transport-links.org/transport-links/filearea/publications/1_851_ORN_5_Final.pdf.

Tullock, G. (1967), 'The general irrelevance of the impossibility theorem', *Quarterly Journal of Economics*, **81** (2), 256–70.

Turpie, J. (n.d.), 'The valuation of riparian fisheries in Southern and Eastern Africa', available at: http://www.iwmi.cgiar.org/assessment/files_new/research_projects/paper_turpie_iclarm.pdf.

Turpie, J. (2003), 'The existence value of biodiversity in South Africa: how interest, experience, knowledge, income and perceived level of threat influence local willingness to pay', *Ecological Economics*, **46** (2), 199–216.

United Nations Industrial Development Organization (UNIDO) (1972), *Guidelines for Project Evaluation*, New York: United Nations.

United Nations Industrial Development Organization (UNIDO) (1978), *Guide to Practical Project Appraisal*, New York: United Nations.

United Nations Industrial Development Organization (UNIDO) (1980), *Practical Appraisal of Industrial Projects*, New York: United Nations.

Urama, K. and I. Hodge (2006), 'Are stated preferences convergent with revealed preferences? Empirical evidence from Nigeria', *Ecological Economics*, **59**, 24–37.

Van Beukering, P., L. Brander, E. Tompkins and E. McKenzie (2007), *Valuing the Environment in Small Islands: an Environmental Economics Toolkit*, Joint Nature Conservation Committee, London: DEFRA.

Van de Walle, D. (1998), 'Assessing the welfare impacts of public spending', *World Development*, **26** (3), 365–79.

Van de Walle, D. (2002), 'Choosing rural road investments to help reduce poverty', *World Development*, **30** (4), 575–89.

Van Pelt, M. (1994), 'Sustainability oriented appraisal for agricultural projects', in N. Maddock and F. Wilson (eds), *Project Design for Agricultural Development*, Aldershot: Avebury, pp. 143–72.

Varian, H. (1996), *Intermediate Microeconomics: A Modern Approach*, New York: W.W. Norton and Company.

Vawda, A., P. Moock, J. Gittinger and H. Patrinos (2003), 'Economic analysis of World Bank education projects and project outcomes', *International Journal of Educational Development*, **23** (6), 645–60.

Venables, A. (2007), 'Evaluating urban transport improvements: cost–benefit analysis in the presence of agglomeration and income taxation', *Journal of Transport Economics and Policy*, **41** (Part 2), 173–88.

Vousden, N. (1990), *The Economics of Trade Protection*, Cambridge: Cambridge University Press.

Weiss, J. (1987), 'Approaches to estimating national economic parameters: Jamaica, Nepal and Ethiopia', *Project Appraisal*, **3** (4), 21–30.

Weiss, J. (1988), 'An introduction to shadow pricing in a semi-input–output approach', *Project Appraisal*, **3** (4), 181–9.

Weiss, J. (ed.) (1994), *The Economics of Project Appraisal and the Environment*, Aldershot, UK and Northampton, MA, USA: Edward Elgar Publishing.

Weiss, J. (1996), 'Project failure: the implications of "a 25% rule"', in C. Kirkpatrick and J. Weiss (eds), *Cost–Benefit Analysis and Project Appraisal in Developing Countries*, Cheltenham, UK and Brookfield, VT, USA: Edward Elgar Publishing, pp. 172–86.

Weiss, J. (2003), 'Poverty objectives and economic analysis of health projects', in D. Potts, P. Ryan and A. Toner (eds), *Development Planning and Poverty Reduction*, London: Palgrave Macmillan, pp. 231–45.

Weiss, J. (2004), 'Reaching the poor with poverty projects: what is the evidence on social returns?', *ADB Institute Discussion Paper*, 9.

Weiss, J. (ed.) (2005), *Poverty Targeting in Asia*, Cheltenham, UK and Northampton, MA, USA: Edward Elgar Publishing.

Weiss, J. and R. Adhikari (1989), 'Estimates of national economic parameters for China', Development and Project Planning Centre, University of Bradford (mimeo).

Weitzman, M. (1998), 'Why the far distant future should be discounted at its lowest possible rate', *Journal of Environmental Economics and Management*, **36** (3), 201–8.

Weitzman, M. (2001), 'Gamma discounting', *American Economic Review*, **91** (1), 260–71.

Wen, H., S. Jia and X. Guo (2005), 'Hedonic price analysis of urban housing: an empirical research on Hangzhou, China', *Journal of Zeijiang University Science*, **6A** (8), 907–14.

Whitehead, J. and G. Blomquist (2006), 'Use of contingent valuation in benefit–cost analysis', in A. Alberini and J. Kahn (eds), *Handbook on Contingent Valuation*, Cheltenham, UK, and Northampton, MA, USA: Edward Elgar Publishing.

Whitehead, J., T. Haab and J. Huang (1998), 'Part–whole bias in contingent valuation: will scope effects be detected with inexpensive survey methods?', *Southern Journal of Economics*, **65** (1), 160–68.

Whittington, D., D. Lauria and X. Mu (1991), 'A study of water vending and willingness to pay for water in Onitsha, Nigeria', *World Development*, **19** (2/3), 1779–98.

Willig, R. (1976), 'Consumer's surplus without apology', *American Economic Review*, **66** (4), 589–97.

Winch, D. (1975), *Analytical Welfare Economics*, Harmondsworth: Penguin.

Woodall, M. (2004), *Cost Benefit Analysis in Educational Planning*, Paris: UNESCO IIEP.

World Bank (1990), *World Development Report 1990*, Washington, DC: World Bank.

World Bank (1995), *Priorities and Strategies for Education: A World Bank Review*, Washington, DC: World Bank.

World Bank (2000), *World Development Report 2000/2001: Fighting Poverty*, Washington, DC: World Bank.

World Bank (2001a), *What is the Program on Targeted Interventions?*, Washington, DC: World Bank.

World Bank (2001b), *2000 Annual Review of Development Effectiveness*, Washington, DC: Operations Evaluation Department, World Bank.

World Bank (2005a), 'Valuation of time savings', *Notes on the Economic Evaluation of Transport Projects*, TRN-15, Washington, DC: World Bank Transport Economics, Policy and Poverty Thematic Group.

World Bank (2005b), 'Valuation of accident reduction', *Notes on the Economic Evaluation of Transport Projects*, TRN-16, Washington, DC: World Bank Transport Economics, Policy and Poverty Thematic Group.

World Bank (2005c), 'Treatment of induced traffic', *Notes on the Economic Evaluation of Transport Projects*, TRN-11, Washington, DC: World Bank Transport Economics, Policy and Poverty Thematic Group.

World Bank (2005d), 'Projects which may have substantial restructuring effects', *Notes on the Economic Evaluation of Transport Projects*, TRN-19, Washington, DC: World Bank Transport Economics, Policy and Poverty Thematic Group.

World Bank (2005e), 'Distribution of benefits and impacts on poor people', *Notes on the Economic Evaluation of Transport Projects*, TRN-26, Washington, DC: World Bank Transport Economics, Policy and Poverty Thematic Group.

World Bank (2007), *World Development Report 2008: Agriculture for Development*, Washington, DC: World Bank.

World Bank (2010), *World Development Indicators*, Washington, DC: World Bank.

World Health Organization (WHO) (2002), *World Health Report 2002, Reducing Risks and Promoting Healthy Life*, Geneva: WHO.

World Health Organization (WHO) (2010), *World Health Report 2010, Health Systems Financing: the Path to Universal Coverage*, Geneva: WHO.

Wren, C. (2005), 'Regional grants: are they worth it?', *Fiscal Studies*, **26** (2), 245–75.

Yaffey, M. (1997), 'Modified discounting revisited', *Project Appraisal*, **12** (1), 79–88.

Yamaguchi, K. (2008), 'Re-examination of stock price reaction to environmental performance: a GARCH application', *Ecological Economics*, **68** (1–2), 345–52.

Yang, Z. (2002), 'Dual rate of discounting in dynamic economic-environmental modelling', *Economic Modelling*, **20**, 941–57.

Zander, K. and A. Drucker (2008), 'Conserving what's important: using choice model scenarios to value local cattle breeds in East Africa', *Ecological Economics*, **68**, 34–45.

Zhao, H., P. You and C. Li (2009), 'Study on the estimating model of shadow prices for national economy evaluation of construction projects', *Management and Service Science, 2009. MASS '09. International Conference*, available at: http://ieeexplore.ieee.org/xpls/abs_all.jsp?arnumber=5303338&tag=1.

Zhongmin, X., C. Guodong, Z. Zhiqiang, S. Zhiyong and J. Loomis (2003), 'Applying contingent valuation in China to measure the total economic value of restoring ecosystem services in Ejina region', *Ecological Economics*, **44** (2–3), 345–58.

Zweifel, P. and H. Telser (2009), 'Cost–benefit analysis for health', in R. Brent (ed.), *Handbook of Research on Cost–Benefit Analysis*, Cheltenham, UK and Northampton, MA, USA: Edward Elgar Publishing.

Index